A HISTORY OF MARXIST PSYCHOLOGY

An illuminating and original collection of essays on 20th century Russian psychology, offering unparalleled coverage of the scholarship of Vygotsky and his peers.

Yasnitsky et al. challenge our assumptions about the history of Soviet science and the nature of Soviet Marxism and its influence on psychological thinking. He significantly broadens the discussion around Vygotsky's life and work and its historical context, applying theories of other notable thinkers such as Alexander Luria and the much-neglected philosopher/psychologist Sergei Rubinstein, alongside key movements in history, such as the pedology and psychohygiene. A diverse range of researchers from countries such as Argentina, Brazil, Canada, France, Russian Federation, Switzerland, Ukraine, and the UK, give this book a truly global outlook.

This is an important and insightful text for undergraduate and postgraduate students and scholars interested in the history of psychology and science, social and cultural history of Russia and Eastern Europe, Marxism, and Soviet politics.

Anton Yasnitsky, Ph.D. (University of Toronto), is an independent researcher who specializes in the Vygotsky–Luria Circle. He is the author of *Vygotsky: An Intellectual Biography* (2018). He has also edited *Questioning Vygotsky's Legacy: Scientific Psychology or Heroic Cult* (2018) and *Revisionist Revolution in Vygotsky Studies* (2015).

A HISTORY OF MARXIST PSYCHOLOGY

The Golden Age of Soviet Science

Edited by Anton Yasnitsky

Routledge
Taylor & Francis Group

LONDON AND NEW YORK

First published 2021
by Routledge
2 Park Square, Milton Park, Abingdon, Oxon OX14 4RN

and by Routledge
52 Vanderbilt Avenue, New York, NY 10017

Routledge is an imprint of the Taylor & Francis Group, an informa business

British Library Cataloguing-in-Publication Data
A catalogue record for this book is available from the British Library

Library of Congress Cataloging-in-Publication Data
Names: Yasnitsky, Anton, 1972– editor.
Title: A history of marxist psychology: the golden age of Soviet science / edited by Anton Yasnitsky.
Description: 1 Edition. | New York: Routledge, 2020. | Includes bibliographical references and index.
Identifiers: LCCN 2020020851 (print) | LCCN 2020020852 (ebook) | ISBN 9780367340063 (paperback) | ISBN 9780367340094 (hardback) | ISBN 9780429323423 (ebook)
Subjects: LCSH: Psychology—Soviet Union—History. | Communism—Soviet Union—Psychological aspects. | Communism and psychology—Soviet Union—History. | Vygotskiĭ, L. S. (Lev Semenovich), 1896–1934.
Classification: LCC BF108.S65 H57 2020 (print) | LCC BF108.S65 (ebook) | DDC 150.947—dc23
LC record available at https://lccn.loc.gov/2020020851
LC ebook record available at https://lccn.loc.gov/2020020852

ISBN: 978-0-367-34009-4 (hbk)
ISBN: 978-0-367-34006-3 (pbk)
ISBN: 978-0-429-32342-3 (ebk)

Typeset in Bembo
by Apex CoVantage, LLC

MIX
Paper from
responsible sources
FSC
www.fsc.org   FSC® C013985

Printed in the United Kingdom
by Henry Ling Limited

CONTENTS

Introduction

A NEW HISTORY OF PSYCHOLOGY

Soviet, Russian, Marxist

Anton Yasnitsky

No news is good news, they say. Then, here it is: yet another "new history". It is not clear yet if this is good news, but some clarifications and explanations are definitely needed right now.

Indeed, the news of a "new history" emerges from time to time, the "new" stays for a while in order to become an "old" one in due time, then, another "new history" emerges. This seems to be a natural course of events in historiography, and one should not be too excited by a proclamation of a novelty of the kind. This is a normative rule of the game: history keeps rewriting itself. The rhetoric pronouncements of a novelty come and go. Sometimes it even happens so that something proclaimed as "new" turns out to be not so new, or even entirely not new. Yet, the attribution "new" remains. After all, one is once again reminded of the *Pont Neuf* – allegedly, the New Bridge, according to its French title – which is the oldest standing bridge across the river Seine in Paris, France. The ancient Book of Ecclesiastes seems to be an eternal and ever novel source for inspiration for thinking along these lines.

So, in order to understand the novelty of this proposal and why anyone might be interested in it, we need to get the answers to these two questions: What is this book about? And, then: What is new in this "new history"?

What is this book about?

Time and space have arguably caused most of the problems to humankind so far. Particularly, our interpretation of the time and space juncture – the "chronotope", for the lack a better genuinely English word – is especially painful and troublesome.

This book is about one of those time-space junctures. The geographic land is the territory of the former Russian Empire, at least most parts of it. Yet, it is not as simple as it seems first: the land does not exist by itself and is circumscribed by other lands. Then, the period is, roughly, a couple of decades of the 1920s and 1930s. This is not so simple either: the period is also surrounded by other times that in many ways influenced or were influenced by the events that occurred then. Things get even further complicated when we start thinking about those people who lived there and then (and whose lives spanned well beyond this territory and period), but also got caught into the human networks of their predecessors, contemporaries and successors across other times and spaces. Yet another complication is added with our interest of the intellectual sphere – the "noosphere" if one prefers a smart-looking word of seemingly Greek origin – as the world of abstract ideas in their concrete material manifestations travelling across time, space and the people moving within, along or across them.

The primary focus of the book is the world of ideas, specifically, in the field of the "psychology" in its historical development. Therefore, the book seems to qualify as an "intellectual history". Our interest in psychology as a scientific discipline makes it also a "disciplinary history". Yet, as all the book's contributors certainly realize, no scientific discipline exists by itself, but deeply in the social context of its time and place. Thus, this is also a "social history". Finally, the abstract human networks at the closest zooming-in fall apart into an array of individual persons' portraits and idiosyncratic faces of the actors (in the sociological sense of the word) or protagonists (if one tends to think about them as of a narrative or theatric drama characters). Therefore, this book can also be construed as a set of "biographies". The last point is particularly true, given the number of memoir texts and reminiscences the reader will find inside.

So, the book is about psychology, in most general terms. Then, the word demands an attribute attached to it. We have four immediate options. These are: "Russian", "Soviet", "Vygotskian" or "Marxist" psychology. Let us discuss them one by one.

First, "Russian psychology". This might refer to some kind of mystical "Russian soul" or "Russian spirit" (like the one that is presumably represented by the characters of Fiodor Dostoyevsky or Anton Chekhov), but this is not about psychology as a scientific discipline and definitely not what this book is about. Alternatively, this might mean a scientific discipline of psychology as it developed from the earlier times of the Russian Empire throughout the Soviet period and until the contemporary Russian Federation. A shorter version of this story (that for obvious reasons did not include the post-Soviet period) can be found in a thick volume *Russian Psychology: A Critical History* by David Joravsky that covers roughly a century of what can be described as Russian psychological thought (Joravsky, 1989). This kind of story is not ours. Then, a curious blend of the two options is a story about the allegedly "special way" of "Russian science" – particularly, psychology – dramatically distinct from a "non-Russian" one due to its essential "spirituality" and "sacrality", therefore, superior to the deprived of "spirit" and "eternal values" equally inhuman and godless "Western science" (for a discussion, see Chapter 1, by

Leonid Radzikhovskii). This kind of perspective and worldview can be found in one of the programmatic works of the genre composed by Soviet–Russian author Mikhail Yaroshevskii (Yaroshevskii, 1996) as well as in quite a few contemporary publications of the last couple of decades within the Russian Federation. Yet, this is certainly not "our way" and not what this book has to offer its readers. Finally, "Russian psychology" can be operationalized on purely linguistic grounds as any scholarship that ever existed published in the Russian language. That would also include Russian translations of foreign works. This approach seems to be quite productive for studies of some kind and has recently been explored in a study on a disciplinary history of this field of knowledge in the first half of 20th century (Yasnitsky, 2015). However, this book is of a very different kind and covers a much broader set of topics, problems and perspectives.

Second, "Soviet psychology". This phrase was quite popular and widely used in publications in the previous century, especially after WWII. Many Western scholars would travel "back to the USSR" in order to get familiarized with the great achievements of state-sponsored Soviet science – especially, after the most impressive and even shocking (from the Westerner's perspective) first launch of an artificial Earth satellite, the Soviet *sputnik* (in 1957) and, then, first ever journey of a human into outer space: Yury Gagarin, a Soviet citizen, in 1961. These two events alone (not to mention the competition in the Cold War nuclear weapons armament) triggered a space race between the two Superpowers and attracted huge investments in Western science and related social practices, including psychology – such as industrial, organizational, developmental and educational psychologies – and, even more importantly, education. Thus, the primary motivation for the Western intellectuals' construction and construal of the "Soviet science narrative" was the need in support of their domestic research from their local governments, and this goal was successfully achieved. The victorious image and the success story of the "Soviet psychology" developed mainly under the impression of these exciting (and threatening, for some) achievements of the first socialist state and was shaped in a set of article and book publications that came out mostly in 1960s and 1970s. Some examples of this attitude can be found in the Cold War era classics of the genre (Bauer, 1962; Cole & Maltzman, 1969; McLeish, 1975; O'Connor, 1966; Rahmani, 1973; Simon, 1957). Since then, however, the glory of the Soviet social and scientific project has withered and does not appear now as obvious and fascinating as it used to. It is, perhaps, for this very reason the attribute "Soviet" does not quite fit as the main defining characteristic of psychology as it is treated in this book. Interestingly, the Anglophone narratives about "Soviet psychology" that widely proliferated in mid-20th century typically passed by (i.e., merely ignored) the "legacy of Vygotsky the Genius" (and considerably underplayed the proclaimed Marxist philosophical foundations of the Soviet science). This observation immediately leads to the next option to consider.

Third, "Vygotskian psychology". Lev Vygotsky (1896–1934) has long been regarded as the most prominent and the most famous Russian (and Soviet) psychologist, a "genius" (Yasnitsky, 2018) and the "Mozart of psychology" (Toulmin, 1978), apart from Ivan Pavlov (1849–1936) and, to a much lesser extent, Vladimir Bekhterev (1857–1927): both physiologists rather than psychologists proper, well known for their research on reflexes and the higher nervous system. Another famous Russian scholar is Alexander Luria (1902–1977), nowadays known primarily for his contributions to the study of the human brain and its relation to human behavior and psychological functioning. Yet, outside the specialized field of neuropsychology, Luria's fame in many ways is closely associated with Vygotsky, with whom he most closely collaborated in the 1920s and early 1930s. Still only the names of Pavlov, Luria and Vygotsky made it to the list of the top 100 most influential psychologists in America, according to a comprehensive study published in early 2000s (Haggbloom et al., 2002).

Yet, from mainstream Western psychology's vantage point, Vygotsky's (and "Vygotskian") legacy is Russian/Soviet psychology's main claim to fame today, in the 21st century. This conclusion is indirectly corroborated by a relatively recent, albeit somewhat dated study of the "coverage of Russian psychological contributions in American psychology textbooks" (Aleksandrova-Howell et al., 2012). Indeed, out of the six Russian scholars' names that made it to the top of the most well-known Russian celebrities in the field (i.e., alphabetically, Bekhterev, Luria, Pavlov, Sechenov, Vygotsky and Zeigarnik) it is the name of Lev Vygotsky that most occurs in the very text of the article with its 28 appearances as opposed to mere 7, 13, 12, 6 and 4 instances for Bekhterev, Luria, Pavlov, Sechenov and Zeigarnik, respectively. Notably, three persons on the list, Bekhterev, Pavlov and Sechenov, are 19th–early 20th century practitioners and scholars primarily in the fields of medical studies and physiology. They are considered the classics of biomedical sciences, but hardly qualify as psychologists proper. The other three, Vygotsky, Luria and Zeigarnik, were closest associates and belonged to the same "Vygotsky-Luria Circle" (Yasnitsky, 2016b), which is interpreted as yet another confirmation of Vygotsky's prominence. There is also an array of other reasons to believe that the image of Vygotsky and "Vygotskian psychology" has largely overclouded and surpassed the entire collective "Russian" or "Soviet psychology" in popular opinion by now. In contemporary psychological and, especially, educational discourse "Vygotskian psychology" is typically positioned as the main and the most important contribution a Russian-speaking scholar ever made into the international psychology. At least, it is safe to claim that Russian psychologists and educators other than Vygotsky (apart from those mentioned as the most popular ones in the "coverage of the Russian contributions" overview) are usually hardly known at all internationally. Consider the fact that the overwhelming majority of the top (i.e., most read and most cited) publications in contemporary journal *Journal of Russian and East European Psychology* (also well known as *Soviet Psychology*, renamed after the collapse of the Soviet Union) are Vygotsky's own papers, articles authored by his former direct associates (such as Lidia Bozhovich, Aleksei N. Leontiev or Daniil El'konin) and their colleagues and students (such as Vasilii

Davydov, Aleksandr Zaporozhets, Piotr Gal'perin or Piotr Zinchenko), or discuss issues directly related to and stemming from Vygotsky's writings such as the topics of the "zone of proximal development", the "social situation of development" or "involuntary remembering". Thus, "Vygotskian" would until quite recently virtually equate with either "Soviet" or "Russian" as long as psychology is concerned. However, not anymore.

It turns out that "Vygotskian psychology" appears to be in a deep crisis these days. If only Google Scholar citation rate is indicative and trustworthy enough, the crisis manifests itself in the number of references to Vygotsky's works that kept steadily growing from the end of 1970s throughout 1980s (Valsiner, 1988) and until most recently. However, as documented by Google, Vygotsky citation rate reached its peak in 2017 and started its rapid and steady decline ever since.[1] Should this conclusion prove ultimately correct in the long run, it would be safe to claim that we are currently observing the "Vygotsky bubble" (Yasnitsky, 2019) in its initial phase of shrinking. The reasons are not entirely clear for this truly tectonic shift in the world of ideas – as reflected in the researchers' and authors' social practices such as citing their scholarly sources, in this particular case. Yet, there are a couple of possible explanations and interpretations of the currently observed phenomenon.

Historically, the social function of the popular conception of "Vygotskiana" was the restoration of North American teachers in their rights as a leading force in the classroom, which were considerably undermined during the concurrent processes of 1960s–1970s of the "cognitive revolution" (Jerome S. Bruner being the most illustrious representative in educational and developmental psychology), the popular proliferation of the ideas of humanistic psychology (exemplified by such figures as Carl Rogers and Abraham Maslow). These processes and events triggered the advent of the "constructivist" education and "child-centered curriculum" that was introduced in opposition to the "traditional" instruction based on the methods of teacher-controlled drills (and related ones) and the positivist educational philosophy of behaviorism. The notion of the "zone of proximal development" (Vygotsky's own yet somewhat distorted phrasing of a very vague idea of roughly the last two years of his life, borrowed from the publications in the United States in the 1960s and 1970s made under Vygotsky's name) was instrumentally used as a forceful argument in the educational field and widely spread among the educationists in support of their claim to getting back the control over learning and instruction. This was promoted under the label of "social constructivism" – as opposed to the older notion of "constructivism" associated with the name of Swiss thinker and researcher Jean Piaget and the child – and the learner-centered movement in education. An explication of this sentiment can be found, for instance, in a recently

---

1 To this effect see, for instance, the link to Vygotsky's Google Scholar profile: https://scholar.google.com/citations?user=L4S0dT0AAAAJ and compare it with those of, for instance, Albert Bandura: https://scholar.google.com/citations?hl=en&user=muejNL8AAAAJ or Sigmund Freud: https://scholar.google.com/citations?hl=en&user=N80kIiYAAAAJ.

published book very characteristically titled *The Right to Teach: Creating Spaces for Teacher Agency* (Ostorga, 2018). Now that American teachers have presumably overcome the problems associated with the de facto loss of their status of the leading force in the classroom and Vygotsky's writings have already played their historical role, one might assume that invocation of his name and work is not so much in demand as it used to be a few decades ago. An alternative (or an additional) explanation of this phenomenon is that references to Vygotsky have typically occurred in support of the claim that children develop in their social context, as trivial and self-evident as it might appear to some (Valsiner & Van der Veer, 2000). Perhaps, this claim has eventually become so obvious to everyone nowadays, in the time of the global computer-mediated social networks of the 21st century that reference to the works of a long gone Russian scholar is not needed anymore. For a further substantial discussion to this effect see Yasnitsky (2019).

In addition, there is another plausible explanation of the presumably growing disappointment in and dissatisfaction with Vygotsky in yet another of his manifestations. This is his persona of "Vygotsky the Marxist". The name of Lev Vygotsky and the brand of "Vygotskian" science has also been long used (and abused) as an umbrella term for the leftist, post-Marxist political-scientific agenda by the left-leaning intellectuals in their scientific and social activities in order to promote their social and political stance (Laine-Frigren, 2020). This situation can be equally observed in different forms and under diverse disguises in North America, in the countries of the Western Europe and, more recently, in other regions, such as the Spanish-speaking world and perhaps even more notably in Portuguese-speaking Brazil (Aguilar, 2016; García, 2016; IJzendoorn et al., 1981; Mecacci, 2015; Métraux, 2015; Ratner & Silva, 2017; Stetsenko, 2016; Yasnitsky et al., 2016; Zazzo, 1982, 1989). A discussion can be found in Chapter 5 that presents the situation in Brazil as viewed through the eyes of the insiders.

The interest of the international community in "Vygotsky the Marxist" is not incidental (Ratner & Silva, 2017). It is based on quite a number of Vygotsky's texts in which he on various occasions quotes from Marx and Engels. Moreover, there is a lengthy discussion of the topic of Marxism in its potential application in psychology, education and related scientific disciplines and social practices. This fragment can be found in one of his earlier unfinished manuscripts of his mechanistic "instrumental" period of 1920s titled variably "The (historical) meaning of crisis in psychology" (Zavershneva & Osipov, 2012a, 2012b). It was not published until after Vygotsky's death and is well known (Vygotsky, 1997). Yet, the actual manuscript was abandoned by its author, and there is no evidence he was ever going to publish it or develop it any further. But this is far from the only obstacle to "Vygotsky's Marxism".

In any single Vygotsky work, there is no trace of any sufficiently well-developed distinctly Marxist research methodology deeply grounded in systematic analysis of the works of Karl Marx and Friedrich Engels. What we have instead are only bits and pieces and occasional quotes unsystematically scattered throughout a range of texts. Furthermore, there are even instances when Vygotsky either contradicted his own "Marxist" proclamations and promises (like his call for application of Marx's method of "reverse analysis" from most developed forms to the less developed ones that he actually never followed in any of his works) or rejected them altogether (like his mechanicist "instrumental method" of the 1920s that he explicitly renounced as erroneous and "reactological" in early 1930s) (Yasnitsky, 2018). Finally, the last argument, Vygotsky's declaration of his personal "Nicene Creed" (or a "symbol of faith"): a major theoretical work on "psychological materialism" that, by analogy with "historical materialism" for Marxist history and sociology, contemporary psychology direly needs as its methodological foundation. This remained only a slogan, mere proclamation and a statement of intent at best: Vygotsky failed to ever write such a book or create a comparable Marxist methodological legacy of this magnitude and importance. And even that is not all. A surprising discovery has been made in a study of Vygotsky's and Luria's experimental research conducted in 1931–1932 in Central Asia. The analysis of correspondence, documents and publications revealed the superficial, reductionist and "vulgar Marxist" essence of Vygotsky's (and his allies') understanding of the foundations of Karl Marx's and Friedrich Engels's philosophical and social teaching even in the most advanced and mature stages of Vygotsky's thinking development in 1930s, until virtually right before his death in 1934 (Lamdan & Yasnitsky, 2016; Yasnitsky, 2018). Thus, Vygotsky's status of a leading Marxist thinker and psychologist has been recently questioned and considerably undermined.

It is hardly possible to tell which of these factors or whether any combination of them (and if any of these) is in play in this situation. In any case, the "Vygotsky crisis" and the related "Vygotsky bubble" are likely to become an intriguing phenomenon in the history of science, to be further explored in the years to come. Yet, in sum, the cumulative scholarship on "Russian psychology", "Soviet science" and "Vygotskian legacy" has left a considerable gap in our knowledge about the real content and social meaning of the intellectual project as it was developed for a number of decades in the Soviet Union, its political satellite countries and their supporters all around the world. This conclusion virtually inevitably suggests the fourth option.

Fourth and the last: "Marxist psychology". After all, this is the real gap in our understanding the Soviet psychological project in its historical development. Indeed, we are still unfortunately lacking the knowledge about (a) distinctly Marxist (but decidedly non-Vygotskian), (b) Soviet and Russian (c) psychology (and the range of closely related disciplines) as (d) inseparable unity of philosophy, theory, scientific research methodology and, finally, social practice. This is the answer. As the reader of this book, who had a chance to have a look at its cover, already knows this is the choice we made. This is perhaps the main reason why this book had to be designed, materialized and released to the public. This is the book, and this is what it is about.

Now, following the logic of Vygotsky's proposal of the mid-1920s, here is what we have:

> The *direct* application of the theory of *dialectical materialism* to the problems of natural science and in particular to the group of biological sciences or psychology is *impossible*, just as *it is impossible to apply it directly* to history and sociology. . . . Like history, sociology is in need of the intermediate *special theory* of historical materialism which explains the *concrete* meaning, for the given group of phenomena, of the abstract laws of dialectical materialism. In exactly the same way we are in need of an as yet undeveloped but inevitable theory of biological materialism and psychological materialism as an intermediate science which explains the concrete application of the abstract theses of dialectical materialism to the given field of phenomena. Dialectics covers nature, thinking, history – it is the most general, maximally universal science. The theory of the psychological materialism or dialectics of psychology is what I call general psychology. In order to create such intermediate theories – methodologies, general sciences – we must reveal the *essence* of the given area of phenomena, the laws of their change, their qualitative and quantitative characteristics, their causality, we must create categories and concepts appropriate to it, in short, we must create our *own Das Kapital*. It suffices to imagine Marx operating with the general principles and categories of dialectics, like quantity-quality, the triad, the universal connection, the knot [of contradictions], leap etc. – without the abstract and historical categories of value, class, commodity, capital, interest, production forces, basis, superstructure etc. – to see the whole monstrous absurdity of the assumption that it is possible to create any Marxist science while bypassing by *Das Kapital*. Psychology is in need of its own *Das Kapital*-its own concepts of class, basis, value etc. – in which it might express, describe and study its object.
>
> *(Vygotsky, 1997, p. 330)*

Vygotsky's uncharacteristically clear and straightforward prose in this specific paragraph is quite instructional and thought-provoking. Let us analyze what Vygotsky suggests in these programmatic lines. First, he claims that Marxism (i.e., its philosophical part, the dialectical materialism) cannot directly be applied to psychology: an intermediary theory is needed. Second, by analogy with historical materialism as in intermediary theory for history, Vygotsky proposes "psychological materialism" as such a theory, and compares it with its own *The Capital*, but for the discipline of psychology. Third, in order to create such theory, a great deal of interpretative intellectual work is needed that would determine and reconceptualize the entire system of basic psychological concepts strictly in agreement with Marx's intellectual system. Yet, each abstract notion and concept requires a specific word or a phrase in order to express it with concrete verbal means of communication. Therefore, fourth and last, the conceptual change of such magnitude will apparently require considerable phraseological and terminological revision that would materialize conceptual apparatus of the "new psychology" with the help of a new terminological toolkit.

Now, let us proceed to Vygotsky's next thesis on Marxism in psychology:

> There is a special difficulty in the application of Marxism to new areas. The present concrete state of this theory, the enormous responsibility in using this term, the political and ideological speculation with it – all this prevents good taste from saying "Marxist psychology" *now*. We had better let others say of our psychology that it is Marxist than call it that ourselves. We put it into practice and wait a little with the term. In the final analysis, Marxist psychology *does not yet exist*. It must be understood as a historical goal, not as something already given. And in the contemporary state of affairs it is difficult to get rid of the impression that this name is used in an unserious and irresponsible manner. An argument against its use is also the circumstance that a synthesis between psychology and Marxism is being accomplished by more than one school and that this name can easily give rise to confusion in Europe.
>
> *(Vygotsky, 1997, p. 340)*

And not only in Europe, as one could remark, given the recent publications on the topic such as Ratner and Silva (2017). In any case, the message is well taken here: no Marxist psychology exists as of the end of 1920s, according to Vygotsky. It seems this conclusion is correct even if applied to the situation in psychology almost 100 years later: the beginning of the 2020s.

The last programmatic fragment is remarkable for its most curious twist of Vygotsky's thought. On the one hand, he declares the necessity of Marxist psychology as a requirement of any scientific psychology. No psychology other than Marxist can exist. And then, immediately after that, he seemingly relieves the reader from this onerous requirement when he suggests that, in fact, any psychology that is strictly scientific, regardless of its proclaimed goals and philosophical foundations, will inevitably become Marxist. This might appear as a circular or, probably, self-contradicting argument to some, but Vygotsky prefers not to notice that. Quite a few of his devoted followers prefer to do the same:

> Our science will become Marxist to the degree that it becomes truthful and scientific. And we will work precisely on making it truthful and to make it agree with Marx's theory. According to the very meaning of the word and the essence of the matter we cannot use "Marxist psychology" in the sense we use associative, experimental, empirical, or eidetic psychology. Marxist psychology is not a school amidst schools, but the only genuine psychology as a science. A psychology other than this cannot exist. And the other way around: *everything* that was and is genuinely scientific belongs to Marxist

psychology. This concept is broader than the concept of school or even current. It coincides with the concept *scientific* per se, no matter where and by whom it may have been developed.

(Vygotsky, 1997, p. 341)

These quoted fragments seem to fully and best represent everything of value that Vygotsky ever said or wrote on the topic of Marxism in psychology. The rest either repeats itself or does not add much to this. Now that we have finally resolved the issue of Marxism in Vygotsky the psychologist, it is interesting to see how this matter is addressed in this new book.

The whole first section "Theory" that immediately follows this very Introduction is dedicated to the discussion of Marxism in psychology: as it was practiced in the social and cultural realities in the Soviet Union in the 20th century and how it might be manifested and implemented in international psychology in the 21st century. The first chapter is the ideas and the text of Leonid Radzikhovskii that he generated on various occasions from late 1980s until up to now. The chapter is really interesting in many respects. First, it gives the reader a first-hand insider's account of Soviet Marxism in psychology in its dogmatic and hypocritical forms during the late Soviet Union era until its eventual and eventful collapse in 1991. This narrative is necessarily personal and auto-biographical. Second, the author also shares his ideas on the ways the unfulfilled promise of Marxist psychology could be realized in psychological theory. These lines, originally written in the late 1980s and somewhat revised recently, seem to be of much interest these days and might suggest a few promising avenues for further scholarly exploration in the nearest future.

Then, the second chapter of the book focuses on the truly gigantic figure of a thinker, philosopher and psychologist Sergei Rubinstein. He was the actual founder of the systemic Marxist thinking in Soviet psychology, widely and unquestionably acknowledged as such by the entire scholarly community of psychologists in that country in the 1940s–1950s, but remains virtually unknown to the contemporary international scholarly community worldwide. This is definitely a great shame and major loss. The chapter is based on a close reading of Rubinstein's programmatic article of 1934 that paved the way to truly Marxist thinking to his peers and played a great role in the disciplinary and institutional establishment of psychology in the Soviet Union in the long run. The analysis of the text is accompanied by an overview of Rubinstein's life and career, and discussion of the reliable sources on his life and legacy, and sketches the fate of his legacy against the background of the later developments in Soviet psychology after Rubinstein's death in 1960, particularly in the context of the allegedly Marxist "activity approach" (also known in certain circles as "activity theory", even worse, "cultural-historical activity theory"). This discussion is focused particularly on a historical episode that took place in 1969 in Moscow within the "inner circle" of top-most researchers of the former "Vygotsky-Luria Circle" such as Aleksandr Luria, Aleksei N. Leontiev, Piotr Gal'perin, Daniil

El'konin, Aleksandr Zaporozhets and, finally, a son of another member of the Circle (Piotr Zinchenko, deceased by then), Vladimir Zinchenko, a noted Soviet and Russian psychologist in his own right. The meeting was fateful, its outcomes are certainly as profound as shocking and sensational from the standpoint of what most of us have known and believed about this Soviet (and international) intellectual movement until now.

Psychology as social practice

In contemporary academic literature, it is not unusual to come across the discussions of the merits of the ideas and theoretical postulates of Russian and Soviet scholarship. Regrettably, though, these discussions have virtually always been alienated from the discussions of the related real world social practices that not only implemented these ideas, but also in many ways shaped and determined the ideas and the course of their development. In other words, the intrinsic unity of theory and social practice is all too often ignored in most of the contemporary publications on the topic of Russian psychology and allied sciences. The standpoint of the "ivory tower" of the pure reason might be appropriate in some, very special contexts, yet it is hardly acceptable in many others. One might argue that there is a wealth of publications on the "social history" of Soviet science, specifically, psychology. Yet, most of these focus on the "social" aspect only, and, which is worse, present the influence of the "social" in the light of the "oppressed science" already discussed above. An increasing volume of recent studies that overcome the age-old biases of the "oppressed science" paradigm and traditional separation of "purely intellectual" and "social" histories bring new light on the idiosyncratic unity of theory and practice of psychology in a Soviet context. A few of these studies are presented in this book.

The whole second section of the book presents the concrete practical applications of psychology in the spheres of medical and educational social practice. These were manifested in the self-proclaimed quasi-disciplines and related practices of "psychohygiene" and "pedology". Both originated in the West in parallel in America and in Europe, yet their greatest success was in the Soviet Russia, more precisely, in the entire Soviet Union, where they proliferated as all-Union mass movements that spread widely across the entire country. From a methodological standpoint, this is a very important issue: due to their disciplinary attribution other than "psychology" proper, these social phenomena that were promoted under different social labels frequently get ignored and avoided by the historians of this field of knowledge. This is a grave mistake that the authors of Chapters 3 and 4, Grégory Dufaud and Andy Byford, efficiently correct. Their stories about "psychohygiene" and "pedology", respectively, importantly complement our understanding of Soviet psychological Marxism in its practical application in social practice. It is up to the reader, though, to make a decision as to how notable in this practice was any Marxism whatsoever.

Transnational psychology

Geographically, most of historiographical research on Russian and Soviet psychology deals with Moscow (predominantly) or, to considerably lesser extent, St. Petersburg (historically, also known as Petrograd in 1914–1924 and Leningrad in 1924–1991). The studies of the history of psychological science in other regions and localities of the former Russian Empire – with a few exceptions such as the history of the "Kharkov school of psychology" (Yasnitsky & Ferrari, 2008a, 2008b; Yasnitsky & Ivanova, 2011) – are notably rarer, fragmentary and carry the flavor of "provincialism", in any sense. In sum, one might argue that the entire history of Russian psychology until quite recently virtually equated with the history of this discipline in the two historical capitals of the State. Furthermore, perhaps due to the Cold War legacy, the "history of national psychology" (as opposed to "foreign psychology") has long dominated in the historiographic accounts in the works of Soviet and, even now, Russian scholars. The radical separation between the "our" and "their" science is the trademark of both Soviet tradition and the great many of the Cold War period Western narratives on this science in the USSR in the 20th century. In other words, the history of Soviet/Russian psychology has long been considered as virtually immanent and self-contained "noumenon", or a "Thing-in-itself" (*Ding an sich*), as the great German philosopher Immanuel Kant might have termed it. Not anymore.

In contrast, quite recently the trend has changed. There are two dimensions to this methodological shift that can be expressed by just one word: "transnational" ("transnationalism"). Interestingly, the word has two meanings that reflect the two dimensions of the recent scholarship's groundbreaking innovation. First (and traditional in the literature), the notion means the focus of research on phenomena, events, processes and entities that equally belong to different national localities, such as international professional unions, scientific congresses, informal networks and cross-border communications of scholars, their joint projects, etc. Typically, the "transnational histories" involve subjects that deal with more than one state (David-Fox, 2012; Heilbron et al., 2008; Krementsov, 2000; Van der Veer & Yasnitsky, 2016; Yasnitsky, 2016a). Yet, as applied to the history of Russia, the world's largest country with its truly enormous vast space and, importantly, the history of a few territorial gains, losses and collapses (most notably, in 1917–1921 and in 1991), the notion of "transnationalism" acquires another meaning. Thus, the second dimension of the "transnational history of Russia" deals with the larger processes across the entire Euro-Asia that lays under the rule of the current Russian government. The analysis of the interplay between the three – the capital city of Russia, its distant localities and the foreign world outside – presents a truly exciting challenge to a researcher. First few steps in this direction have been made as illustrated by the majority of this book's chapters.

The reader is reminded about the second meaning of "transnationalism" in the two chapters on the social practices of Soviet psychology in their application in medicine and education as the All-Union mass movements of "psychohygiene" and "pedology". Yet, this dimension is underdeveloped in these texts that give a relatively sketchy overview of the history of these quasi-disciplines in the Soviet Union of the interwar period. The multitude of places and the richness of details of the geographical localities of the USSR can be found, though, in other works on Soviet "applied psychologies" in the works of these authors, Grégory Dufaud and Andy Byford, and some other scholars, who work on these and related topics.

Yet, "transnational" dimension in its first sense can be found in many other chapters of the book. Thus, the mentioned "psychohygiene" and "pedology" are not exclusively idiosyncratic Soviet inventions, but much larger, truly global transnational research projects. Particularly, this point is emphasized in Dufaud's chapter that highlights the cross-border trips, international exchange of ideas and "knowledge circulation" between various geographic and cultural localities. The same is true of Sergei Rubinstein, the eternal traveler – in the geographical and intellectual sense – between different times and places in Ukraine, Germany and Russia, as it is presented in Chapter 2. Apparently, the topic of "transnationalism" is so huge and essential that it deserved a special section within the structure of the book. The reader is invited to help themselves for the intellectual treats of the complexities of the transnational Brazilian reception, accommodation and application of Soviet psychological knowledge, especially, the Vygotskian legacy in Lusophone South America (Chapter 5, authored by Gisele Toassa, Flávia da Silva Ferreira Asbahr and Marilene Proença Rebello de Souza), and the deeply personal story of the transnational virtual dialogue between the Western researcher and the author of Chapter 6, Alexandre Métraux, and his distant Soviet peer Alexander Luria.

The deliberately personal dimension of thinking about psychology and its history is yet another major innovation of the "new history" that needs our discussion and clarification.

Personality: the "Romantic science"

The main problem with both Soviet "Marxist psychology" as we have known it by now and the multiple narratives about its history is that the person was ultimately lost, even in the biographic and, counter-intuitively perhaps, auto-biographical accounts of psychology and its actors in the Soviet era. What we have had instead was a series of rather abstract, dry, depersonalized or, in case of biographies, biased (when the biographers have been the students, followers, relatives, etc. of the scholar, whose life story they narrated) or cautiously self-censored (in case of autobiographies). Yet, as Chapter 2 reminds us, personality is both the starting point and ultimate goal of any psychology whatsoever. The same holds true of the history of this field of knowledge. It is for this very reason that this book is so rich with personal accounts, in various disguises.

An exciting and thrilling Chapter 1 by Leonid Radzikhovskii can largely be characterized as a memoir. Furthermore, this is clearly declared from the onset as "reminiscence". This standpoint is echoed in Alexandre Métraux's Chapter 6, presented as a "personal account". The two voices of the authors of the chapters not only involve the reader in personal stories, but seem to engage in a virtual dialogue within the book itself, as its first and last numbered chapters, This personal dimension of these two chapters is complemented with Piotr Gal'perin's voice as it is expressed in Chapter 2 in his recorded direct speech at one of those "inner circle" meetings of late 1960s with its excitingly revealing disclosures to our contemporaries and painfully disclosing revelations to the contemporaries of the speaker.

The authors of Chapter 5 from the very beginning importantly acknowledge that theirs is "necessarily personal history of psychology and Marxism in Brazil", by virtue of them being an integral part of the history as insiders and active participants of the described events and the processes. This acknowledgement is very important from the methodological standpoint: in their attempt to present their story as objectively and in a non-partisan manner as possible the authors must inevitably realize and come to terms with their own stance and perspective, their "party-ness" in Soviet Communist parlance. Otherwise, a non-biased account of history of science, even the making of science as such, is hardly possible.

The genre of a memoir is definitely not a novelty, including the historiography of science, and numerous "oral histories" only prove that. Yet, we are dealing with something different in this case, it seems. For psychology (and the related field of human science) from the times of "introspectionism" (discussed by Sergei Rubinstein in Chapter 2) this is also a powerful instrument for getting insight about the "inner side" of the soul, its depths and hidden recesses. This is so much true of the Sigmund Freud, his clinical method and intellectual legacy, and proves to be his main claim to fame as a psychologist of all times. Yet, the acute interest in personality is characteristic of many others, including the protagonist of Chapter 6, Alexander Luria. His famous clinical studies on his patients Shereshevskii and Zasetskii were published in Russian, translated into dozens of languages and made it to the lists of best-sellers, ultimately serving as very promising models of psychological story-telling for future generations of authors, such as Oliver Sacks, a renowned neurologist, whose books can be found now in virtually every book store on the specialized "Psychology" book shelves. In turn, Sacks was not only an ardent admirer of Luria, but also his active correspondent for a number of years during mid-1970s. He described his life experiences and exchanges with Luria on many occasions, for instance, in one of his last publications, his book chapter that came out a couple of years before his death in 2016 (Sacks, 2014). It is there that Sacks reflects on Luria's (and his own) distinct approach to the craft of an intellectual and practitioner in human sciences that he, following Luria, refers to it as "Romantic science". So, let us once again witness direct speech:

> To write true stories, to construct true lives, to present the essence and sense of a whole human life – in all its living fullness and richness and complexity – this must be the final goal of any human science or psychology. William James saw this, in the 1890s, but could only dream of its accomplishment. . . .

We ourselves are very privileged, because we have seen, in our own century, with the profound "unimagined portraits" constructed for us by Freud and Luria, at least the beginnings of this ultimate achievement. "This is only the beginning," Luria would always say, and, at other times, "I am only a beginner." Luria devoted the whole of a long life to reaching this beginning. "It has been my life's wish," he once wrote, "to found or refound a Romantic Science" (personal communication, letter dated July 1973). Luria, surely, accomplished his life's wish, and indeed founded or refounded a totally new science – the newest science in the world, in a way, and yet the first, and perhaps the oldest of all.

(Sacks, 2014, p. 527)

We are standing on the shoulders of giants. It is our solemn duty to keep it this way. The show must go on!

References

Aguilar, E. (2016). Vygotski en México: Una travesia bibliográfica y otros temas breves. In A. Yasnitsky, R. Van der Veer, E. Aguilar, & L. N. García (Eds.), *Vygotski revisitado: Una historia crítica de su contexto y legado* (pp. 361–373). Buenos Aires: Miño y Dávila Editores.

Aleksandrova-Howell, M., Abramson, C. I., & Craig, D. P. A. (2012). Coverage of Russian psychological contributions in American psychology textbooks. *International Journal of Psychology, 47*(1), 76–87.

Bauer, R. A. (1962). *Some views on Soviet psychology.* Washington, DC: American Psychological Association.

Cole, M., & Maltzman, I. (Eds.). (1969). *A handbook of contemporary Soviet psychology.* New York: Basic Books.

David-Fox, M. (2012). *Showcasing the great experiment: Cultural diplomacy and western visitors to the Soviet Union, 1921–1941.* Oxford, UK: Oxford University Press.

García, L. N. (2016). Before the "boom": Readings and uses of Vygotsky in Argentina (1935–1974). *History of Psychology, 19*(4), 298–313.

Haggbloom, S. J., Warnick, R., Warnick, J. E., Jones, V. K., Yarbrough, G. L., Russell, T. M., . . . Monte, E. (2002). The 100 most eminent psychologists of the 20th century. *Review of General Psychology, 6*(2), 139–152.

Heilbron, J., Guilhot, N., & Jeanpierre, L. (2008). Toward a transnational history of the social sciences. *Journal of the History of the Behavioral Sciences, 44*(2), 146–160.

IJzendoorn, M. V., Goossens, F. A., & Van der Veer, R. (1981). *Kritische psychologie: Drie stromingen.* Baarn: Ambo.

Joravsky, D. (1989). *Russian psychology: A critical history.* Cambridge, MA: Blackwell.

Krementsov, N. (1997). *Stalinist science.* Princeton: Princeton University Press.

Krementsov, N. (2000). Lysenkoism in Europe: Export-import of the Soviet model. In M. David-Fox & G. Peteri (Eds.), *Academia in upheaval: Origins, transfers, and transformations of the communist academic regime in Russia and east central Europe* (pp. 179–202). New York: Garland Publishing Group.

Laine-Frigren, T. (2020). Marxist influences in psychology. In *Oxford research encyclopedia of psychology.* Oxford University Press. http://dx.doi.org/10.1093/acrefore/9780190236557.013.612

Lamdan, E., & Yasnitsky, A. (2016). Did Uzbeks have illusions? The Luria – Koffka controversy of 1932. In A. Yasnitsky & R. Van der Veer (Eds.), *Revisionist revolution in Vygotsky studies* (pp. 175–200). London and New York: Routledge.

McLeish, J. (1975). *Soviet psychology. History, theory, context*. London: Methuen & Co.

Mecacci, L. (2015). Vygotsky's reception in the West: The Italian case between Marxism and communism. *History of the Human Sciences, 28*(2), 173–184.

Métraux, A. (2015). Lev Vygotsky as seen by someone who acted as a go-between between eastern and western Europe. *History of the Human Sciences, 28*(2), 154–172.

O'Connor, N. (1966). *Present day Russian psychology. A symposium by seven authors*. London: Pergamon Press.

Ostorga, A. N. (2018). *The right to teach: Creating spaces for teacher agency*. Lanham, MD: Rowman & Littlefield Publishers, Inc.

Payne, T. R. (1968). A. V. Petrovskij's 'history of Soviet psychology'. *Studies in Soviet Thought, 8*(2–3), 181–187.

Petrovskii, A. V. (1967). *Istoriia sovetskoi psikhologii. Formirovanie psikhologicheskoi nauki [History of Soviet psychology. The formation of psychological science] Год издания М.: Просвещение*. Moscow: Prosveschenie.

Petrovsky, A. (1990). *Psychology in the Soviet Union*. Moscow: Progress Publishers.

Rahmani, L. (1973). *Soviet psychology: Philosophical, theoretical, and experimental issues*. Oxford: International Universities Press.

Ratner, C., & Silva, D. N. H. (Eds.). (2017). *Vygotsky and Marx: Toward a Marxist psychology*. London and New York: Routledge.

Sacks, O. (2014). Luria and 'romantic science'. In A. Yasnitsky, R. van der Veer, & M. Ferrari (Eds.), *The Cambridge handbook of cultural-historical psychology* (pp. 517–528). Cambridge: Cambridge University Press.

Simon, B. (1957). *Psychology in the Soviet Union*. Stanford, CA: Stanford University Press.

Stetsenko, A. (2016). *The transformative mind: Expanding Vygotsky's approach to development and education*. Cambridge, UK: Cambridge University Press.

Toulmin, S. (1978). The Mozart of psychology. Mind in society: The development of higher psychological processes by L.S. Vygotsky, edited by Michael Cole, by Vera John-Steiner, by Sylvia Scribner, by Ellen Souberman, the psychology of art by L.S. Vygotsky, Soviet developmental psychology: An anthology edited by Michael Cole. *The New York Review of Books, 25*(14), 51–57.

Valsiner, J. (1988). *Developmental psychology in the Soviet Union*. Brighton, Sussex: Harvester Press.

Valsiner, J., & Van der Veer, R. (2000). *The social mind: Construction of the idea*. Cambridge: Cambridge University Press.

Van der Veer, R., & Yasnitsky, A. (2016). Translating Vygotsky: Some problems of transnational Vygotskian science. In A. Yasnitsky & R. Van der Veer (Eds.), *Revisionist revolution in Vygotsky studies* (pp. 143–174). London and New York: Routledge.

Vygotsky, L. S. (1997). The historical meaning of the crisis in psychology: A methodological investigation. In R. W. Rieber & J. Wollock (Eds.), *The collected works of L. S. Vygotsky: Vol. 3. Problems of the history and theory of psychology* (pp. 233–344). New York: Plenum Press.

Yaroshevskii, M. G. (1996). *Nauka o povedenii: Russkii put' [The science of behavior: The Russian way]*. Moscow: Institut prakticheskoi psikhologii.

Yasnitsky, A. (2015). Distsiplinarnoe stanovlenie russkoi psikhologii pervoi poloviny XX veka [Disciplinary formation of Russian psychology of the first half of 20th century]. In A. N. Dmitriev & I. M. Savel'eva (Eds.), *Nauki o cheloveke: Istoriia distsiplin* (pp. 299–329). Moscow: Izdatel'skii Dom NIU VShE.

Yasnitsky, A. (2016a). A transnational history of 'the beginning of a beautiful friendship': The birth of cultural-historical Gestalt psychology of Alexander Luria, Kurt Lewin, Lev Vygotsky, and others. In A. Yasnitsky & R. Van der Veer (Eds.), *Revisionist revolution in Vygotsky studies* (pp. 201–226). London and New York: Routledge.

Yasnitsky, A. (2016b). Unity in diversity: Vygotsky-Luria circle as an informal personal network of scholars. In A. Yasnitsky & R. Van der Veer (Eds.), *Revisionist revolution in Vygotsky studies* (pp. 27–49). London and New York: Routledge.

Yasnitsky, A. (2018). *Vygotsky: An intellectual biography*. London and New York: Routledge.

Yasnitsky, A. (2019). Vygotsky's science of superman: From utopia to concrete psychology. In A. Yasnitsky (Ed.), *Questioning Vygotsky's legacy: Scientific psychology or heroic cult* (pp. 1–21). London & New York: Routledge.

Yasnitsky, A., & Ferrari, M. (2008a). From Vygotsky to Vygotskian psychology: Introduction to the history of the Kharkov school. *Journal of the History of the Behavioral Sciences*, *44*(2), 119–145.

Yasnitsky, A., & Ferrari, M. (2008b). Rethinking the early history of post-Vygotskian psychology: The case of the Kharkov school. *History of Psychology*, *11*(2), 101–121.

Yasnitsky, A., & Ivanova, E. F. (2011). Remembering for the future: Grigorii Sereda in the history of Kharkov school of psychology. *Journal of Russian and East European Psychology*, *49*(1).

Yasnitsky, A., Van der Veer, R., Aguilar, E., & García, L. N. (Eds.). (2016). *Vygotski revisitado: Una historia crítica de su contexto y legado*. Buenos Aires: Miño y Dávila Editores.

Zavershneva, E., & Osipov, M. E. (2012a). Primary changes to the version of "The historical meaning of the crisis in psychology" published in the collected works of L.S. Vygotsky. *Journal of Russian and East European Psychology*, *50*(4), 64–84.

Zavershneva, E., & Osipov, M. E. (2012b). Sravnitel'nyi analiz rukopisi '(Istoricheskii) Smysl psikhologicheskogo krizisa' i ee versii, opublikovannoi v t. 1 sobraniia sochinenii L.S. Vygotskogo (1982) pod redaktsiei M.G. Yaroshevskogo [Comparative analysis of the manuscript '(Historical) Meaning of psychological crisis' and its version that was published in vol. 1 of collected works of L.S. Vygotsky (1982) under the editorship of M.G. Yaroshevskii]. *PsyAnima, Dubna Psychological Journal*, *5*(3), 41–72.

Zazzo, R. (1982). Necrologie. Alexis Leontiev. *L'année Psychologique*, *82*(2), 537–544.

Zazzo, R. (1989). Vygotski (1896–1934). *Enfance*, *42*(1–2), 3–9.

PART I
Theory

1

REMINISCENCE ABOUT FUTURE MARXIST PSYCHOLOGY

One hundred years of solitude

Leonid Radzikhovskii

First I got amused, then I got amazed. I was amused by the invitation that I received from the editor of this volume to contribute a new chapter that would be based on my 30-year-old paper that I once published in Russian academic journal *Issues of Psychology* (*Voprosy psikhologii*, in original Russian) amid the so-called *perestroika* ("reconstruction") period in the latest history of the Soviet Union. On the surface, the editor's offer appeared very unusual and utterly weird, to say the least. And only then it was that, upon rereading this virtually forgotten text, I got amazed by realizing how contemporary this old paper looks now, 30-something years later, at the close of the second decade of the 21st century. Indeed, virtually nothing has changed since then and it is as if time has stopped for Russian psychology, from the perspective of Marxist thinking in this field of knowledge, at least. That said, one cannot but acknowledge quite a few changes that took place in Russian psychology in a number of other respects over the last 30 years. These I am going to somewhat sketchily overview in the initial, newly written part of this chapter. Then, I will proceed to the considerably revised "prequel" of the story that reflects the state of the art in the field as of the end of the 1980s as it was reflected in my earlier publication (Radzikhovskii, 1988). Yet, before I proceed any further, a personal comment on my place in this story – rather, a history – of Soviet and Russian psychology is in order.

1970s–1980s: the portrait of the author in social context

The author of these lines graduated in 1975 from the Department of Psychology of Moscow State University and soon thereafter, at the age of 26, officially defended his doctoral (more precisely, "Candidate of Sciences") dissertation in the field of the history of psychology in 1979, specifically, on the scientific legacy of Lev Vygotsky (1896–1934). Given that his 226 pages long doctoral research topic was dedicated to the pioneering exploration of the topic of "main stages of scientific creativity of Lev Vygotsky" (Radzikhovskii, 1979b), he seems to qualify as one of the pioneers in the field of the "Vygotsky Studies", a new and emerging subfield of scientific inquiry back then, and a burgeoning field of knowledge now, the field of research that is currently undergoing a "Revisionist Revolution" of the 21st century (Yasnitsky, 2012, 2019a; Yasnitsky & Van der Veer, 2016b; Yasnitsky et al., 2016). Besides, not only was he an established authority in Vygotsky's legacy, its history and historiography (Radzikhovskii, 1979a) and one of the key organizers of the first conference on Vygotsky's legacy in the Soviet Union in June, 1981 (Davydov et al., 1981), but also a scientific researcher at the Institute of Psychology in Moscow (more precisely, the Scientific Research Institute of General and Pedagogical Psychology of the Academy of Pedagogical Sciences of the USSR, as it was officially titled at the time) well-known by the names of a few of its former employees, including a few academic celebrities: Lev Vygotsky and his collaborators and members of the "Vygotsky-Luria Circle" such as Leonid Sakharov (the author of the famous "Vygotsky-Sakharov test"), Alexander Luria, Mark Lebedinskii, Viktor Kolbanovskii, Aleksei N. Leontiev and many others. Thus, it does not come as a surprise that the author of this chapter was appointed as a secretary of editorial board of the forthcoming six-volume project of Lev Vygotsky's "Selected Works" that were published in Russian in 1982–1984. It was this very edition that was subsequently translated and published in English in 1987 (first volume that included "Thinking and speech") and then, after a pause, in 1993 and 1997–1999 (cumulatively, other five volumes).

Editing Vygotsky: how I wrote Leontiev's famous chapter

My duties and responsibilities in my capacity of scientific and editorial secretary included a wide range of activities and assignments, including the lion's share of textological work, preparation of indexes and compiling bibliography. In retrospect, one of those assignments appears particularly curious and strange. Thus, I distinctly remember the situation when Vasilii Davydov (1930–1998), my direct administrative supervisor as the Institute's Director (in 1973–1983, then, again, in 1991–1992), scientific collaborator (Davydov & Radzikhovskii, 1980, 1981, 1985) and one of the chief members of editorial board of the project, approached me and assigned the task of writing an Introduction to the six-volume collection of Vygotsky's texts, which would present an outline of Lev Vygotsky's life and historical development of his legacy. There was nothing curious or strange in that, given my scholarly interests and expertise at that time, and I successfully accomplished the job some time by early January 1981, when the whole manuscript of the first book was submitted to the publisher. That also implied its prior authorization by Soviet official censoring agency, which was preoccupied with its hard work and granted publication of the volume by the Christmas, in December, 1981. This very text was published as its introductory chapter in the first volume of the Collected Works in 1982. Yet, curiously and strangely enough, it was signed not by its author's name, but the name of Aleksei Nikolaevich Leontiev (1903–1979), who outlived the closest Vygotsky ally Aleksander Luria (1902–1977), but was, in turn, slightly outlived by another former immediate collaborator of Vygotsky, who, I would claim, for a long time remained the main active force behind the project: Aleksander Zaporozhets (1905–1981), a notable Soviet psychologist and prominent administrative authority in Soviet psychology and education in his capacity of the founding director (from 1960) of the Moscow's Scientific Research Institute of Preschool Upbringing of the Academy of Pedagogical Sciences of the USSR. Thus, my chapter – albeit under Leontiev's name – came out in Russian in 1982 and, once again, in English translation, in 1993.

I can hardly remember specific discussions that I must have had with my superiors or the explanations of the situation that I was given on this matter prior the publication. I guess, the main argument ran somewhere along the lines that "Leonid, you should understand, Aleksei Nikolaevich [Leontiev] is the first, the best and the most devout student of Vygotsky, his major intellectual heir, and, furthermore, he is the founder and the Dean of the Department of Psychology of Moscow State University, therefore, it is Aleksei Nikolaevich only, who could have written this introductory chapter of utmost importance for the whole six-volume collection, but Aleksei Nikolaevich is really not feeling well and, besides, for a long time already cannot find time to contribute this important piece of writing, etc." – or something of the kind. In any case, as I junior scientific worker at the very start of my career in the stagnating Soviet Union in early 1980s I was not given much choice or freedom of discussion or action. Yet, I would like to emphatically state here that – as strange as might appear today – at the time it never crossed my mind to blame anyone for anything (pretty much like I am not inclined to accuse and blame anyone personally now) as the whole situation was perceived as absolutely normal by all sides involved, and totally fitting the dominant scientific ethos in Soviet scientific practice of the time, the idiosyncratic "archetype of Soviet psychology" and the contemporary age-old "Stalin model" in Soviet and Russian science, as it was described recently (Yasnitsky, 2015, 2016). Like every psychologist around me, I was a part of this system, shared its values and never questioned the accepted practices. Furthermore, I was really glad and proud to have received such a flattering and honorable assignment as a junior researcher, whose work turned out good enough to be signed by the name of a Great Man such as Aleksei N. Leontiev. This is how I truly felt and perceived the situation then.

Yet, the situation was quite strange indeed, and it took another couple of decades for important memoir interviews to be published of the key direct witnesses to the inside activities of the top-rank administrative and scholarly authorities in Soviet psychology (Shchedrovitskii, 2001; Zinchenko, 2003) that shed light on what had chiefly remained hidden from the lower-rank researchers like myself. From these memoirs we know about the considerable resistance among the top-rank Soviet psychologists (including Vygotsky's former students and allies) to the very idea and initiative of publishing the works of Vygotsky after 1956. Georgii Shchedrovitskii (1929–1994) reminisced that it was only due to Aleksander Zaporozhets' open interference at one of the ritualistic critical public discussions that helped him to counter the critique and defend the prospective Russian publication of Vygotsky's works volume in 1960 (Vygotskii, 1960). Yet, this was the last major publication of Vygotsky's works that would come out under the editorship of a psychologist in Soviet Union during the following two decades. The end of this period was witnessed and discussed by the other memoirist, Vladimir Zinchenko (1931–2014), who recalled Aleksei N. Leontiev, the official heir to Vygotsky's legacy and the founder of the "activity theory", who not only resisted, but also apparently deliberately delayed the release of the six-volume "Collected Works of L.S. Vygotsky", in preparation since the late 1970s, at least as long as my involvement in the project is concerned. According to Zinchenko, one of the techniques Leontiev used to indeterminately postpone the conclusion of the project was his presumed "solemn duty" and eternal promise to contribute an introductory chapter, yet always avoiding actually writing it. The problem seemed to have promised to keep remaining endlessly, and it was in this very situation that Vladimir Zinchenko suggested his friend and colleague Vasilii Davydov assign the task of writing this introductory chapter to a young Vygotsky expert and prolific author Leonid Radzikhovskii. This is how, it seems, this chapter, confirmed and signed by Leontiev, made it into the first volume of the collection, which eventually gave the green light to the publication. Further, Zinchenko remarked that it looked as if Leontiev so much resisted the idea of publication that he did not live up to seeing that: Leontiev died in 1979, roughly three years before the first volume actually saw the daylight.

The purpose of this episode in the history of Soviet psychology within this chapter and the main reason for me telling it here is to provide an illustration of how everyday life of a psychologist in the typical social milieu in the Soviet Union might have sometimes looked like; yet also to give the reader an idea of the kind of events and processes the author of this chapter was involved in during his career as an academic psychologist "back in the USSR", the land that does not exist anymore. In fact, my career of an insider in academic psychology lasted until the very end of the decade of 1980s, since when I radically changed my lifestyle and professional orientation from a purely academic "ivory tower" thinker to the career of a journalist and a practitioner. Therefore, from the early 1990s I have remained a psychologist (in some sense), but only an external observer of the directions and trends in this discipline in Russian Federation as the newly emerged state after the collapse of the Soviet Union. Perhaps, this turn of events deprived me from certain first-hand experiences and observations from within the academy, but, on the other hand, provided me with an advantageous vantage point of an outsider. It is, thus, exactly from this position that I am going to provide, albeit in a few strokes, a history of Russian psychology as it developed in the Russian Federation after its formation in 1991 following the collapse of the Soviet Union.

1990s: away from the "triumph of Marxism-Leninism" to the "oppressed science" and the "Russian way" in psychology

The most curious, perhaps, transformation that psychology underwent in this country over the last half a century or so, is its most decisive abortion of virtually any Marxist references whatsoever. This is particularly amazing given that until the very end of the 1980s Marxism was proclaimed as the leading intellectual force in this field of knowledge and references to the founders of Marxism-Leninism and the programmatic materials and decisions of the leadership (e.g., Politburo or the Congresses) of Communist Party of the Soviet Union abounded Soviet psychological publications until the mid-1980s. The mystery of this disappearance can be relatively easy explained.

The most important and acute strategic issue for all Soviet psychologists during the so-called *perestroika* ("reconstruction", in English) in the mid-end 1980s – as well as for any other national or international psychological community, for that matter – was the adjustment of their field of knowledge to the pressing needs and requirements of the *Zeitgeist*, the time period it belonged to. Perhaps, this claim can be disputed among the academics in the contemporary industrially developed "West". Yet, in the USSR of the 1980s it was plain obvious that psychology was diseased with the same sickness as the rest of Soviet social sciences. The main problem was that social sciences hardly reflected the actual life problems of contemporary social reality and, instead, dealt with abstract schemes and abstract images of idealized people as they "should be" as opposed of the real people in the concrete settings of the their socialist social environment in the Soviet Union.

Therefore, the main goal of *perestroika* in social studies in the Soviet Union – including psychology, of course – was to turn (rather, return) research towards practice and transform it in the genuine humanist spirit in the sense of making it accountable for and capable of solving the problems of the real individuals, the citizens of the country and the social groups populating the land in their effort to solve their mundane problems. The key question was, though, to what extent the actual academic psychology of the time was in principle up to the challenge and capable of solving these problems. Specifically, an open question was what exactly in the contemporary intellectual legacy and related practices required to be changed first-hand. A rational discussion of the topics of "practicality" of science was complicated by a number of idiosyncratic local circumstances that considerably slowed down the development of psychological knowledge in the USSR. The challenge confronted with manifold personal and group ambitions supplemented by the related administrative resources dispersed between these groups of scholars, which had considerable impact on decision-making in Soviet science. In other words, one is safe to claim that "the 1980s was a period of diversification and of increasing numbers of academic psychologists, with psychologists tending to show loyalty to subgroups rather than to one artificially maintained unified field" (Sirotkina & Smith, 2012, p. 438).

Yet, perhaps the major handicap in bringing the actual life problems to the light of critical discussion was the age-old dogmatism seemingly deeply ingrained in the minds of my contemporaries and colleagues. All Soviet grand psychological theories and lesser-scale projects were invariably referred to as "Marxist" ones, according to the Marxist doctrine that was officially proclaimed and imperative for all scholars in the country from early 1930s (Todes & Krementsov, 2010), but not only that. Another major factor that played a considerable role in sustaining the dogmatism and stagnation in social sciences was the great extent of the scholars' loyalty to the regime, servility, "political correctness" and voluntary and conscious self-censorship. A critical discussion of Marxist legacy – including psychological theoretical and methodological ideas and approaches that were supposed to embody Marxist ideology in academic practice – would be considered as potentially vulnerable to the accusation in subversive activity, betrayal of the Marxist ideals and even the conspiracy against the foundations of the state and regime. Thus, the revision of the Marxist fundamentals was not apparently an option. It was way easier – and way more pleasant and self-satisfying to the Soviet scholars in the times of the rapidly disintegrating state and official ideology – to denounce any Marxism altogether. This was triumphantly accomplished roughly by the end of the decade of the 1980s. A few solitary exceptions only prove the rule.

A case study: the life and ideas of Mikhail Yaroshevskii (1915–2001)

Yet, "one does not waste a sacred space", as an old Russian proverb goes. The transformation was swift and seemingly miraculous. The place of Marxism in Russian psychological thinking was pretty fast taken by another general and overpowering idea: the predominance of the uniquely Russian "special way" in world psychology. This transformation can be best illustrated, perhaps, with a glimpse on one of the gurus and, according to one of the recent publications (Sirotkina & Smith, 2012), the "reform-minded" leader of the historiography of Russian and Soviet psychology, Mikhail Yaroshevskii (1915–2001). Thus, in one of his major publications, a textbook on history of psychology that was published in 1985, Yaroshevskii clearly and authoritatively stated:

> Without any exaggeration one can claim that its renaissance in the USSR in 1920s psychology owes to Marxism since, as it has been noted, this was the time of the dominance of reflexological theories that denied the very possibility of objective and deterministic investigation of the consciousness (i.e. the internal world of the human subject) and, therefore, the possibility of the genuine science about the humans. . . . The achievements of the Soviet psychology of 1920s and 1930s determined its development in the subsequent period. Having mastered the richness of the ideas of Marxist-Leninist teaching about the psyche and the consciousness and having harmoniously merged [Marxist-Leninist] methodological orientation with the practice of

the formation of the personality of socialist society, Soviet psychological science succeeded in participating in solving actual tasks of the Communist construction [of personality and society].

(Yaroshevskii, 1985)

Yet, only a decade later (a decade that included the fall of the Berlin Wall, the collapse of the Soviet Union and the downfall of its Communist Party), another text by the same author came out. The change in the tonality is radical and startling. Here is a characteristic example of new discourse:

American psychologists borrowed the ideas of Russian researchers of behavior. But their paths considerably differed. To transform humankind as a whole being so that its biological set up (*"tvarnaia organizatsiia"*, in Russian original) would be driven by the highest spiritual values – that was the Russian over-precious idea (*"russkaia sverkhtsennaia ideia"*). A great historical task, it guided the minds of the naturalists to the service of the people, who were fighting against their slavery. This idea stirred these minds, in the country that was regarded as delayed and wild, to the creation of the innovative programs that would integrate the revolutionary events in biology. A holistic perspective on a human being, that was the over-task (*"sverkhzadacha"*) of Russian thought. The contradistinction between the sciences of the organism and the sciences of consciousness undermined the attempt to tackle this task. That was a dead-end. The exit was in the establishment of the science of behavior. . . . Russian thought that discovered the problem of behavior and created the categorical scheme of its development did not substitute either physiology or psychology with this problem. Russian thought was in search for the ways of integration of its discoveries with the historically developed categories that defined the object of research in these disciplines. Different was (under the influence of the philosophy of positivism) the strategy of the researchers of behavior in the United States. In this country, the reduction of behavior to the relation "stimulus – reaction" has led to the conception that this relation – as the core and the only equivalent of a strictly scientific psychology – must be devoid of both mentalist (i.e., directed to the subject's consciousness) and physiological "admixtures". [American] psychology, as it was said about its last leader B. F. Skinner, turned into the science of an "empty organism". But that was yet un-Russian way.

(Yaroshevskii, 1995)

This radical change in discourse certainly reflected the "wind of changes" and the post-*perestroika* mainstream Zeitgeist in Russian culture and society of this époque. Yet, having pronounced this, Yaroshevskii was one of the first in his country at the end of the 20th century to open the discussion of the "national question" and its impact on the "Russian style" in scientific research. The cited article of 1995 was followed by the 1996 publication of a book titled *The Science of Behavior:*

The Russian Way and authored by the same author (Yaroshevskii, 1996), who – along with his soul-mates and spiritual "soul-lovers" – seems to have opened the Pandora box. Indeed, this line of reasoning awoke the old demons and let them out, which has led to the proliferation of a wide range of conservative, isolation-ist, as well as religion- and ethnic-centric discussions and theories getting as far as proclaiming the "Russian Christian-Orthodox Psychology", some adherents and leaders of which belong to the older generations of the well-established formerly Soviet scholars of highest distinction, who have their strongholds even in the old-est and, presumably, the best national universities in St. Petersburg and Moscow (for instance, in Lomosov Moscow State University, the oldest and, according to all academic ratings, the most prestigious university in Russian Federation) (Bra-tus', 1995; Slobodchikov, 2019; Vasilyuk, 2015). Thus, for instance, a paper that came out recently in the Russian Psychological Society's and Psychology Faculty of Lomonosov Moscow State University's own *National Psychological Journal*, accord-ing to its English abstract, presents

> the first attempt to consider cultural and historical background of the new scientific direction of Christian psychology in the post-Soviet Russia. It shows the continuity of this trend with the works of the Tsar Russia period, and the connection with the works on the psychology of faith by foreign scientists. The reasons for reviving the interest in the psychological issues of spiritual development and religious outlook are described. Despite the fact that certain ideas and attitudes to the issues mentioned above appeared at the Soviet time, the possibility of the open movement arose only at the decline of Soviet ideology. The interest in the study of personality and individuality was increasing on a par with the issues of man's inner world, which is unthinkable without spiritual and religious aspects of human mind. The main milestones of Moscow school of Christian psychology development are highlighted: Seminar on Christian Psychology and Anthropology at the Department of Psychology, Lomonosov Moscow State University (1990), Laboratory of Philosophical and Psychological Foundations of Human Development (actually Christian psychology laboratory) at the Psychological Institute of RAS [i.e., Russian Academy of Sciences], new specialty "Psychology of Religion" at the Department of Psychology, Lomonosov Moscow State University (early 1990s), the first Russian edition of textbook "Christian Psychology" for high schools (1995), "Chelpanovskye readings" in the Psy-chological Institute of RAO [i.e., Russian Academy of Education], which touched on Christian issues. Several departments of the Institute of Educa-tional Innovations RAO start practicing Christian education and psychology. International conferences of the late 1990s – early 2000s on the psychology of religion and the implementation of other facts of the Christian ideas of psychology at educational and practical activities in Russia are mentioned.
>
> *(Bratus', 2015)*

The transformation of the former ardent and loyal "Marxist-Leninist psychologists" into the advocates of the distinctly spiritual "Russian way" in science and "Russian Orthodox psychologists" is truly remarkable, puzzling and startling. I am certainly not going to get into an in-depth analysis, a full-blown "deconstruction" of these two kinds of very dissimilar ideas, ideologies and discourses that implement them. This would be too long of a discussion, hardly of interest to the readers of this chapter, and is a research topic of its own. Yet, a couple of observations are in order concerning interesting and not so obvious similarities rather than apparent dissimilarities of these two texts and the ideology behind them. The first similarity is the authors' – such as Yaroshevskii and many others – emphasis on the uniqueness, excellence and idiosyncrasy of "our", domestic psychological thought whether it is framed in terms of the "unique path" of "progressive" Marxist-Leninist psychology of its Soviet interpretation or the distinctly and exclusively "Russian" science as a representation of a special kind of "innate spirituality" of the nation and the "mysterious Russian soul", which immediately brings us back to the 19th century with its Romantic and idealistic speculations about the "psychology of the nation", the *Völkerpsychologie*, in original German. This argument is vulnerable to pretty obvious criticism.

The "uniqueness" of the former – that is, the progressive and worldwide leading "Soviet Marxist psychology" – might well be disputed by the admirers of other variations of Marxism in psychology, for instance, those that developed under the influence of Antonio Gramsci in Italy, Georges Politzer and Henri Wallon in France and the francophone world, the philosophers of the Frankfurt School in Germany and German-speaking countries, or the Austrian version of psychological Marxism as it is represented in the work of Alfred Adler or Wilhelm Reich and their followers. Then, the uniqueness of the latter, namely, the "special spirituality" of the Russians can be easily undermined by a simple argument of arguably each nation's distinct historical pathway and cultural legacy, coupled with its own "spirit" and "spirituality", equally perplexing and mysterious. In fact, any variation of nationalism with its geopolitical, cultural and linguistic claims would firmly stand on the argument of this kind.

The second similarity between the two seemingly radically different positions is way more interesting, subtle and thought-provoking, though. This is the cluster of loosely interrelated ideas such as the teleological construction of personality; emphasis on the consciousness; rejection of the mechanically understood "cognition", "mind" or even "psyche" (in favor of the "spirit" or "soul"); and the image of people fighting against their "slavery" or suffering. All these seem to be the rudiments of the line of thinking with its roots in the post-Revolutionary 1920s, perhaps most notably exemplified by Vygotsky's utopian version of Soviet futuristic and avant-garde "science of Superman" (Yasnitsky, 2019b). This line of thinking, stripped from its utopian, idealistic and spiritualistic undertones, of course, is of considerable promise, it seems, and opens new horizons for meaningful and productive discussion of psychology's potential as contemporary scientific theoretical and practical activity in the context of the 21st century.

Yet, back to Yaroshevskii and his kind. Some people say, a life story and the actual deeds of a person truly complement his (or her) words. In this sense, the life story of Yaroshevskii was truly remarkable. Born in a provincial town Kherson in the southern Russian Empire in 1915 (Ukraine now), Yaroshevskii graduated and started his post-graduate studies under Sergei Rubinstein in Leningrad in 1937, then was briefly arrested, yet released in 1939 and defended his post-graduate thesis in Moscow in 1945. Following the launch of the anti-Semitic campaign in late 1940s, Yaroshevskii left Moscow for Soviet Central Asia and soon thereafter (a year before Joseph Stalin's death in 1953) published a couple of papers under the characteristic titles "Cybernetics, the science of obscurantists" and "The answer of I.P. Pavlov to American reactionary psychologists" (one can access these immortal monuments of later Stalinist discourse online). In the mid-1960s Yaroshevskii left Central Asia for Moscow, where he headed a department in the Institute of the History of Natural Sciences and Technology of the Academy of Sciences of the USSR and published the first edition of his *History of Psychology* (1966), the book that survived another two Soviet editions of 1976 and 1985: above, we have already enjoyed a quote from this text with the statement on the role of "Marxist-Leninist teaching" and "Communist construction" in the development of Soviet psychology. A contemporary Russian author claims that Yaroshevskii's *History of Psychology* "was the main textbook used for psychological education in Soviet universities" and that "all psychological education in the USSR, since the first faculties of psychology were opened in Moscow State University and Leningrad State University in 1966, was grounded on his books on history of psychology". Furthermore, this very author asserts that it was Yaroshevskii, who "laid the foundations of the Russian school of the history of psychology", but then, for unclear reason, regrets his obscurity to the non-Russian readers and, strangely enough, calls Western readership to study the scientific legacy of this classic of quasi-Marxist and highly dogmatic Soviet version of the history of this scientific discipline (Mironenko, 2016). In the 1980s, Yaroshevskii lauded the great and "progressive" Marxist-Leninist psychology and edited the six-volume "Collected Works of L.S. Vygotsky" that introduced systematic censorship and massive falsifications of the author's original text; for perhaps the most outrageous example of these falsifications that took place in Vygotsky's and Luria's "Tool and sign" see the meticulous textual analysis and critical discussion in (Van der Veer & Yasnitsky, 2016; Yasnitsky, 2017). Then, in 1990s he lamented the brutally "oppressed science" of the Soviet past; glorified the unique and mysterious "Russian way" of national psychology; and published, in 1993, a book on Vygotsky, which curiously reflected both his fascination with and transition from Marxism-Leninism and the triumph of distinctly Soviet science to the search of "Russian roots" in the pre-Revolutionary Imperial past of the so-called Silver Age of Russian culture. Finally, the last episode of this life story took place at the very end of the last century. People make their choices of the way they live and act. Yet, this was a strikingly "un-Russian way", as Yaroshevskii would say, indeed: just a couple of years after his "special Russian way" publication, in

1998, for health reasons Mikhail Yaroshevskii immigrated to the United States of America. There he died in 2001 in Los Angeles, California.

Generations and cultures of Soviet (and Russian) psychologists: mind the gap!

In retrospect, I have been long thinking about this seemingly magic and mysterious transformation of the entire framework of Soviet psychology that occurred within just a few years immediately preceding the collapse of the Soviet Union. I have already mentioned here a text titled "The archetype of Soviet psychology: From the Stalinism of the 1930s to the 'Stalinist science' of our time" (Yasnitsky, 2016). The author presents his discussion of what he refers to as the "Stalin model of science" that was firmly established at the end of 1930s in the Soviet Union and, despite a series of reforms and mutations, has allegedly remained in many respects in the social, institutional and intellectual make-up of science in contemporary Russian Federation to these very days. The main argument runs along the lines of analysis of the demography of Soviet psychologists in the 20th century, particularly, with respect to their control over power and intellectual agenda in this scholarly discipline in the Soviet Union. Yet, I would like to make a point that the "demographic argument" is not uniquely Yasnitsky's invention. Thus, a famous paper comes to my mind. This is Stephen Toulmin's book review about Lev Vygotsky characteristically (and very conveniently for some of his early advocates and proponents of his legacy) titled "The Mozart of Psychology" (Toulmin, 1978), used in support of the claim of "Vygotsky the genius", frequently cited, but seemingly never read. In this paper, Toulmin touches upon a "generation gap" in Soviet psychology that emerged in 1935–1955, and this is exactly when the new scholarly tradition got established.

Similarly, the author of "The archetype of Soviet psychology: From the Stalinism of the 1930s to the 'Stalinist science' of our time" follows a contemporary historian of Soviet science Nikolai Krementsov and claims that "Stalinist science" (Krementsov, 1997) – or, somewhat milder put somewhere else, the "Stalin model of science" (Yasnitsky, 2015) – gradually developed in the Soviet Union from late 1920s and was eventually solidified and inaugurated by 1939 with an openly symbolic act: on December 22, 1939, Joseph Stalin was elected an Honorary Member of the Academy of Sciences of the USSR. The model as such was established and institutionalized in Soviet academia mostly by the representatives of the older pre-Revolutionary generation of Soviet scholars, born at the end of 19th–beginning of the 20th century and bearers of the "old-school" scholarly traditions, such as good gymnasium education, knowledge of a few foreign languages and high academic standards of international science. A few of them would have completed their university education abroad: these are the cases of highly prominent "old-school" Soviet psychologists of the 20th century such as Sergei Rubinstein (1889–1960) and Dimitri Uznadze (alias Usnadze, 1886–1950), who wrote and defended their doctoral dissertations in philosophy in Germany before WWI.

Then, the author argues that the continuity of this "Stalin model" tradition to these very days was safeguarded by the "generation of the 1920s-30s": that would, more precisely, include the individuals born in the second half of 1920s and the first half of 1930s. Born in the interwar period between WWI and WWII, they were mostly young enough to be drafted in the army and perish at the war, but sufficiently grown-up to take school studies – very much weakened, disrupted and deficient in many ways due to the war situation behind the front lines or, even worse, in the evacuation (e.g., to the regions of the Urals, Central Asia, Volga region, etc.). Then, this very generation would graduate from universities and complete their doctoral studies in the Late Stalinism and early Cold War era and typically have virtually no knowledge of foreign languages and have minimal familiarity with international science. One of the major formative experiences for this generation of young Soviet scholars was the V.I. Lenin All-Union Academy of Agricultural Sciences of the Soviet Union (the VASKhNIL) Session of August, 1948 and its aftermath: this was a major event in the history of the whole Soviet science that established the new ground rules of the game and reset the "social contract" between the scientific community in the Soviet Union and the state's power. It further enforced the state-party control over scientific research; introduced the de facto mandatory assumed national priority in virtually all scientific disciplines and the cult of ethnically Russian "Founding Fathers" in scientific disciplines; and reinterpreted the three-fold requirement of the "Marxsism", "party-ness" and the "practicality" in science (Krementsov, 1997).

Perhaps the most important episode in the history of Soviet psychology of this period was the "Pavlovization" of this academic discipline and scholarly community that took place in 1950–1951 during a couple of official public events at the highest administrative level of administration in Soviet human science: the Academy of Sciences, the Academy of Medical Sciences (June–July, 1950), the All-Union Society of Neuropathologists and Psychiatrists (October, 1951) and the Academy of Pedagogical Sciences (March, 1952). Another major factor that considerably shaped social thought during this period was an unofficial, yet effective (and, unfortunately, very much efficient) state-sponsored Anti-Semitism and, on the other hand, neo-Imperial Russian chauvinism in all spheres of social life, behaviors and practices, especially in personnel selection, university admission and hiring policies (Krementsov, 1997).

This might have been yet another exercise of their survival skills for the mature and experienced representatives of the "old-school" high-ranking Soviet psychologists, but at the same time it was definitely the most considerable formative experience for the younger generation of scholars. They got enculturated within the characteristic Stalin model of science of the era and would earnestly perpetuate it well into the subsequent decades to come, until the very end of the Soviet Union in 1991. This way it turned out that the next generation of Soviet psychologists would pick up this idiosyncratic "ethos of Stalinist science" in their university years and post-graduate early careers and would continue the tradition into the post-Soviet era after their overtake of top administrative positions in psychological institutions of various sorts from the mid-1960s up until roughly the end of the 1980s.

This is how the author's argument goes. To this, I would add that perhaps the most characteristic example of a career of a "late Stalinist generation" was the life path of Boris Lomov (1927–1989), a researcher in industrial psychology (and related fields), high-ranking state-party bureaucrat and the "big boss" of the official Soviet psychology of its last period, who, according to a 1985 Western publication, concentrated all administrative power and control over this field of knowledge in the USSR in his hands and whose closest associates and allies determined and shaped virtually the entire intellectual landscape of Soviet psychology in the 1980s:

> Professor Boris Lomov acts like a man in charge – and, in fact, he is. Since the deaths of Luria and Leont'ev in the last decade [in 1977 and in 1979, respectively], Lomov has become the most powerful Soviet psychologist. In Western terms, he is "Mr. Psychology"; in the Soviet Union, as one of his Russian colleagues told me, "He is now a figure." Not only is he the chairman of the Soviet Psychological Society but he is also the director of the influential Academy of Sciences Institute of Psychology, located in Moscow. He organized a principal scientific journal (*Journal of Psychology*) in psychology and serves as its editor. His research and books (especially Man and technology) are widely read and cited in the USSR.
>
> *(Solso, 1985)*

Another telling characterization was given in Lomov's obituary that came out in the journal *American Psychologist* in 1991:

> Lomov was a controversial figure. Some disagreed bitterly with his strong management of psychology in the USSR. Others remember Lomov as an individual who, out of his own sheer strength of character and personal determination and dedication, built USSR psychology into its present state.
>
> *(Solso & Brushlinsky, 1991)*

Personally, I find this depiction quite adequate and mostly true to how it appeared to me, an eye-witness and the contemporary of those historical events and processes. Furthermore, I would like to extend this line of reasoning and reflect on the next generation of Soviet scholars (specifically, psychologists), the one to which I belong myself. This is a postwar generation of those born in 1945–1955 or so, who graduated between 1967 and 1977 (this decade includes the first graduates of the fully independent Departments of Psychology that were officially launched for the first time in the Soviet Union in Moscow and Leningrad State Universities in 1966) and – those of them, who would subsequently make their careers in the academia – typically defended their Candidate of Sciences dissertations by the early 1980s. Thus, the model is perfectly reflected in the life paths of the earlier-mentioned contemporary advocates of "Russian Orthodox Christian Psychology" – Boris Bratus, Viktor Slobodchikov and Fyodor Vasilyuk – all three former students of the "old-school" classics of Soviet Marxist psychology such as the renowned Bluma Zeigarnik (1901–1988), Aleksei N. Leontiev (1903–1979) and Daniil El'konin (1904–1984). In terms of political standpoint, the intelligentsia of this generation was quite loyal and obedient. No doubt, among us there were a few furious dissidents highly critical of the state-party regime of the USSR as well as, on the other hand, a few individuals were (or presented themselves as) militant and zealous supporters of the ruling order. From my experience, the representatives of both extremes would be perceived with caution and suspicion, albeit for different reasons. Nevertheless, despite all their sincere or demonstrative loyalty and political correctness, the majority of the representatives of my generation (among Soviet intelligentsia, at least) clearly saw the hypocrisy and demagoguery of official propaganda with its proclamations of the "next generation of Soviet people living in Communism", the "new Soviet man" of our mundane "advanced socialism", and the progressive role of the Communist Party of the Soviet Union in the social progress and the triumph of the "invincible doctrine of Marxism – Leninism". Yet, all references to the founders of Marxism – Leninism were being duly, sometimes ironically and somewhat cynically made on the first pages of published works, wherever – and until – necessary and unavoidable.

In 1991 the Union of Soviet Socialist Republics collapsed. All formal and hypocritical references to Marxist authors in psychological publications were not considered as mandatory anymore, and therefore were swiftly dropped, seemingly forever. Yet, we still have unfinished business here, it seems. One is once again tempted to quote from Stephen Toulmin's "The Mozart of Psychology":

> unless behavioral scientists in the West begin to develop a more general theoretical frame of their own which has something approaching the scope and integrative power that "historical materialism" has had for the Russians, our own arguments are doomed (I believe) to remaining split down the middle. On the one hand, there will be those who see all human behavior as one more phenomenon of Nature: who are concerned, that is, to discover in human behavior only "general laws," dependent on universal, ahistorical processes and so free of all cultural variability. On the other hand, there will be those who see Culture as a distinct and entirely autonomous field of study, set over against Nature: a field within which diversity and variety are the rule, and "general laws" are not to be looked for. For myself, I find this continued polarization a depressing prospect. It was fair enough, at the turn of the century, to press the special claims of the *Geisteswissenschaften* (or "moral sciences"), if only as a counter to the vulgar, mechanical materialism of much earlier non-Marxian thought. Today, however, many of the most important and fascinating questions about behavior – whether within developmental

psychology or psycholinguistics, epistemology or moral philosophy – arise precisely at the boundaries between Nature and Culture, and so between the natural sciences and the moral sciences.

(Toulmin, 1978)

Thus, it appears we now have all reasons and motivation for a revision of the Soviet (and Russian) case of psychology in its century-long desperate and lonely search for Marxism.

Marxist psychology: back to the future

It is common knowledge that the slogan of Marxist psychology was introduced in this country in the early 1920s by Pavel Blonskii (1884–1941) and Konstanin Kornilov (1879–1957), the students and once allies of Georgii Chelpanov (1862–1936), a pre-Revolutionary proponent of experimental Wundtian psychology as an "objective" and independent (from either philosophy or physiology) scientific discipline, who was the founding director of the Institute of Psychology in the Imperial Moscow University (Kozulin, 1985; Radzikhovskii, 1982). During the first post-Revolutionary years Chelpanov strongly resisted the idea of psychology determined by any philosophy whatsoever, but later gradually softened his views and offered his view on a possibility of Marxist psychology, although limited by the relatively narrow confines of social psychology only (Chelpanov, 1924). Regardless of true intentions of Chelpanov in his public support of Marxist social psychology and criticism of the possibility of implementation of Marxists principles in all other spheres of psychological theory and research, the first attempts at the establishment of an overarching Marxist psychology by his opponents seem to confirm the rationale of his critical stance. In the works of Kornilov, Blonskii and their associates the findings of the concrete psychological investigations, their goals, methods and experimental data interpretations existed independently of the proclaimed Marxist principles and notions, such as the determination of the social consciousness by social life conditions, reflexive function of the psyche, social nature of human being, etc. In terms of rhetoric and style, the two domains and their discourses existed by themselves. The connection between them was established rhetorically only and through the logically unnecessary conjunction "and". The philosophical part of these works and their concrete psychological content had very different functions, served different purposes and were formulated with the use of very dissimilar vocabulary. The philosophical and the concrete psychological aspects of analysis remained effectively autonomous.

Yet there was also certain positive effect of the first works of self-proclaimed Soviet Marxist psychologists. These first attempts at implementation of Marxism in psychology brought awareness to the acuteness of the problematic juxtaposition of the two aspects of analysis. This key methodological problem was subsequently addressed in the late 1920s–early 1930s in works of Lev Vygotsky and Sergei

Rubinstein. Both formulated their understanding of this problem and demonstrated the potential impact of Marxism on the future development of Soviet psychology. Unfortunately, their methodological quest did not receive proper development in the subsequent period. Thus, in the mid-1970s, Aleksei N. Leontiev wrote:

> It is necessary, however, to acknowledge that in the following years the attention of psychological science to *methodological* problems weakened somewhat. This, of course, does not mean in any way that theoretical questions became of less concern, or that less was written about them. I have something else in mind: the acknowledged *carelessness in methodology* of many concrete psychological investigations, including those in applied psychology. . . . They almost leave an impression of dichotomy: On the one hand there is the sphere of philosophical – psychological problematics, and on the other, the sphere of specific psychological, methodological questions arising in the course of concrete investigations (emphasis added, Leontiev, 1975, pp. 2–3). [Furthermore, there appears] an illusion of "*demethodologizing*" of the sphere of concrete research results, which increases even more the impression of a breaking up of the internal connections between fundamental theoretical Marxist bases for psychological science and its accumulation of facts.
>
> *(Leontiev, 1975, p. 4)*[1]

Leontiev's assessment of the state of the art in Soviet psychology in the mid-1970s, curiously enough, well resonates with Stephen Toulmin's opinion that he expressed in the mentioned essay "The Mozart of Psychology". In 1978, Toulmin exclaimed apparently in astonishment, "just as Western psychology is beginning to escape from its earlier positivism, Russian academic psychology is, ironically, beginning to look more like the American experimental psychology of the intervening forty years!" (Toulmin, 1978).

Facts, theory and philosophy: interrelations and "disconnections"

Running the risk of yet further sharpening these acute criticisms, one might come to the following conclusions. First, Marxist psychology and its initial yet intense development should be dated 1920s–1930s, but in the 1940s–1970s (not to mention the *perestroika* of 1980s, even less the subsequent three decades of post-*perestroika*, post-Communist and post-Soviet period) no considerable progress in this direction was achieved. Indeed so, and it is no surprise that Soviet psychologists (and contemporary Russian ones and their traditionalist peers abroad) keep persistently

---

1 The translation of 1975 introduced an error: the word "demythologizing" was used instead of "demethodologizing" (*demetodologizatsiia*), as it stands in the original Russian. The mistake along with a couple other relatively minor ones have been duly corrected here.

returning to the works of Lev Vygotsky and Sergei Rubinstein, written almost a century ago in the 1920s–1930s. Similarly, in the West, the call to the return to the Marxist ideas of "historical materialism" sounds as contemporary and challenging as it sounded in Toulmin's proposal that

> unless behavioral scientists in the West begin to develop a more general theoretical frame of their own which has something approaching the scope and integrative power that "historical materialism" has had for the Russians, our own arguments are doomed (I believe) to remaining split down the middle.
>
> *(Toulmin, 1978)*

It is obvious that no solutions were found in the works of Soviet and Russian psychologists to these challenges of psychological methodology and theoretical problems that would approach in magnitude to the proposals of Soviet scholars such as Rubinstein and Vygotsky. Quite a different matter is how one should assess some of the proposed solutions and theories available to date. In these, some might see a logically accomplished implementation (or implementations) of a Marxist methodology in psychology; on the other hand, others might regard these only as first attempts to the solution of the problem.

Second, it seems that the actual understanding of the interconnections, in Leontiev's terms, between "philosophical – psychological problematics" and the contemporary "sphere of specific psychological, methodological questions arising in the course of concrete investigations" still remains extremely poor and is in fact reduced to *illustrating* the famous Marxist ideas by concrete psychological empirical data. The "disconnection" of the ties between the facts and the philosophical foundations of psychology means that facts seemingly can be obtained and meaningfully interpreted in psychological terms regardless of the related philosophical theory. Yet then it is not clear: in what sense can a philosophical theory count as a "foundation" for these facts? This is a central question.

In psychology, as well as in other sciences, a theory is nothing else but an instrument for obtaining and explaining the facts (Fleck, 1979). In this sense, any working and valid theory is interrelated with the facts, and there can be no "disconnection": facts can contradict a theory, but theory, by definition, cannot exist regardless of an array of facts, the foundation of which this theory is. The whole history of psychology illustrates such interrelation between theory and facts: each major psychological theory (for instance, Gestalt psychology, psychoanalysis, etc.) is rigidly bound with a very distinct set of facts. Thus, there can be a confirmation or refutation along the line "facts – theory", but there can be no theory which does not produce any facts whatsoever. Speculations that, in principle, do not lead to facts do not qualify as a scientific theory.

Yet, a whole different issue is the connection of a concrete scientific theory and philosophy. A world view or a philosophical system does not directly and automatically lead to any concrete scientific system. The connection along the line "philosophy – concrete science" is way less rigid and straightforward than the connection between theory and facts within the frontiers of a concrete scientific discipline. Each concrete theory (and inseparably related to it hypotheses and facts) certainly can be interpreted in the context of this or that philosophical system.

However, one is not allowed to *directly* assume (or deny the possibility of) the existence of facts or *directly* produce scientific theories, hypotheses, etc. only on the grounds that a specific philosophical system has been adopted. For instance, there is a fact: mind-body (alternatively, psychophysical or psychophysiological) correlation. A dualist philosopher interprets it as the evidence of psychophysiological parallelism, whereas a monist would see it as the evidence of the unity of the world. Then, there is a fact of psychosocial correlations (interactions), such as, for instance, conformity. A dualist would regard it as psychosocial parallelism and the preordained alienation of a person and social world. In contrast, a monist would interpret the fact as the unity of a person with their own psyche (mind) and the larger society. Thus, the interrelations between philosophy and specific scientific theory (or even scientific movement) are not relations of content *generation*, but the relations of meaningful *interpretation*. These are not internal (intrinsic), but external (extrinsic) relations. For instance, among psychoanalysts there have been those who would identify themselves as Marxists and advocate for psychoanalysis (or post-Freudian tradition in general) as a variation of Marxist psychology. On the other hand, there have been those Freudians (or Sigmund Freud's actual or former followers) who have been the opponents and even contenders of Marxist ideas in psychology. Similarly, there have many among Marxist philosophers who consider the post-Freudianism as compatible or incompatible with Marxism. These interpretations notwithstanding, all of them operate the same set of facts and the same theory, the dissimilarity between them being the idiosyncratic differences in the interpretation of the facts.

Therefore, the adoption of a philosophical system alone does not automatically lead to the adoption of specific psychological theory as an instrument for the production or refutation of facts, but it can only facilitate or, or the contrary, hinder the interpretation and, thus, adoption of scientific theories and facts as those "confirming" or "contradicting" the given philosophical system. This means that there is a real objective possibility of certain "disconnection" – yet it exists along the line "concrete psychological theory – Marxist philosophy". Hence follows a question: to what extent can this "disconnection" be minimized?

Vocabulary and phraseology of psychology and philosophy

In my opinion, one of the main reasons for the gap between philosophy and psychological theory and practice is the *fundamental difference in the vocabularies* (therefore, the problematics) *of philosophy and psychology*. An utterance, a statement has psychological sense and belongs to psychological discourse when it directly expresses a certain conscious or unconscious subjective state (or lived-through experience) or when this very statement – even if indirectly – correlates with a subjective lived-through experience (for instance, the principles of psychophysics, social-psychological patterns, etc.).

The wealth of subjective states and lived-through experiences (*Erlebnis* in German, *perezhivanie* in Russian, etc.) reflected in the corresponding vocabulary and phraseology constitute cumulatively the basis and the true essence of distinct *discourse* of the discipline of psychology. On the other hand, philosophers have not properly discussed and interpreted all the potential richness of Marxist philosophy in its contribution to the problems of subjective lived-through experiences: no Marxist philosophical anthropology has been established, and the notion of subjective lived-through experience has not found its place in the system of discourse of our philosophy. That is the main reason why the transition from Marxist philosophy to psychological theory is particularly difficult, keeping in mind that direct extrapolation of philosophical ideas on psychological theory is impossible. The task is, thus, to discover some other, indirect way of transition from Marxist philosophy, the *dialectical materialism*, to psychological theory.

It was Lev Vygotsky, who as early as in the 1920s clearly understood that here lies the very essence of the establishment of Marxist psychology – or, for that matter, any other scientific discipline – in the making:

> The *direct* application of the theory of *dialectical materialism* to the problems of natural science and in particular to the group of biological sciences or psychology is *impossible*, just as it is *impossible* to apply it directly to history and sociology. . . . Like history, sociology is in need of the intermediate *special theory* of historical materialism which explains the *concrete* meaning, for the given group of phenomena, of the abstract laws of dialectical materialism. In exactly the same way we are in need of an as yet undeveloped but inevitable theory of biological materialism and psychological materialism as an intermediate science which explains the concrete application of the abstract theses of dialectical materialism to the given field of phenomena.
>
> *(Vygotsky, 1997a, p. 330)*

Each psychological theory obviously has a set of notions that it uses to express, describe and investigate its object, and each theory's terminology is different. Yet, following Vygotsky's logic, the goal of Marxist psychology is to establish a *new system of notions* that would include those with real psychological meaning and those that reflect the key principles of Marxist philosophy. This requires not the mechanical conjunction with the help of quotations (within formally same psychological discourse) of philosophical and psychological notions that have in principle different sense, but the discovery of their "lowest common denominator" and meaningful translation of philosophical notions into the useful terminological toolkit of psychology. This, in turn, requires a major reconstruction of the entire discourse of psychological science. In other words, this implies the establishment of the special conceptual apparatus, or *metadiscourse*, which would integrate two discourses: that of psychology and of Marxist philosophy. The most important challenge, though, is the genuine integration, the establishment of new interconnections, the emergence of a logically homogenous system of a new scientific discourse.

Pioneers of Marxist psychology of the 1920s–1930s advocated for the reinterpretation of this scientific discipline into a logically homogenous system that would, by virtue of applying general and universal scientific laws, unite all psychological theories and explain all their phenomena and facts. Frankly, this somewhat utopian goal is still quite far from its realization. The topic of the "crisis in psychology" is not very popular among academic psychologists, as the "crisis" seems to have turned into the norm of the "psychologies" of our days (Diriwächter & Valsiner, 2008; Toomela & Valsiner, 2010). Apparently, the time for universal theories and psychological laws – those that the pioneers of Marxist psychology were dreaming about and those that would integrate all these "psychologies" into a unified scientific discipline of Psychology – has not come yet.

In my opinion, one of the paths for the search of the solution is the already mentioned idea: the *development of metadiscourse* that would integrate the philosophical notions and the psychological ones. The historical heritage of Soviet and Russian psychology in its search for general psychological system reveals great heuristic potential for the intellectual work in this direction. Let us consider just two examples: the theory of Lev Vygotsky and the theory of Aleksei N. Leontiev. Yet, let us keep in mind that a great potential can also be found in a few other Soviet attempts at creating a unified general psychology such as the theories of Sergei Rubinstein, Dimitri Uznadze and Vladimir Miasischev. All these excellent psychologists, prominent in the Soviet Union albeit virtually unknown nowadays in the West, had their distinct and equally interesting variations of this idea realization.

In search of solution: Vygotsky's attempt

Lev Vygotsky proceeded from one of the most foundational principles of Marxist philosophy, according to which the essence of humans is not inherently individual, but collective, a reflection of the sum total of social relations. In his attempt to reformulate this principle in psychological discourse, Vygotsky wrote:

> Paraphrasing the well-known thesis of Marx, we could say that the psychological nature of human being represents the totality of social relations transferred inside and turned into functions of the personality and the forms of the structure of personality. We do not want to say that this is exactly the meaning of Marx's postulate, but we see in this postulate the fullest expression of everything that the history of cultural development leads us to.
>
> *(Vygotskii, 1983, p. 146)*

True, yet one is tempted to wonder how exactly we can understand and describe the "totality of social relations transferred inside and turned into functions of the personality", given that social relations are expressed in terms of one kind of discourse and "psychological functions" are expressed in another kind of discourse, the two being very different in principle. And a further question emerges as to how one can establish any correspondence between the two kinds of discourse.

There is a way to establish the external, objective correlations that would demonstrate how psychological processes change depending on the social factors. Curiously, these abstract *factors* are way more concrete than also abstract *social relations*. But such a mechanistically performed demonstration of the correlation of parallelism between the social and the psychological gives no clear way of understanding the internal "sociality" of the mind and its structure, the social essence of human psyche, or what is the totality of social relations transferred "inside" human mind. It also certainly does not lead to the development of the mediating metadiscourse.

In order to translate the category of "social relations" into the discourse of psychology, Vygotsky in fact makes two substitutions. First, he changes "social relations" into "interpersonal relations": psychological "functions initially are formed in a collective in the form of relations between the children, then they become psychological functions of the personality" (Vygotskii, 1983, pp. 146–147). Second, he postulates that there is a special process, the process of "interiorization" (alias: "internalization"), the outcome of which is the transfer of the structure of the interpersonal relations that occurs inside the human psyche (i.e., in Vygotsky's terms, the same as a psychological function that exists "between people" in the inter-psychic, or inter-mental plane). Somewhere else Vygotsky occasionally described this schematic process as "growing inside", "in-growing" or the emergence of "intrapsychological" processes from "interpsychological" ones.

These linguistic manipulations allowed Vygotsky to narrow the gap between "social relations" and "psychological functions": "The mechanism itself that forms the basis of higher psychological functions is a mold from the social. . . . Even left all alone, a human preserves the functions of [interpersonal] communication" (Vygotskii, 1983, p. 146).[2] In other words, as the foundation for his general psychological metadiscourse in the making Vygotsky utilized the notion of "interpersonal communication": *obschenie*, in Russian, a cognate word of a same-root adjective *obschii* that means "common" with its implicit connotation of "community", "communal", "communication", etc., but, importantly, completely unrelated to "Communism" – *kommunizm*, in Russian. Vygotsky's "interpersonal communication", *obschenie* is, by the way, equally unrelated to and far from another politically charged notion, the idiosyncratic "Soviet commune" or "Soviet community", which is rendered in Russian with just one word *kollektiv*, "a collective" in English.

---

2 These quotes were translated from the Russian original. The reason is obvious: the comparison between the original and the published English translation available in its edition of 1997 revealed considerable distortions and digressions from the real meaning of the original. For the sake of comparison see the corresponding places in (Vygotsky, 1997b, pp. 106–107).

Alternatively, one may legitimately interpret this notion of "interpersonal communication" in terms of "dialogue": an originally Greek word composed, in turn, of two other Greek words *dia* and famously extremely reach in its semantics *logos*, meaning "through" or "by means of" (the former) and the wide range of "word", "speech", "discourse", "account", "opinion", "reason", "plea", "expectation", "ground" and "proportion" (the latter). Quite erroneously, this word, "dialogue", is sometimes interpreted as stemming from "two" (and on this ground contrasted to the monstrous "polylogue" as a dialogue between more than two persons) or related to "dialectics", which in essence has nothing in common with "communicating" or "interpersonal exchange" – at least, in its meaning as it is used in philosophy.

Then, taking for granted the "interpersonal communication" (*obschenie*) or "dialogue" as a foundation of new psychological metadiscourse, one is legitimately allowed to establish the following continuity of notions: social relations – interpersonal relations – "interpersonal communication" – internal dialogue. Internal dialogue is, thus, an individual psychological equivalent of the totality of all social relations, following Vygotsky's logic. For justice's sake, tracing Vygotsky's logic to its historical roots, we cannot but acknowledge Vygotsky's fundamental dependence on the age-old Romantic tradition of Continental thought and give the credit for this line of reasoning and the ideas on "dialogue", "inner speech" and, furthermore, the essentially dialogic nature of language to the German philosophical-philological tradition originated with the great intellectual and state's servant Wilhelm von Humboldt (1767–1835) and the subsequent linguistic, psychological and philosophical tradition. This tradition came down to Vygotsky through the mediation of his compatriots such as Aleksandr Potebnia (1835–1891) and Lev Yakubinskii (1895–1945) (Bertau, 2014a; Naumova, 2004; Van der Veer & Zavershneva, 2018).

It is important to point out that dialogue does not have to be exclusively a verbal exchange: neither exchange (e.g., in case of inner speech) nor the use of words is its defining feature. Indeed, following Vygotsky's logic, dialogism is a universal phenomenon characteristic of any psychological process, including non-verbal ones, and this is the common structural foundation of all psychological phenomena. This postulate, though, was not expressed by Vygotsky with unambiguous clarity and is the result of some kind of "advancement" and interpretation of his views on psychology as they were presented in the most mature period of his thinking, roughly a few months before his death in 1934 (Radzikhovskii, 1991). Yet, it seems, this interpretation is quite legitimate and has very interesting perspectives in contemporary context (Bertau, 2014b). This approach orients academic research towards theoretical and experimental investigation of hidden dialogical dimensions of psychological processes. Then, in the field of clinical and applied psychology and psychotherapy, a practically positive outcome of research and practice can be achieved by artificial unfolding of a psychological process into a dialogue, the "splitting of what is now [i.e., in the structure of a given psychological phenomenon] merged into a unity [i.e., each psychological phenomenon is intrinsically a 'dialogical unit'], the experimental unfolding of a higher psychological process into the drama that occurs among people" (Vygotskii, 1983, p. 145).

However, despite the promise of this approach that seems to open new pathways into psychological research in terms of a "dialogical science", this innovation first needs to meet quite a number of challenges in order to turn into a full-fledged program of mainstream psychological investigations. Among these challenges is the establishment of a typology of dialogues as verbal and non-verbal as well as more or less reduced and developed (along the scale of external – internal), etc. Furthermore, the "dialogical discourse" requires an analysis as such. Specifically, one could argue that dialogue in principle does not allow for a formal logical description and analysis on the grounds that such kind of analysis inevitably annihilates the psychological essence of a dialogue. Were this assumption correct, the problem arises of the interrelation of dialogical discourse with any "normal" scientific discourse that is presumably constructed in agreement with the laws of formal logic (Radzikhovskii, 1991).

One final remark on Vygotsky's "dialogism" is in order. Despite the heuristic promise of this program of research and theoretical generalization, it was neither accepted nor realized in the history of Soviet psychology. Furthermore, very different authors (including Leontiev) criticized Vygotsky exactly for his innovation and axiomatic basis. First, he was criticized for substituting social relations with the interpersonal ones. This was interpreted as the deviation from a specifically Marxist approach on the grounds that interpersonal relations are studied by all those who regard them as an expression of the social nature of psychological functioning of people. These researchers include psychologists, anthropologists, sociologists, etc., and, even worse (in the opinion of Vygotsky's critics), not necessarily of Marxist creed. One is free to believe that interpersonal relations embody and express social relations, otherwise, to altogether disregard any social relations whatsoever in the Marxian sense – in either scenario the analysis of interpersonal relations in terms of a dialogue (expressed, or rather implied in Vygotsky's writings) remains unaffected and intact. Therefore, in the transition from "social relations" to "interpersonal relations" the distinctly Marxist dimension is lost and there occurs the "disconnection" of philosophical and psychological discourses. Vygotsky's second assumption was also criticized. It concerned the notion of "interiorization" (or "internalization") that Vygotsky merely postulated as a real psychological process and illustrated its outcomes, but never conducted full-fledged concrete psychological studies on the internal dynamics and the mechanisms of this alleged psychological process.

Leontiev's "Marxist alternative"

In many ways on the basis of the criticisms towards Vygotsky's theorizing, Aleksei N. Leontiev developed his variation of a Marxist psychology: the so-called general psychological theory of activity. One specific Marx's postulate played the key role for Leontiev, who grounded his theory in its interpretation and translation in psychological terms. This idea is expressed by Marx's famous dictum that "the history of *industry* and the *objective* existence of industry as it has developed is the *open* book of the *essential powers of man*, man's *psychology* present in tangible form" (Marx, 1992, p. 354).

However, this "open book", as it was presented in Marx's works, was written in social-economic terms. The task was, thus, to translate it into the discourse of psychology without losses in its contents and meaning, or, in other words, to create a metadiscourse that would integrate the objectivist-economic discourse with the subjectivist-psychological one.

Leontiev introduced the notion of "psychological activity" (that in many ways reflected and corresponded with Marx's socio-economic notion of "labour") and made an attempt to develop the metadiscourse on the basis of this notion. Activity is an organic system that includes a subject (i.e. a person, an individual) and an object of his or her activity. According to Leontiev, an interchange occurs between the subject and the object in the course of activity. Leontiev criticized the traditional psychology of his time for separating the subject from activity and treating the subject and the object as separate entities. Instead, Leontiev advocated for viewing the subject within the system of inseparable unity of subject – object interrelations within activity. From this methodological standpoint the entire psychology would be reconceptualized and reinterpreted in terms of the "metadiscourse of activity". This would allow developing a new, objective method of psychological research and revealing undiscovered, systemic properties of human psychological performance. The idea appeared splendid in plan, yet it stumbled upon the same old problem as the one that had earlier challenged Vygotsky. The problem was how exactly one can describe "psychological activity" in perfectly psychological terms in order to avoid yet another "psycho-activity" parallelism.

Activity as a general scientific category is not exclusively and specifically psychological one, since it denotes human social activity in general, which is not an attribute of an individual, but a universal unity considerably broader that the totality of individual actors and their actions. Thus, it is not the individual actors who produce activity, but on the contrary, it is social activity that involves individuals and urges them to act in certain ways. From this standpoint, a description of psychological processes as those involved in activity means, therefore, to deprive psychology of its genuinely psychological meaning and to establish a very different field of knowledge that might be referred to as "praxeology", or the "science of activity". When I first expressed this idea in Russian more than 30 years ago (Radzikhovskii, 1988), I could have hardly anticipated how true it would eventually turn out at the end of the second decade of the 21st century (Spinuzzi, 2019).

Yet, how is one supposed to express in psychological terms the discourse that describes activity? One option is to focus on an individual's activity, and, then, for the sake of the analysis of the individual's actual activity, on the person's subjective lived-through experiences, intentions, motives, etc. In this case, one is bound to eventually get back to the traditional empirical psychology that uses the notion of "motive" in order to describe a vague intermediary variable that presumably determines the behavior of a human. The quintessentially Marxist distinction of the activity approach immediately disappears hereby.

Leontiev made an attempt to explain and overcome this contradiction. As a psychologist, he appealed to the activity of an individual that is determined by a motive. Yet, the motive as such is interpreted, according to Leontiev, not from the traditional, subjective vantage point. He idiosyncratically interpreted psychological terminology and, fully in accordance with the principle of the inseparable unity of the subject and the object of activity, proposed to consider the object of activity as its genuine motive. Leontiev wrote: "According to the terminology I have proposed, the object of an activity is its true motive" (Leontiev, 1975, p. 62).

However, Leontiev is quite right when he points out that he merely "proposed terminology". The real problem remained. It makes no problem to juxtapose the words "motive" and "object" and equate one with the other in principle, but one cannot stop just here and claim an established metadiscourse that would integrate the discourses of the "psychologies" and the "praxeologies" (or any other scientific discipline that describes and studies the objective processes of social activity).

Leontiev's students clearly realized this problem. For instance, it was Lidia Bozhovich (1908–1981), Vygotsky's former student and long-time collaborator of Leontiev from the 1920s and 1930s, who critically and sarcastically observed:

> Generally, in Leontiev's conception – as well as in the speculations of many other psychologists – the issue of the analysis of distinctly psychological process . . . – that is, the process of their transition into qualitatively new forms – has remained beyond the scope of his discussion. He attempts to solve this problem in the abstract-theoretical plane, with the use of the arguments of *istmat* [i.e. "historical materialism"] in those instances when he has not enough concrete psychological data. And this can be easily explained given that there are only a few experimental studies in this field of knowledge in which he could have grounded his work.
>
> *(Bozhovich, 1972, p. 12)*

The criticism of Bozhovich reveals two important issues and acute problems with Leontiev's approach and achievement. First, Leontiev's writings abound with quasi-Marxist abstract speculations, "the arguments of *istmat*", instead of systematic psychological theoretical work. Second, Bozhovich was an experimental developmental psychologist specifically interested in motivational and volitional spheres of personality development in children and adolescents. Leontiev's excessive *istmat* speculations, in her view, reflected the fundamental deficiency of well-developed distinct methodology of scientific research and the studies of "psychological activity" conducted on its basis.

The criticisms of the kind give a hint at some relatively vague perspectives of the future development of a truly organic system of new psychological discourse, in which the psychological motive, the object of activity and subjective image would correspond as the notions of the same order and dimension and would equally be based on subjective lived-through experiences. Yet, in the classic version of Leontiev's "activity theory" (as it is known now) the "disconnection" between the two discourses remained largely unacknowledged and undetermined: the objective description of activity exists in Leontiev's (and a few of his "activity theory" followers' texts) by itself and separated from the subjective description of psychological processes and internal psychological world exists by itself.

Thus, we have just covered the two specific attempts at the establishment of Marxist theory in Soviet psychology. Although neither of the two achieved the higher global goals their authors claimed they would, the studies of both Vygotsky and Leontiev and their associates produced non-trivial results and provoked considerable intellectual stir among psychologists worldwide. The negative outcomes of their work can be attributed mainly to the only reason: the imprecise, exaggerated depiction of these historical figures and their legacies, and the canonization and dogmatization of their scholarship. This is what objectively restrains and slows down the solution of the truly historical task of eventually establishing a general psychological science on the basis of dialectical materialism.

The contribution of the "revisionist revolution in Vygotsky studies"

A recent contribution should be mentioned, without which this discussion would be somewhat incomplete. This contribution comes from the corpus of research works associated with the "revisionist revolution in Vygotsky Studies", a set of which was published in a programmatic namesake book (Yasnitsky & Van der Veer, 2016b). This thought-provoking book and related literature not only shred to pieces the traditionally over-inflated and at times notably mythologized images of the super-heroes of Soviet psychology, but also provide meticulous analyses of the texts and their histories in the social contexts of the time – but not only that. In its concluding chapter, the Epilogue, the authors followed the lead of Ekaterina Zavershneva, another contributor to the book and a well-known Vygotskian researcher, who had earlier done a very nice research on the notion of the "consciousness" in Vygotsky's legacy of the last decade of his life and meticulously and critically analyzed the three phases of Vygotsky's thought evolution. The importance of this notion for Vygotsky can hardly be overestimated, since it always remained among the central foci of his theorizing, although it underwent a series of important mutations along the way (Zavershneva, 2014). Furthermore, the unfinished "theory of consciousness" was what Vygotsky ultimately came up to in his intellectual work in psychology, according to his words that he expressed on a few occasions in his last private notes and publications (Yasnitsky, 2018; Zavershneva & Van der Veer, 2018).

Yet, the full meaning of "consciousness" for Vygotsky and his Russian-speaking associates, followers and the readers of their texts apparently escapes the

English-speaking readers of his works, mostly for linguistic reasons. Thus, the two authors of the Epilogue provide a nice analysis and detailed discussion of the semantic field of the Russian words (and cognate ones). For the details of this splendid analysis I would refer to the chapter that bears a self-explanatory title "'Lost in translation': talking about sense, meaning, and consciousness" (Yasnitsky & Van der Veer, 2016a). Yet, I would like to render the main message and the key discovery presented in this work. The chapter's authors highlight three important points.

First, "consciousness" (*soznanie*, in Russian) can have a derivative verb that denotes an active action in Russian, like in some other languages, for instance, in German. This is pretty obvious to a Russian-speaker, yet quite counter-intuitive to an English-speaker. Thus, for a Russian-speaker, there is a chain of highly interconnected nouns, adjectives, verbs, adverbs, etc., such as: *soznanie – (o)sozna(va)t' – osoznannyi – (o)soznaiushchii – osoznanie – soznatel'nyi – soznatel'no – soznatel'nost'*. All these clearly indicate the broad range of different aspects of "consciousness" as interpreted by a Russian-speaker on the basis of a given system of vocabulary and linguistic means of this language. This multitude is definitely hidden from a non-speaker of the language.

Second, "consciousness" (*soznanie*) in Russian is closely related in its meaning to another noun: "meaning" or rather "sense" (*smysl*, in Russian). This appears quite counter-intuitive even to a Russian-speaker, who never thought about the words, what they mean and how they are interconnected. At first look, the two words are quite different. Yet, the authors convincingly demonstrate that all differences disappear in the cognate verbs: Russian *osoznavat'* and *osmyslivat'* respectively that in many contexts can be (and actually are) used virtually as synonyms. This is a very interesting and thought-provoking idea indeed. Thus, the authors advance this point by demonstrating that – in parallel with the derivatives and cognate words of "consciousness" (*soznanie*) – there is another, quite similar chain of Russian words with the stem "sense" (smysl): *smysl – osmysli(va)t' – osmyslennyi – osmyslivaiushchii – osmys(h)lenie – osmyslivanie – smyslovoi – osmyslenno – osmyslennost'*. Quite a few of these are synonymous or, at least, very close in their meaning to the chain of the "consciousness" (*soznanie*) cognate and derivative ones.

Third, the authors make another very important observation. The linguistic means readily available in English do not allow us easily and without the loss of meaning to converse on such matters; therefore, in order to provide such means, the authors in fact deliberately and artificially construct the terminological network of English words that enable one to productively engage with truly Vygotskian thinking on these matters in English. This work, however, implies compromises and minor violations of the intuitively accepted norms of the given language, in which a new terminological network is to be created. Thus, for instance, the authors propose that for the lack of a better solution readily available within the English language, we need to accept the convention, according to which "consciousness" as a noun that denotes a psychological phenomenon is related with a verb with admittedly related meaning. On the ground that Russian *soznanie* is a composite of *so-* and *znanie*, which, from the standpoint of the etymology, means "knowing/knowledge together" (pretty much like in the original Latin "con-" and "sciencia") the authors propose an English word (and its many derivatives), which could be used as an equivalent for Russian terminological richness. The word is "cognize" and all its derivatives such as: cognizing (sth.), conscious (of) or cognizant (of), cognizance (of sth.). The obvious advancement is that now we have a verb with the meaning of "getting aware of", which allows us to discuss "consciousness" not as an entity, but as a process and, furthermore, an action – passive and receptive, or even deliberate and proactive (the closest analogue for a speech action, for instance, would be the active action of "speaking" and the passive action of "listening"). Then, all these, according to the terminological convention, will be acknowledged as closely related to the set of words and phrases that stem from "meaning" and "sense", such as: (to) make sense (of sth.), sense-making or making sense (of sth.), semantic (e.g. analysis) or meaningful (e.g. activity), meaningfulness. Unless this (or a similar) linguistic and terminological convention is deliberately and systematically accepted as a metadiscursive basis of this research program, no productive development of these ideas in this domain will predictably occur, not in the English language, at least.

This would require systematic and voluntary following of terminological convention that rigidly binds the entire terminological system of the metadiscourse of a new psychology as a strict and discursively consistent system of knowledge. Yet, here also lies the main problem: something that is artificially constructed – rather than naturally belongs to the given system (in this particular instance, the system of natural language as it is now) – is vulnerable and tends to disintegrate, fall into parts and constitutive elements, and eventually die out. Science is truly an international intellectual enterprise and its laws work equally well all over the globe. On the other hand, the linguistic bounds, the Babel Tower problem creates a curious linguistic and intellectual paradox, according to which scientific research is at the same time international and valid regardless of nations or localities, and, on the other hand, is hardly adequately and fully translatable. This is, perhaps, one of the greatest challenges to the metadiscourse of the future general psychology in its ambition of overtaking the numerous "psychologies" of our days.

Marxist psychology: one hundred years of solitude

"In retrospect we see the debris, only debris", as Russian Noble-prize-winner in Literature Joseph Brodsky wrote once. Like another great poet wrote, "midway upon the journey of our life I found myself within a forest dark". This is more or less where I am now.

I am a humble man, not a fighter or a dissident. I could have never written, like did Alexander Etkind (formerly of Cambridge, currently Mikhail M. Bakhtin

Professor of History of Russia-Europe Relations at the Department of History and Civilization, European University Institute in Florence, Italy):

> Vygotsky was *not the solitary hero of Nietzschean-Bolshevik mythology*: and even more, he was *no messiah, arriving out of nowhere to save psychology and imme-diately finding faithful apostles*. He was a man of culture, an intellectual, who operated in the mainstream of the esthetic, philosophical, political, and sim-ple vital ideas of his time. He was *not the founder of new principles that he scooped from the inner core of his own talents*, but one of those representatives of the most modern tendencies who captured the minds of his generation. He *was no miracle child, born a Marxist*, but a literary personage of the post-symbolist era, who had come to psychology and Marxism by way of difficult but typi-cal paths. He was *not the "Mozart of psychology,"* but a man of his times, who successfully applied his cultural experience to a new and unexpected domain.
> *(emphasis added; Etkind, 1994, p. 32)*

Given the age-old (and contemporary) "cult of Vygotsky" and the zeal of his self-proclaimed followers and admirers, one would need to possess a great deal of courage and self-determination in order to state anything like that. Never did I – with an exception of a couple of occasions or so, perhaps. Yet, I am not a brave man, and I would never get involved in fighting for ideas or principles. A child of my generation, I have always been somewhat of a romantic, mostly a cynic, and would ever be up to compromises of various sorts. I have nobody or noth-ing to blame. In fact, by virtue of having been involved in the production of the considerably falsified six-volume collection of Vygotsky's works, I am sharing the responsibility for what has been done. For that – as well as for any other mistakes of the kind that I knowingly or unknowingly made – I am humbly taking the blame on me.

I am definitely not a hero. I am also not a revolutionary, a visionary or an inno-vator: neither in science nor in politics. I am not even a psychologist anymore, at least, certainly not in a traditional meaning of the word. Yet, I do know something and still believe in something. A part of what I know and believe in is what I have presented here, in this very text. And, regardless of who I am and what I ever did, I still believe that this science, the science of psychology, deserves much better than what we have now in its place. The psychologies must go, and the "new psychol-ogy" must come instead. This, however, will never happen until the united "new psychology" finds its own distinctive vocabulary, language, discourse and metadis-course. In order not to turn into mere speculations, demagoguery and propaganda, all these will be intrinsically related to empirical practice of lab experimentation and applied knowledge production in the real, social world. Finally, in order to succeed and not to get "lost in translation", it must be developed enough from the linguistic standpoint and possess a sophisticated and rich means of inter- and transnational communication and knowledge production. I firmly believe this is possible, whether this will happen with Marx or even – *horribile dictu* – without him. Where there's a will there's a way. And vice versa: there is no other way, but this one and unless a will is there.

References

Bertau, M.-C. (2014a). Inner form as a notion migrating from West to East: Acknowledging the Humboldtian tradition in cultural-historical psychology. In A. Yasnitsky, R. Van der Veer, & M. Ferrari (Eds.), *The Cambridge handbook of cultural-historical psychology* (pp. 247–271). Cambridge: Cambridge University Press.

Bertau, M.-C. (2014b). The need for a dialogical science: Considering the legacy of Russian-Soviet thinking for contemporary approaches in dialogic research. In A. Yasnitsky, R. van der Veer, & M. Ferrari (Eds.), *The Cambridge handbook of cultural-historical psychology* (pp. 474–487). Cambridge: Cambridge University Press.

Bozhovich, L. I. (1972). Problema razvitiia motivacionnoi sfery rebionka. In L. I. Bozhovich (Ed.), *Problemy formirovaniia lichnosti*. Moscow: Institut prakticheskoi psikhologii.

Bratus', B. S. (Ed.). (1995). *Nachala khristianskoi psikhologii [Foundations of Christian psychology]*. Moscow: Nauka.

Bratus', B. S. (2015). Khristianskaia psikhologiia kak nauchnoe napravlenie: K istorii voprosa [Christian psychology as a scientific direction: On the history of the issue]. *National Psychological Journal, 19*(3), 4–14.

Chelpanov, G. I. (1924). *Psikhologiia i marksizm [Psychology and Marxism]*. Moscow: Russkii knizhnik.

Davydov, V. V., & Radzikhovskii, L. A. (1980). Teoriia L.S. Vygotskogo i deiatel'nostnyi podkhod v psikhologii [Vygotsky's theory and activity-oriented approach in psychology]. *Voprosy Psikhologii, 6*, 48–59.

Davydov, V. V., & Radzikhovskii, L. A. (1981). Teoriia L.S. Vygotskogo i deiatel'nostnyi podkhod v psikhologii [Vygotsky's theory and activity-oriented approach in psychology]. *Voprosy Psikhologii, 1*, 67–80.

Davydov, V. V., & Radzikhovskii, L. A. (1985). Vygotsky's theory and the activity-oriented approach in psychology. In J. Wertsch (Ed.), *Culture, communication, and cognition: Vygotskian perspectives* (pp. 35–65). New York, NY: Cambridge University Press.

Davydov, V. V., Zinchenko, V. P., Munipov, V. M., & Radzikhovskii, L. A. (Eds.). (1981). *Nauchnoe tvorchestvo L.S. Vygotskogo i sovremennaia psikhologiia. Tezisy dokladov Vsesoiuznoj konferentsii. Moskva, 23–23 iiunya 1981 g. [Scientific legacy of L.S. Vygotsky and contemporary psychology. Proceedings of the All-Union conference. Moscow, June 23–25, 1981]*. Moscow: APN SSSR.

Diriwächter, R., & Valsiner, J. (2008). *Striving for the whole: Creating theoretical syntheses*. New Brunswick, NJ: Transaction Publishers.

Etkind, A. M. (1994). More on L.S. Vygotsky: Forgotten texts and undiscovered contexts. *Journal of Russian and East European Psychology, 32*(6), 6–34.

Fleck, L. (1979). *Genesis and development of scientific fact*. Chicago: University of Chicago Press.

Kozulin, A. (1985). Georgy Chelpanov and the establishment of the Moscow institute of psychology. *Journal of the History of the Behavioral Sciences, 21*(1), 23–32.

Krementsov, N. (1997). *Stalinist science*. Princeton: Princeton University Press.

Leontiev, A. N. (1975). Introduction. In *Activity, consciousness and personality* (pp. 1–9). Englewood Cliffs, NJ: Prentice-Hall, Inc.

Marx, K. (1992). Economic and philosophical manuscripts (1844). In *Early writings* (pp. 279–400). London: Penguin.

Mironenko, I. (2016). History for 'polycentric' psychological science: An 'outsider's' case. In S. H. Klempe & R. Smith (Eds.), *Centrality of history for theory construction in psychology* (pp. 111–121). Cham: Springer.

Naumova, T. (2004). Das problem des dialogs: A. A. Potebnja, L. P. Jakubinskij, L. S. Vygotskij, M. M. Bachtin. In K. Ehlich & K. Meng (Eds.), *Die Aktualität des Verdrängten. Studien zur Geschichte der Sprachwissenschaft im 20. Jahrhundert* (pp. 211–225). Heidelberg: Synchron.

Radzikhovskii, L. A. (1979a). Analiz tvorchestva L.S. Vygotskogo sovetskimi psikhologami [Analysis of L.S. Vygotsky's legacy by Soviet psychologists]. *Voprosy Psikhologii*, 6, 58–67.

Radzikhovskii, L. A. (1979b). *Osnovnye etapy nauchnogo tvorchestva L.S. Vygotskogo [Main stages of scientific creativity of L.S. Vygotsky]* (Unpublished Kandidat psikhologicheskikh nauk dissertation). Ordena trudovogo krasnogo znameni nauchno-issledovatel'skii institut obschei i pedagogicheskoi psikhologii, Moscow.

Radzikhovskii, L. A. (1982). G. I. Chelpanov – Organizator Instituta psikhologii [G. I. Chelpanov – The organizer of the Institute of Psychology]. *Voprosy Psikhologii*, 5, 47–59.

Radzikhovskii, L. A. (1988). Diskussionnye problemy marksistskoi teorii v sovetskoi psikhologicheskoi nauke [The acute problems for discussion on the Marxist theory in Soviet psychological science]. *Voprosy Psikhologii*, 6, 124–131.

Radzikhovskii, L. A. (1991). Dialogue as a unit of analysis of consciousness. *Soviet Psychology*, 29(2), 8–21.

Shchedrovitskii, G. P. (2001). *Ya vsegda byl idealistom [I have always been an idealist . . .]*. Moscow: Put'.

Sirotkina, I. E., & Smith, R. (2012). Russian federation. In D. B. Baker (Ed.), *The Oxford handbook of the history of psychology: Global perspectives* (pp. 412–441). Oxford: Oxford University Press.

Slobodchikov, V. I. (2019). The formation of Russian Christian psychology. Problems and prospects for future development. *Russian Social Science Review*, 60(3), 221–229.

Solso, R. L. (1985). An interview with Boris Lomov. *Soviet Psychology*, 24(1), 3–23.

Solso, R. L., & Brushlinsky, A. V. (1991). Boris Fiodorovich Lomov (1927–1989): Obituary. *American Psychologist*, 46(3), 245.

Spinuzzi, C. (2019). From superhumans to Supermediators: Locating the extraordinary in CHAT. In A. Yasnitsky (Ed.), *Questioning Vygotsky's legacy: Scientific psychology or heroic cult* (pp. 137–166). London and New York: Routledge.

Todes, D. P., & Krementsov, N. (2010). Dialectical materialism and Soviet science in the 1920s and 1930s. In W. Leatherbarrow & D. Offord (Eds.), *A history of Russian thought* (pp. 340–367). Cambridge: Cambridge University Press.

Toomela, A., & Valsiner, J. (2010). *Methodological thinking in psychology: 60 years gone astray?* Charlotte, NC: Information Age Publishing, Inc.

Toulmin, S. (1978). The Mozart of psychology. Mind in society: The development of higher psychological processes by L.S. Vygotsky, edited by Michael Cole, by Vera John-Steiner, by Sylvia Scribner, by Ellen Souberman, the psychology of art by L.S. Vygotsky, Soviet developmental psychology: An anthology edited by Michael Cole. *The New York Review of Books*, 25(14), 51–57.

Van der Veer, R., & Yasnitsky, A. (2016). Vygotsky the published: Who wrote Vygotsky and what Vygotsky actually wrote. In A. Yasnitsky & R. Van der Veer (Eds.), *Revisionist revolution in Vygotsky studies* (pp. 73–93). London and New York: Routledge.

Van der Veer, R., & Zavershneva, E. (2018). The final chapter of Vygotsky's thinking and Speech: A reader's guide. *Journal of the History of the Behavioral Sciences, 54*(2), 101–116.

Vasilyuk, F. E. (2015). Prayer, silence, and psychotherapy. *Journal of Russian and East European Psychology, 52*(1), 59–65.

Vygotskii, L. S. (1960). *Razvitie vysshikh psikhicheskikh funktsii. Iz neopublikovannykh trudov [Development of psychical functions. From unpublished works]*. Moscow: Izdatel'stvo Akademii pedagogicheskikh nauk.

Vygotskii, L. S. (1983). Istoriia razvitiia vysshikh psikhicheskikh funktsii [The History of development of higher mental/psychic functions]. In *Vygotskii, L. S. Sobranie sochinenii. Tom tretii. Problemy razvitiia psikhiki* (pp. 5–328). Moscow: Pedagogika.

Vygotsky, L. S. (1997a). The historical meaning of the crisis in psychology: A methodological investigation. In R. W. Rieber & J. Wollock (Eds.), *The collected works of L. S. Vygotsky: Vol. 3. Problems of the history and theory of psychology* (pp. 233–344). New York: Plenum Press.

Vygotsky, L. S. (1997b). The history of the development of higher mental functions. In R. W. Rieber (Ed.), *The collected works of L. S. Vygotsky* (Vol. 4, pp. 1–252). New York, NY: Plenum.

Yaroshevskii, M. G. (1985). *Istoriia psikhologii [History of psychology]*. Moscow: Mysl'.

Yaroshevskii, M. G. (1995). Nauka o povedenii: Russkii put' [The science of behavior: The Russian way]. *Voprosy Psikhologii, 4*, 5–19.

Yaroshevskii, M. G. (1996). *Nauka o povedenii: Russkii put' [The science of behavior: The Russian way]*. Moscow: Institut prakticheskoi psikhologii.

Yasnitsky, A. (2012). Revisionist revolution in Vygotskian science: Toward cultural-historical Gestalt psychology. Guest editor's introduction. *Journal of Russian and East European Psychology, 50*(4), 3–15.

Yasnitsky, A. (2015). Stalinskaia model' nauki: Istoriia i sovremennost' rossiiskoi psikhologii [Stalin model of science: The history and the state of the art of contemporary Russian psychology]. *PEM: Psychology. Educology. Medicine, 3–4*, 407–422.

Yasnitsky, A. (2016). The archetype of Soviet psychology: From Stalinism of the 1930s to the 'Stalinist science' of our days. In A. Yasnitsky & R. Van der Veer (Eds.), *Revisionist revolution in Vygotsky studies* (pp. 3–26). London and New York: Routledge.

Yasnitsky, A. (2017). 'Orudie i znak v razvitii rebenka': Samaia izvestnaia rabota L.S. Vygotskogo, kotoruiu on nikogda ne pisal ["Tool and sign in the development of the child": The most famous Vygotsky's work, which he never wrote]. *Psikhologiia. Zhurnal Vysshei Shkoly Ekonomiki, 14*(4), 576–606.

Yasnitsky, A. (2018). *Vygotsky: An intellectual biography*. London and New York: Routledge.

Yasnitsky, A. (Ed.). (2019a). *Questioning Vygotsky's legacy: Scientific psychology or heroic cult*. London and New York: Routledge.

Yasnitsky, A. (2019b). Vygotsky's science of superman: From utopia to concrete psychology. In A. Yasnitsky (Ed.), *Questioning Vygotsky's legacy: Scientific psychology or heroic cult* (pp. 1–21). London and New York: Routledge.

Yasnitsky, A., & Van der Veer, R. (2016a). 'Lost in translation': Talking about sense, meaning, and consciousness. In A. Yasnitsky & R. Van der Veer (Eds.), *Revisionist revolution in Vygotsky studies* (pp. 229–239). London and New York: Routledge.

Yasnitsky, A., & Van der Veer, R. (Eds.). (2016b). *Revisionist revolution in Vygotsky studies*. London and New York: Routledge.

Yasnitsky, A., Van der Veer, R., Aguilar, E., & García, L. N. (Eds.). (2016). *Vygotski revisitado: Una historia crítica de su contexto y legado*. Buenos Aires: Miño y Dávila Editores.

Zavershneva, E. (2014). The problem of consciousness in Vygotsky's cultural-historical psychology. In A. Yasnitsky, R. Van der Veer, & M. Ferrari (Eds.), *The Cambridge handbook of cultural-historical psychology* (pp. 63–97). Cambridge: Cambridge University Press.

Zavershneva, E., & Van der Veer, R. (Eds.). (2018). *Vygotsky's notebooks. A selection.* New York: Springer.

Zinchenko, V. P. (2003). 'Da, ochen protivorechivaia figura . . .' ["Very controversial person, indeed . . ."]. *Zhurnal Prakticheskogo Psikhologa, 1–2*, 162–179.

2

SERGEI RUBINSTEIN AS THE FOUNDER OF SOVIET MARXIST PSYCHOLOGY

"Problems of psychology in the works of Karl Marx" (1934) and beyond

Anton Yasnitsky

Sergei Rubinstein (1889–1960) was definitely and undeniably the founder of Soviet Marxist psychology. No doubt, he was not the only one to face the challenge: numerous Soviet psychologists, explicitly or implicitly, sooner or later aligned themselves with the Marxist strand in psychology as early as the beginning of the 1920s. A few of them would go as far as to voluntarily assume the role of the leading creators of the distinctly Marxist psychology and the spokesmen for the entire discipline or any of its subdivisions. These would infrequently be positioned as allied to psychology or even fully independent scholarly disciplines such as well-known internationally applied psychological disciplines and social practices of "psychotechnics", "pedology", "psychohygiene"[1] or unique Soviet home-grown idiosyncratic "reactology" or "reflexology". One should not be misled by Konstantin Kornilov's chapter (1930) that appeared in English in an edited book collection characteristically titled "Psychologies of 1930", which featured a wide range of contemporary psychological theories and reads today as some kind of more or less comprehensive "who is who" in psychology of its time (Murchison, 1930). Kornilov's chapter "Psychology in the light of dialectic materialism" (with its clear Marxist commitment of the contributing author, the proponent of the idiosyncratic "reactology" of his own back at home) might have read as *the* "Marxist Soviet psychology" in the West, whereas in fact it was only *a* Marxist psychology among a few other similar Marxist psychological theories in the Soviet Union. To be precise, by the 1930s there were no Soviet psychologists who would openly oppose Marxism or advocate for any alternative to it.

---

1 For a discussion of the two applied psychological disciplines – "pedology" and "psychohygiene" – and related social practices see Part II of this book.

And yet, it was not until Sergei Rubinstein entered the field in the mid-1930s that a really stable and officially accepted version of Marxist psychology would appear. In other words, the unified project of *the* Soviet Marxist psychology emerged in Rubinstein's works and was forever strongly associated with his name and contribution. Surprisingly enough, this gigantic figure and the creator of Soviet psychological Marxism is virtually unknown in the West to this very day: only a few of his works are available in English (a little bit more are known in non-Anglo-Saxon psychological communities, for instance, in German scholarly community). This seems to be not only sufficient, but also a compelling reason for considerable attention to this Soviet thinker and his ideas, as obscure as they still are for a reader in English. An in-depth analysis of Rubinstein's legacy has once been undertaken in a study of 1960s (Payne, 1968) that is also not so familiar among the Western readers and appears quite outdated by the standards of our time. That is why this chapter is much needed as a long-overdue contribution to the discussion of Rubinstein's heritage in the context of 21st century psychology. Yet, another in-depth analysis would require another major book. Instead, the chapter presents only the highlights of Rubinstein's life and scholarly legacy. Then, it proceeds to the close reading and discussion of Rubinstein's seminal paper "Problems of Psychology in the Works of Karl Marx" that was his first explicitly Marxist work that paved the way for the rest of his compatriots and peers to follow in this field of knowledge.

Reliable sources on Rubinstein's life and legacy

Before we proceed any further, an important discussion of what materials count as scientifically reliable sources on Sergei Rubinstein's life and legacy is in order. This discussion is triggered not only by the requirement of the adherence to the usual high standards of rigid and objective science. There is another, very compelling reason to inspect and overview the available data, on the basis of which an understanding of the real career and scholarly contribution of Sergei Rubinstein can legitimately be made.

Rubinstein was a leading Soviet scholar, whose life spanned seven decades and whose academic legacy has been presented and discussed on quite a number of occasions in multiple publications; most of them took place within the Soviet Union. Yet, there are serious reasons to question these narratives and analyses. A cult figure for some, Rubinstein happened to supervise the work of a number of Soviet scientific workers in 1930s–1950s, who later claimed themselves as intellectual heirs of Rubinstein. Regrettably, though, these individuals were predominantly raised and encultured in academia within the "Stalin model of science" that was firmly established in the Soviet Union in the late 1930s and further solidified during the period of Late Stalinism of the late 1940s–early 1950s. In fact, despite certain historical evolution and a number of important mutations, this model persists in contemporary scientific ethos in Russian Federation to these very days (Yasnitsky, 2015b, 2016).

As long as Rubinstein's postwar students are concerned, the situation is further aggravated by the social and institutional circumstances of their intellectual milieu: the majority of them were associated and affiliated with the Institute of Philosophy of the Academy of Sciences of the USSR, deeply entrenched in dogmatic and scholastic quasi-Marxism. Thus, to give just one example of a direct consequence of Rubinstein's students' partisan involvement, the entire period of Rubinstein's life and his scholarship associated with German "idealist" Neo-Kantianism remained virtually unexplored and greatly omitted in the traditional narratives about Rubinstein's life and legacy – until very recent times. This can be explained by the ideological loyalty and dogmatism of Rubinstein's students, as well as the fact that the overwhelming majority of them did not have the command of the German language (or, for that matter, any other foreign language) sufficient for reading their supervisor's earlier works composed in German. Furthermore, the situation with Rubinstein's intellectual legacy in the 21st century has not improved in any sense, even deteriorated. A handful of Rubinstein's contemporary self-proclaimed followers and interpreters, in addition to the deficiencies of the earlier period, tend to downplay and distance the Marxist core of his writings and speculate on the "humanist" trends in his work – to the detriment of both German Neo-Kantianist and Soviet Marxist foundations of his thinking throughout his entire intellectual life. Apparently, this creates a largely biased and distorted – if not falsified – image of Sergei Rubinstein, the philosopher and psychologist, and his legacy. A somewhat similar situation in Soviet psychology, specifically, in relation to the legacy of Lev Vygotsky, has been observed, described and thoroughly analyzed in the course of the ongoing "revisionist revolution in Vygotsky Studies", most notably featured in programmatic landmark English and Spanish publications (Yasnitsky & Van der Veer, 2016b; Yasnitsky et al., 2016). This is the reason why most of traditional Soviet and Russian publications are highly suspected of a considerable bias and distortion (if not dismissed altogether), and a rigorous "audit" of the documentary materials and sources on Sergei Rubinstein is direly needed.

The main core of Sergei Rubinstein's personal and scholarly archive has been preserved in the V.I. Lenin State Public Library and the Institute of Psychology of Russian Academy of Sciences (RAN) in Moscow; some other archival documents related to Rubinstein are also available in the collections of libraries and institutional archives in St. Petersburg (former Leningrad), Moscow (both in Russian Federation), Odessa, Kharkiv (both in Ukraine) and, possibly, in Germany. Regrettably, the personal file of Rubinstein as a student in Marburg (Germany) was reported missing (or misplaced), according to a recent publication (Dmitrieva & Levchenko, 2015).

Perhaps, the earliest albeit somewhat dated trustworthy source on Rubinstein's life and scholarship is the book by T. R. Payne titled *S. L. Rubinštejn and the Philosophical Foundations of Soviet Psychology* (Payne, 1968). The author apparently had working knowledge of Russian and German and perused an impressive number of original sources in these two languages, which is mandatory in the case of

Rubinstein's scholarship. Payne's first-hand knowledge of the sources and acute analysis of the texts make his work a valuable source on Rubinstein until this very day, even despite the book's shortcomings. The author clearly identifies the focus of his research and the scope of its coverage:

> The purpose of this work is to discuss the philosophical foundations of Soviet psychological theory. The treatment of this subject is more expository than critical, though the task of giving a general account of Soviet psychological theory necessarily involves a certain element of evaluation. The method adopted is somewhat unusual. Rather than attempt to give an overall account of the philosophical aspects of Soviet psychological theory, we have chosen instead to study these questions as they are discussed in the works of one particular Soviet writer . . . S. L. Rubinstejn has been chosen as the subject for this study chiefly because he was, until his death in 1960, the most influential writer on psychological theory in the Soviet Union. His works, moreover, cover all the major aspects of Soviet psychological theory, and though it is doubtful if he can be called a "great" philosopher, his writings manifest a depth and originality of thought impressive by any standard.
>
> *(Payne, 1968, p. 2)*

One could only regret that the book has largely remained unnoticed by the larger academic community of those scholars, who are interested in the issues the book covers. To this very day, this book remains the main and virtually the only second-hand source available to an English reader; all other available publications are mostly in Russian. Among these, particularly important are the studies of archival nature that document Rubinstein's life upon his return from Germany in Odessa (Levchenko, 2012; Romenets, 1989), and, then, in Leningrad (Parkhomenko et al., 1989). One should also mention a remarkable collection of papers that also included the original and previously unpublished important materials from Sergei Rubinstein's archive (Lomov, 1989).

Yet, particularly prominent are the studies of Nina Dmitrieva (of Moscow Pedagogical State University), who systematically pursues her research in Neo-Kantian philosophy and has recently published a series of important studies solidly grounded in the critical reading of original texts and archival materials. The author and her studies deal not only with the Marburg school of Neo-Kantian philosophy in its relation to the Russian intellectual milieu and its impact on Russian thought in humanities and social sciences (Dmitrieva, 2007), but increasingly focus on the figure of Sergei Rubinstein, his intellectual biography and the personal network of his peers and interlocutors such as, for instance, Ernst Cassirer (Dmitrieva, 2016a; Dmitrieva & Levchenko, 2015), as a Neo-Kantian scholar in his dialogue with Hegelian thought (Dmitrieva, 2016b). These studies complement the traditional view on Rubinstein as a quintessential Marxist thinker, considerably enrich our understanding of Rubinstein's evolution from German Neo-Kantian philosophy towards Soviet Marxist psychology and dramatically problematize the phenomenon of "Marxist psychology" as an integral part of European Continental intellectual tradition. So, in sum, despite quite a number of Soviet publications on Sergei Rubinstein, it is safe to claim that scholarly rigorous and systematic "Rubinstein Studies" are only in their infancy as a very promising direction of future research and these are the main studies of primary interest as the most reliable publications on life and, generally, the intellectual legacy of Rubinstein.

Finally, this chapter provides a close reading of specific Rubinstein's text: his ground-breaking article of 1933 (published in 1934) on Karl Marx and the problems of psychology (Rubinshtein, 1934). The original edition of 1934 is rare and virtually inaccessible to a contemporary reader; therefore all references to the text in Russian are given here by its later republication, which is relatively reliable from a textological standpoint (1973b). The analysis of the text was supported with its publications in German (1981) and in English (1987). Then, for the references to the original works of Karl Marx and Friedrich Engels the 50-volume English edition of Marx/Engels Collected Works (MECW, 1975–2004) was used. In addition, for the original German texts, the author consulted the editions of 44-volume (in 46 books) *Marx-Engels Werke* (MEW, 1956–1990) and the largest collection, the ongoing *Marx-Engels-Gesamtausgabe* (MEGA2, since 1975; the end of publication projected in 2025).

Sergei Rubinstein: life and legacy

Sergei Rubinstein was born in Odessa, a major city in the south-west Russian Empire, in 1889 in a family of Leonid Rubinstein, a successful and wealthy lawyer. Sergei completed his classical gymnasium education in 1908 with a gold medal (the diploma of the highest distinction), which – along with his father's financial support – allowed him to travel to Western Europe and take a course of university studies in philosophy in Germany. The academic subject of Rubinstein's choice, philosophy, was dominated there by the so-called Neo-Kantian tradition, and the famous names of the leading philosophers of this intellectual movement are Wilhelm Windelband (1848–1915) and Heinrich Rickert (1863–1936) (both in Freiburg im Breisgau, Baden), and Hermann Cohen (1842–1918) and Paul Natorp (1854–1924) (both in Marburg). Also, Ernst Cassirer (1874–1945) was both influenced by and notably contributed to the Neo-Kantianist movement. Rubinstein accomplished his university studies in two cities: first, he studied in Freiburg under Rickert for over a year (in summer of 1909 and winter semester of 1909/1910), and then, somewhat disappointed with his Freiburg studies, in Marburg, both among the oldest (more precisely, top-ten) German-speaking university cities (Dmitrieva, 2007).

In 1912, Rubinstein's mentor Hermann Cohen retired from the university in Marburg and moved to Berlin. The next year, in 1913, Rubinstein completed his university courses and followed Cohen. For about a year he stayed in Berlin, where he took the opportunity to attend the courses of Ernst Cassirer (at the Friedrich Wilhelm University, later renamed Humboldt University of Berlin) and prepared for publication of his doctoral thesis in philosophy titled "A Study on the Problem of Method" (*Eine Studie zum Problem der Methode*): by German academic standards this publication was the requirement and precondition for the defense. In 1914 he published the first part of his dissertation (Rubinstein, 1914); this was immediately followed by successful defense on July 20, 1914 (Sieg, 1994, pp. 383, 487). Thus, just a week before the outbreak of WWI (i.e., July 28, 1914), Rubinstein completed his university studies and, in order not to get interned during the war as a citizen of a belligerent country involved in the military conflict against Germany, Rubinstein left for Imperial Russia.

Thus, in 1914 Rubinstein arrived back home in Russia as a full-grown intellectual and mature philosopher of the Marburg school of German Neo-Kantianism, highly valued by his teacher Hermann Cohen, who considered him as one of his best students and favorites, as evident from Rubinstein's and his peers' in Germany correspondence (Pasternak, 2005, pp. 107–110). It is not entirely clear what exactly he was involved in since then in his home town of Odessa until 1917 since when he is known to have been working as a history instructor in a gymnasium in Odessa. In April 1919 he got a position of *privat-dozent* (roughly, an equivalent of an assistant professor in North America) at the Department of Philosophy of the Novorossiiskii (Odessa) University. He made an impressive fast – albeit brief – career at this institution (that underwent a series of administrative reforms and reorganizations during the period) and even reached the position of Full Professor and the Chair of Department in 1921.

Yet again, under unclear circumstances, in 1922 he switched to an Adjunct (*vneshtatnyi*) Professor at the university (Levchenko, 2010), which was chiefly a teaching (but neither administrative nor research) job, in order to become the Director of the Odessa Scientific Library. He held this position until 1930 when he left his home town in order to assume a position of a Director of Saltykov-Schedrin Central Scientific Library in Leningrad, the former capital of Russian Empire, which was apparently quite a promotion for him (Romenets, 1989). Interestingly enough, even as the top city library administrator Rubinstein never abandoned his intellectual quest and kept profusely writing on various philosophy related topics; quite a few of his manuscripts have been preserved in his archives. Furthermore, he made several attempts at publishing these works on various occasions – at home or abroad – all of them to no avail (Dmitrieva & Levchenko, 2015). This might suggest that the twist of Rubinstein's career and his departure from academia in 1922 was not exactly his voluntary and eager choice.

Thus, in 1930 Rubinstein left Odessa for Leningrad. Soon thereafter, he received an offer for another – presumably, way more attractive from his personal standpoint – position: the Chair of psychology at the Department of Pedology at the local Herzen Leningrad Pedagogical Institute. The offer was accepted. Thus, Rubinstein resumed his scholarly life after a decade of supervisory and administrative work in the Soviet library system, in the academic year of 1931–1932 (Parkhomenko et al., 1989).

An active educational administrator in Leningrad and a sharp thinker, Rubinstein would not publish anything on philosophical or psychological matters ever since his return from Germany – with seemingly the only exception: an early small paper of 1922 on the "principle of creative self-activity" that came out in Odessa in an obscure local collection of scientific papers (Rubinshtein, 1922). So, it was only in 1934 that he debuted as a psychologist with a publication of his seminal paper on the "Problems of psychology in the works of Karl Marx" (Rubinshtein, 1934), which did not make an immediate considerable stir, yet nevertheless it had a profound lasting effect on the entire edifice of Soviet psychology for the years to come. This article was soon followed by an important book publication: Rubinstein's *Foundations of Psychology* (*Osnovy psikhologii*). The book was completed and submitted in late 1934, then, published in 1935 (Rubinshtein, 1935). Five years later, in 1940, another of Rubinstein's book was released. Originally planned as a revised version of his 1935 volume, his *Foundations of General Psychology* (*Osnovy obschei psikhologii*) eventually turned out a whole new book project that accommodated the criticisms of his first Russian book and earned him a reputation of a stellar psychologist, furthermore, the leading specialist in this field in the Soviet Union (Rubinshtein, 1940).

The beginning of the German invasion of the USSR in July 1941 during WWII reached Rubinstein in Leningrad where he stayed even during the German military blockade of the city, famine and mass starvation in 1941–1942. Yet, the year of 1942 was the turning point in his life and career. Indeed, in 1942 Rubinstein was awarded the most prestigious Stalin Prize (of the second degree) for his work on the general psychology. The same year he left Leningrad for Kislovodsk, and soon thereafter for Moscow, in order to become the founding Head of the Chair (*kafedra*) and Department (*otdelenie*) of Psychology affiliated with the School (*fakul'tet*) of Philosophy at the Lomonosov Moscow State University (kept the position until 1945). The following year, in 1943, he became the first Soviet psychologist to become a Corresponding Member of the Academy of Sciences of the USSR (elected on September 29, 1943). Finally, in 1945 Rubinstein became the founding Director of the Sector (*sektor*) of Psychology at the Institute of Philosophy of the Academy of Sciences of the USSR. The impact of the latter appointment can be hardly overestimated: it meant, in effect, that psychology as a scholarly discipline for the first time ever received an official institutional recognition at the highest level of the Soviet nomenclature of scientific disciplines, albeit somewhat subdued to Philosophy as its constitutive sub-field. In 1946 the second, slightly revised edition of his award-winning *Foundations of General Psychology* was released (Rubinshtein, 1946).

Yet, the end of the 1940s was marked by a dramatic shift in the international relations between the geo-political powers well known as the beginning of the period of the Cold War. This change had a profound effect on foreign and domestic policy of the Soviet Union, including its scientific policy (Krementsov, 1997). Thus, as a result of a few waves of political processes of the late 1940s and the beginning of the campaign against the "rootless cosmopolitans" (a Soviet newspeak euphemism for the launch of Anti-Semitic campaign), Sergei Rubinstein was released of all his administrative roles in 1949 at the Sector of Psychology of the Institute of Philosophy and eventually fired from the Moscow State University in 1952, although he retained his membership at the Academy of Sciences of the USSR. In retrospect, this might be interpreted as a relatively reasonable compromise between the dominant trend in the party-state policy and the resistance of the scholarly community to give up its major assets such as Sergei Rubinstein, the philosopher-psychologist and the leading, officially acknowledged intellectual of the time. Yet, the times would dramatically change very soon.

Despite his public ostracism and official removal from virtually all positions that Rubinstein had occupied before the beginning of the Cold War and the related changes in the political and social climate in the country, he would ever remain an intellectual leader and one of the most reputable figures in Soviet psychology. Thus, the Francophone psychologists, who had contacts with their peers in the Soviet Union in the mid-1950s, recall their meetings in Moscow with the group of the Big Five. Apart from Sergei Rubinstein, this group included Aleksandr Luria, Aleksei N. Leontiev, Anatolii Smirnov and Boris Teplov, each of whom – but Rubinstein, of course – would occupy some or another more or less important position in the official nomenclature hierarchy of the Soviet institutionalized psychology of the time (Piaget, 1956; Zazzo, 1982, 1989). Immediately after Joseph Stalin's death in 1953 the policy hardly changed in any radical sense, yet a few further compromises on the part of the regime were made. Thus, during the so-called period of The Khrushchev Thaw (or *khrushchevskaia ottepel'*, called so by Nikita Khrushchev, the new political leader of the Party and the government after Stalin) Rubinstein slightly regained some of his lost positions in the academia: for instance, in 1956 he was reappointed as the Director of the Sector of Psychology at the Institute of Philosophy. In 1957 his earlier book, prepared for publication under the title *Philosophical Roots of Psychology* that was banned by the Late Stalinist censorship in 1947 and, apparently, subsequently somewhat revised, was eventually published under the new title of *Being and Consciousness* (*Bytie i soznanie*), followed by another book of 1959 *Principles and the Ways of Psychology's Development* (*Printsipy i puti razvitiia psikhologii*) (Rubinshtein, 1957, 1959). It turned out, at about the same time Rubinstein was working on yet another book of his, *The Human and the World* (*Chelovek i mir*): this one – not entirely finished monograph – would become his "swan song" and the first posthumous major publication that remained unpublished until an edition of 1973 saw the daylight – by admission of a contemporary author and closest relative of an active and highly involved member of the editorial team, a considerably "adapted" (Slavskaia, 2015, p. 9), that is, edited and falsified, therefore, a highly questionable from textological standpoint publication (Rubinshtein, 1973a). Eventually, in 1959 Rubinstein was quite deservedly nominated for the most prestigious sign of distinction a scholar could have been awarded at that time in the USSR: the Lenin Prize. Yet, he would never receive it: Sergei Rubinstein died on January 11, 1960.

Rubinstein's "Problems of psychology in the works of Karl Marx" (1934): the context of composition and publication

The circumstances of the article's composition are not clear. Yet, the historical context is well researched when Rubinstein's most remarkable and foundational article was written and published. Let us sketch it, thus, even if in a few strokes.

Most of the decade of the 1920s was dominated in the Soviet Union by the New Economic Policy (NEP) that allowed for restoration of private businesses in the country and resulted in the proliferation of an idiosyncratic Soviet "middle class", the "nepmen" (*nepmany*). A definite success in the regime's effort to feed the masses and provide basic services to the country's population, the NEP was perceived by the majority of the Communist Party members and the state bureaucracy as social injustice, a retreat from and the betrayal of the ideals of the Revolution of October 1917 with its pronunciations of the elimination of private property and inequality in favor of the socialist, communal, egalitarian forms of social life and state economy. Complicated with the intricacies of the inter-Party struggle for the power and political leadership, the situation developed to the end of the 1920s, when the official leader of the Party, Joseph Stalin, and his regime in its initial phase of Early Stalinism introduced the inseparable unity of the forced industrialization, collectivization and "cultural revolution" that dramatically impacted the entire system of industry, agriculture and social relations in the country, respectively. The cultural revolution is of primary interest in this context since it had profound effect on the development of the natural, social and human sciences and the scientific policies, discussions and practices in the Soviet Union, particularly in philosophy and psychology. The rupture between the decades of the 1920s and the 1930s was swift and decisive and is well known under the banner of the Great Break that Joseph Stalin announced in 1929.

The entire period before the Great Break was dominated in Soviet philosophy and ideology by the mechanist interpretation of Marxism and its role as the foundation in scientific research. This period is also characterized by continuous and passionate discussions and critique of the mechanist model from the rival group of Soviet Marxist philosophers, who proposed an alternative to Marxist philosophical mechanism, the "dialectical" model. The continuous struggle between the two groups was interrupted by Joseph Stalin's direct intervention in the discussion in the end of 1929 with his critique of the mechanicism, then, again, the end of 1930 with a critique of the alternative group of Soviet Marxists that he dubbed "menshevising idealists" (from the name of the "Menshevik" right faction of Russian Social-Democratic Party, the virtually outlawed by then political opponents of the ruling former Bolshevik faction, renamed the Communist Party). The history of this period is well researched and received impressive coverage in the literature (see, e.g., Bauer, 1952; Graham, 1972; Joravsky, 1961; Todes & Krementsov, 2010).

As far as psychology is concerned, the situation for Soviet scholars in this and allied fields (such as pedology, psychotechnics or psychohygiene) appeared rather frustrating. In their attempt to align with the officially sanctioned version of Marxism, they were considerably disoriented with the rapid changes and the zigzags of the "official course" of Soviet Marxism in its historical evolution and the sequential of both available alternatives: these were pronounced equally banned, and the war against the two was launched under the banner of the struggle against the "mechanicism" and the "menshevising idealism". Clearly, a third option, a politically safe and intellectually robust middle way was needed not only in philosophy, but also in sciences, including psychology. It is exactly against this background that the article emerged of a virtually unknown author in the world of Soviet publications, yet a well-established standing and a reputation of a doctoral graduate in one of Germany's best schools of philosophy and a prominent professor of psychology in Leningrad in 1930s. It seems the combination of the two – the profound training in German philosophy and the long-time involvement with psychology in the Soviet Union was the key to the success of this newbie author of a Soviet psychological paper in his mid-40s.

The text of the paper was finished and submitted for publication on May 31, 1933; the article was not published until the next year. Originally established in 1928 under the auspices of the Moscow State Institute of Experimental Psychology of RANION (former Institute of Psychology, later renamed Institute of Psychology, Pedology and Psychotechnics, the *GIPPiP*, in 1930) as *The Journal of Psychology, Pedology and Psychotechnics*, the three series of the journal soon thereafter split into three independent journals, titled, accordingly, *Psychology*, *Pedology* and *Psychotechnics and Psychophysiology of Labour*. The journals on psychology proper and its educational counterpart, pedology, were closed down upon the decision and the ruling of the supervisory bodies of the party-state in 1932. The journal on psychotechnics survived, but it was reorganized and renamed *Soviet Psychotechnics*, under which title it kept circulating during the last two years of its life.

Rubinstein's seminal paper came out in the first issue of the journal *Soviet Psychotechnics* (*Sovetskaia psikhotekhnika*) of 1934 (Rubinshtein, 1934), then another issue followed and the journal followed the other two psychological journals and was also closed down. This was the last of the three specialized Soviet psychological journals, and the article on the problems of psychology might have turned a "farewell letter" and a "swan song" of this discipline in the country. Yet, as the fate would have it, it definitely was not.

Despite this clearly negative trend in the world of specialized psychological publishing in the country that certainly reflected deeper processes and changing attitudes to this field of knowledge and related social practice among the political and administrative leadership in the USSR, Rubinstein's paper seems to have met the sharp demand in the philosophical interpretation and establishing the ground rules and conceptual foundations of the quintessentially Soviet Marxist psychology in its search of the middle way by boldly navigating between Scylla and Charybdis – that is, the dangers of mechanicism and the "menshevising idealism". This is how, it seems, Sergei Rubinstein's intellectual genius made its truly invaluable and most foundational contribution to the entire discipline of Soviet psychology in the making from the mid-1930s onward. All that the rest of Soviet psychologists had to do after this publication was to follow Rubinstein's lead. And this was exactly what they actually did.

Rubinstein's sources: Marxist and other

Rubinstein's paper was very timely in terms of the pressing demands of the Soviet psychological community in search of its mandatory Marxist foundations at the time of crisis and rapid social and cultural changes. Yet, it was also timely in a very different sense. The paper was almost an immediate reaction to an important publication of Karl Marx's work. The work is probably less known and less popular than the author's monumental three-volume *Capital* (*Das Kapital. Kritik der politischen Ökonomie*, 1867–1883) or the programmatic *The Manifesto of the Communist Party* (*Manifest der Kommunistischen Partei*, 1848). Nevertheless, the importance this highly influential work for the intellectuals and philosophers around the world can be hardly overestimated. The "Economic and Philosophic Manuscripts of 1844", prepared by the Soviet researchers at the Moscow's Marx – Engels – Lenin Institute and first published in 1932 in Berlin (followed by another publication, also in German, in the Soviet Union in 1933), shed light on the earlier thought of young Marx on his way to the later foundational classic Marxian works. These publications of the manuscripts of 1844 provided intellectuals with very promising insights into the ways how Marx's early "humanistic" ideas could be applied in a wide range of contexts, for instance, as a methodological basis of social, human and even natural sciences. Therefore, not surprisingly, slightly over half of the footnotes of Rubinstein's paper refer to this very inspirational early work of Marx that he drafted at the age of 26. At this very age, Rubinstein had already defended his doctoral dissertation and just returned to his home city of Odessa in Imperial Russia, amidst WWI. Now, at the age of 44, a holder of a doctorate in philosophy in Imperial Marburg and a professor of psychology in Soviet Leningrad, Rubinstein debuted with his first psychological publication.

Another third of the remaining number of references in Rubinstein's paper go back to the monumental classics: the first volume of Karl Marx's *Capital*. Then, in 1932 two other important works of young Marx were also published in the same edition of the *Marx-Engels Collected Works* (*Marx-Engels-Gesamtausgabe*, the so-called MEGA1, not to be confused with the ongoing publication project MEGA2 launched in 1975): "Theses on Feuerbach" (*Thesen über Feuerbach*, drafted in 1845, first published in 1888) and "The German Ideology" (*Die deutsche Ideologie*, composed in the spring of 1846, first published in this very edition of 1932). Both works also found their way to Rubinstein's article, although neither of them with their relatively modest three references gave such a remarkable performance in Rubinstein's text as the "Economic and Philosophic Manuscripts of 1844". In any case, these new publications made quite a difference and had quite a revolutionizing impact on the social and methodological thought of the day. In addition, there is also a reference to Engels' "Dialectics of Nature" (*Dialektik der Natur*, an unfinished 1883 work on the philosophy of natural sciences first published in a bilingual German-Russian edition in Moscow in 1925), which concludes the list of all references to Karl Marx's and Friedrich Engels' works. In total, slightly less than three quarters of all cited sources in this text belong to the publications of the founders of Marxism. Then, in addition Rubinstein cited Lenin three times.

Finally, on various occasions the author refered to the publications of contemporary psychologists, mostly in foreign languages. These include: Karl Bühler's "Bericht über die XII Kongress der Deutschen Gesellschaft für Psychologie" (1932) and "Die Krise der Psychologie" (1929), a Russian translation of Theodor Valentiner's report about the X International psychological congress (1933, originally published same year in the *Zeitschrift für Angewandte Psychologie*), a Russian text by Rubinstein's compatriot Nikolai Grot of 1897, another Russian translation – John B. Watson's "Psychology from the Standpoint of a Behaviorist" (1924, Russian publication of 1926), Henri Bergson's "Evolution créatrice" (1911) and Henri Wallon's "Le problème biologique de la conscience" (1929), Friedrich Adolf Trendelenburg's posthumously published "Zur Geschichte des Wortes 'Person'" (1908), David Katz's "Hunger und Appetit" (1932), Édouard Claparède's "La psychologie fonctionnelle" (1933), and, finally, Kurt Lewin's "Vorsatz, Wille und Bedürfnis" (1926). Some of these authors – virtually all of them stellar scholars of their times and lands – are well known until now, some are still remembered by the historians of science only, and some are either well forgotten or even have ever hardly been known to the wider psychological community. Yet, what this list of names and titles shows is the distinct Rubinstein trade-mark erudition, profound knowledge of academic literature in all main languages of science of his time, equal familiarity with the classics and the most contemporary publications of the day, and devotion to systematic knowledge and perpetual learning well beyond the confines of geographical and disciplinary boarders. This characteristic of Rubinstein the thinker and the scholar would remain with him until the very end of his intellectual career and life itself.

One might speculate on the reasons and the causes of the publication of Rubinstein's article in 1934, but in fact the truth might be very simple. It seems Sergei Rubinstein was the main asset of the Soviet scholarly community of psychologists and virtually the only person up to the task. Indeed, Rubinstein's general erudition, profound knowledge of German philosophy and intellectual movements of the time (a part of which Marxian thought undeniably was), his experience of successful post-graduate doctoral training in Germany, therefore, absolute fluency in German and ability to penetrate into the intricacies of Marx's original texts (the first Russian translation of the early works of Marx including his "Economic and Philosophic Manuscripts of 1844" would not appear until a Soviet publication of 1956) – all that made him a natural first-rate candidate for the job. And he splendidly did the job.

The structure of the article

The author did not provide any formal structure of the text, yet the whole paper can be somewhat artificially divided into the following six sections: (a) introduction, (b) discussion of crisis in psychology, (c) overview of the three dominant "psychologies", (d) the rationale for overcoming the crisis, (e) discussion of the interpretation of Karl Marx's ideas in psychological terms and (f) conclusion. For purely rhetorical purposes, let us switch into the present tense as if in order to observe the drama of creation unfolding right now, before our very eyes.

Introduction: Karl Marx and psychology

In the beginning, Rubinstein finds himself in a typical situation of an author writing about another long dead thinker, who left a legacy of some kind that does not quite fit with what exactly the present author is preoccupied with. Yet, for some reason or another, he is obliged or compelled to bridge the gap and revive the writings of the past in the contemporary context. So, he needs to provide the rationale for his interest to the heritage of this old-time intellectual and explain why it can be of interest to anybody else.

Thus, Rubinstein starts with a general claim that Karl Marx has not left any single work that would directly deal with the issues of psychology proper, unlike, for instance, political economy, which is well represented in his critical works. Yet, continues Rubinstein, a range of ideas generously scattered among different Marx's works comprise an internal unity and, if systematized and further developed, "form a single, monolithic whole that permeates the entire worldview of Marx". Therefore, his legacy is not merely of historical or philological value, but is of great importance in the field of psychology: "We must approach him as we would approach the most contemporary of our contemporaries, to confront his thought with the most modern problems" (Rubinštejn, 1987, p. 111).

One might correctly remark that this line of reasoning and argumentation is far from unique. Furthermore, this kind of argumentation is frequently observed in historiographic studies that attempt to promote a relatively obscure or seemingly irrelevant author and advance his (or her) legacy among wider audiences and readerships. Under the circumstances, the advocates of the ideas of some distant in time author would typically employ a set of virtually ritualistic phrases and statements (like, for instance, the claim of the contemporary – or even timeless – importance of the advertised "intellectual product") quite similar to those claims that Rubinstein made in relation to Karl Marx. For a discussion of a similar case of social promotion and "appropriation" see a discussion in a recently published book chapter with a self-explanatory title "On Vygotsky's international celebration, or how to critically appropriate authors from the past" (García, 2019). Furthermore, somebody might argue that this very chapter on Rubinstein is also an example of the same phenomenon.

Crisis in psychology

The next section of this paper deals with the topic of the "crisis in psychology". Rubinstein casually mentions the methodological crisis in other scientific disciplines, specifically in contemporary mathematics and physics, and immediately proceeds to psychology. The crisis in psychology, simply put, is the lack of the common theoretical and conceptual foundation of psychology as a unified discipline, which leads to the coexistence of a wide range of rival "schools". Despite Rubinstein's claim to the contrary, these schools are not necessarily involved in openly fighting one another, but rather have real trouble speaking the same language. Yet, from the perspective of his time, Rubinstein is certainly absolutely right. The representatives of these schools did fight one another back then, and frequent pronouncements of the crisis and, then, the dire need to overcome it where merely commonplace. Rubinstein particularly pinpoints a few notable performances and publications to this effect, such as the mentioned Karl Bühler book of 1927 and his opening statement at the Twelfth Congress of German Psychologists in Hamburg in 1931, when he warned about the "serious need for rethinking of the bases of psychology". This warning was echoed by Wolfgang Köhler, who delivered a speech at the Tenth International Congress of Psychology in Copenhagen in August 1932 and stated that "if we do not find the connecting links within psychology soon, we will be atomized". By "being atomized" Köhler certainly meant the same old problem: the divergence of these different schools to the extent when any dialogue between them would be impossible due to total separation and fragmentation into a range of different quasi-disciplines, even though all these might cumulatively pass under "psychology" as an umbrella term. In retrospect, as we all too well can see this situation now, the warnings were in vain and had eventually minimal – if any – effect on the psychological community. Harsh criticism of contemporary psychology of the 21st century as "fragmented", "atomized" and disoriented in its methodological foundations are, unfortunately, very much not infrequent these days (Toomela & Valsiner, 2010).

The three "psychologies"

Rubinstein agrees with Karl Bühler that the crisis in psychology stems from the three "psychologies" that he refers to as "introspectionism", "behaviorism" and "psychology of spirit". In his discussion of the three, Rubinstein certainly has in mind specific psychological conceptions of his time and authors that are associated with them, yet never explicitly mentions any theories or the names. The paper was published many decades ago and these ideas – albeit in different guises and under a variety of labels – on many occasions have returned into scientific research since then. Thus, it is worthwhile to somewhat digress from too close and too literary reading and employ interpretative analysis of this section of the paper.

What in fact Rubinstein has in mind when he talks about three psychologies is not exactly specific theories and psychological conceptions, but rather the three research methodologies, general perspectives or even three philosophies of psychological research. In doing so, it seems, Rubinstein is quite consistent: ever since his doctoral study "A Study on the Problem of Method" (*Eine Studie zum Problem der Methode*) he was preoccupied with the problem of methodology of scientific research, and this paper provides a nice example of the product of his thinking along these very lines.

So, first comes "introspectionism". As a methodology of psychological research, Rubinstein claims, it rests on two pillars. The first is the acute interest in "consciousness" – whatever that means. True, the meaning of the words that serve as guiding metaphors and, then, turn into the major psychological terms is another important aspect of Rubinstein's approach. He emphasizes that the meaning of the terms is historically grounded and contextualized, and what some authors mean using the terms does not necessarily mean the same to us now. Furthermore, on some occasions, he argues, we should voluntarily and consciously revise the meanings of the words and reintroduce them, yet having invested these old terms with new meanings. "Consciousness" is one of the instances of that.

The second pillar of the "introspectionism" is its reliance on the method of introspection. Differently put, it could probably be also referred to as "self-observation" or even "self-remembering". The object of such observation or remembering is the individual, who reports his (or her) internal psychological processes that become thus "externalized" and, therefore, available to a researcher's analysis and interpretation. The assumption is that the report objectively and correctly represents the inner states of the mind, thus, the phenomenon (the protocol of the participant of the study of his or her inner world) is identical with the essence. Many would argue, though, that such assumption is overly naïve and over-optimistic: as the multiple criticisms of the method go, the verbal protocols of psychological processes more often than not distort the image and are not sufficient for a rigid study of the depths of the human psyche. For instance, one line of criticism of the kind can be found in the fascinating work of Sigmund Freud, who arguably "discovered" the other side of the mind, with all its depths hidden from conscious self-observation. In brief, "everybody lies", as a couple of well-known movie series characters of our times would famously say. And yet, even despite any criticism of "introspection" as the main or even the only method of getting inside the individual psyche, psychological researchers of the past and up to these very days keep getting back to it and productively using it, not infrequently in combination with other methods and techniques of research. In some sense, even the inventor of psychoanalysis, Dr. Freud, can be regarded as using this very method (of "self-remembering" or "looking inside"), although with very different (from the true "introspectionists" in search of the consciousness) analytical tools of profound revision of the obtained protocol data and critical interpretation.

And here enter the second protagonist of the scene: Russian (better known under the labels of "reflexology" or the "theory of higher nervous activity" of Vladimir Bekhterev and Ivan Pavlov, respectively) and American "behaviorism", the fierce opponent of "introspectionism". Rubinstein astutely remarks that what the two psychologies – despite their apparent and multiple differences – have in common is their understanding of "consciousness" as the inner mental world of an individual, separated from anything external, therefore, inaccessible to the researcher unless through the protocol of "self-observation". Yet, here lies the major difference between the two: while the proponents of "introspectionism" fully trust the verbal protocol, the advocates of "behaviorism" are extremely doubtful and suspicious of it; therefore, the latter reject it altogether. Then, along with the method, they also quite logically reject the object of "introspectionist" research: the "consciousness". This move is quite consistent with such interpretation of "consciousness" as isolated within an individual, hidden from objective observation by another party and inaccessible to a rigid scientific analysis. Instead, another object of research is proposed: the "behavior". Then, the method is naturally chosen: observation, in most general terms (which includes various opportunities for uninvolved observation, intervention, artificially designed experimental investigation, etc.). Here Rubinstein in his paper of 1934 makes another astute terminological remark: external "behavior" (*povedenie*) can be termed otherwise "activity" (*deiatel'nost'*). Someone might contest this claim and insist on the essential differences between these two terms. Yet, to Rubinstein (in his treatment of the matter in this very paper, at least), the two words are different, but their meanings are virtually identical. At this point we really need to get back to the text as close as possible, and there are two compelling reasons for that. First, Rubinstein expresses a set of very interesting and extremely important ideas on "behavior", "activity" and "consciousness". Second, although an English translation of Rubinstein's Russian text exists (translated from Russian by T.J. Blakeley of Boston College "with the editorial help of" Alex Kozulin, of Boston University back then), for some reason this very fragment has never been translated into English – despite its utmost importance for understanding his argument and, counter-intuitively, a great deal of the subsequent history of Soviet psychology. This stipulates the need for the rendering of this fragment here, for the first time in English:

> The first operation that behaviorist psychology performed with human activity – in order to free itself from the connection with consciousness ([that it] excommunicated from psychology) and to establish it [i.e., activity] as an object of psychological research – was interpreting human activity as a set of

interpreted consciousness and human psyche. Not in that was the mistake of behaviorism that it aspired to explore people in their activity, but first of all in how it interpreted such activity. And the confusion of psychology of spirit is not in the acknowledging the essence of consciousness as mediated by its relation to culture, to ideology, but in how it interprets this relation. Therefore, the way to overcoming the crisis cannot be in rejecting consciousness altogether on the basis of the erroneous introspectionist interpretation of consciousness and – like behaviorism – attempting to build psychology without psyche or trying – like subjectivist psychology of consciousness – to build psychology without taking into account human activity or, finally, making an effort to correct the mistake of erroneous interpretation of consciousness by merging it with another mistake – the erroneous interpretation of human activity, etc. There can be only one way of overcoming the crisis as demonstrated by the struggle between these conceptions: only the radical revision of the interpretation as such of both consciousness and human activity, which is inseparably connected with the new interpretation of their interrelations. Only such radical revision can lead to the correct revealing of the object of psychology. It is exactly this way – and this is our foundational principle – that with absolute definitiveness is indicated in the psychological claims of Marx. They clearly suggest an alternative interpretation of both consciousness and human activity, which overcomes the split in its roots and establishes the basis for the development of Marxist-Leninist psychology as a "a genuine, comprehensive and *real*" [in the original German, "zur wirklichen inhaltvollen und *reellen* Wissenschaft werden", the author's emphasis] science.
(Rubinshtein, 1973b, p. 24)

Nothing can be added to these beautiful words, it seems.

Marxism as method: inventing the new language for psychology

Basically, the lion's share of Rubinstein's positive program is implicitly contained in his critical discussion of the three psychologies: introspectionism, behaviorism and the "psychology of spirit". Now we proceed to the section of the paper where Rubinstein provides his sketch of Marxist psychology in its explicit form as it is presented in the system of psychological insights and ideas scattered in the writings of Karl Marx, especially in his "Economic and philosophic manuscripts of 1844".

Let us have a look at the table of contents of this work, which is the most cited source in Rubinstein's paper. What we encounter here is the mind-blowing list of words and expressions such as: capital, wages of labour, profit of capital, the rule of capital over labour and the motives of the capitalist, the accumulation of capitals and the competition among the capitalists, rent of land, estranged labour, antithesis of capital and labour, landed property and capital, private property and labour, private property and Communism, human needs and division of labour under the rule of private property, the power of money, critique of the Hegelian dialectic and philosophy as a whole.

When a psychologist or an educationist (and let us think especially about, for instance, a professional in early childhood education or clinical psychology) sees that, she might think: all this may be a good subject for a highly intellectual speculation about neoliberalism, postcolonialism, feminism, capitalism, power, liberation, emancipation, mind, brain, culture, social activism and their interrelations, but what does it all have to do with what I deal with in my profession? Indeed, the gap is more than obvious, and a great deal of interpretative mind work and translation of the terms is needed to bring all this intellectual capital closer to the realities that practitioners (or even intellectual workers) in human sciences are challenged with every day in their mundane work. In fact, providing this kind of interpretation is the goal of this part of the chapter.

One should also realize that Rubinstein's goal was very different: he made his analysis and wrote his paper with a very different readership in mind. This was the readership of two main kinds: first, the official Soviet philosophers who were socially positioned as the supreme judges and the supervisors over the politically (and philosophically, of course) correct interpretation of the works and ideas of Marxist classics in their application in science; and only then, the second group was the psychological community in search for the "new language" of their discipline, acknowledged and approved as truly Marxist by those in power. The reference to "power" is not incidental. The reader should also realize that, unlike the content of concrete theories and ideas characteristic of a knowledge field in a specific scientific discipline, the Marxist legacy was quite well explored by virtually every top-rank Communist Party member in power, well versed in most foundational principles of this doctrine. For them, Marxism was the intellectual tool that led them to power and guided their actions in their fight for a better society, and therefore, was a political issue of primary importance.

Therefore, certain liberties in analysis of this fragment of Rubinstein's paper in contemporary context are not only forgivable, but also advisable. In order to impress and convince the philosophers, the author eagerly peruses philosophical sources, copiously quotes and incidentally gets involved into arguments with the contemporary psychological scholarship, not necessarily of relevance from the standpoint of our time. Many of these are largely abbreviated or omitted in this chapter. After all, the text is available in translation and any reader with a special interest in philosophy and desire to get really deep into the details on Rubinstein's line of reasoning is invited to get acquainted with it in English, better – in German, yet better – in original Russian. What follows is a somewhat simplified and reorganized presentation of Rubinstein's take on application of Karl Marx's ideas in psychology. It seems, for our current rhetorical purposes it is most beneficial to start from the end, that is, from where Rubinstein came in the conclusion of his analysis of Marx and psychology.

Psychology studies personality as a whole, and not isolated psychological phenomena, processes or functions: this is the mandatory requirement for a Marxist psychology, claims Rubinstein. This claim is supported with Marx's statement that Rubinstein gives in a somewhat abbreviated form. The longer version of the paragraph runs thus:

> Man appropriates his comprehensive essence in a comprehensive manner, that is to say, as a whole man. Each of his human relations to the world – seeing, hearing, smelling, tasting, feeling, thinking, observing, experiencing, wanting, acting, loving – in short, all the organs of his individual being, like those organs which are directly social in their form, are in their objective orientation, or in their orientation to the object, the appropriation of the object, the appropriation of human reality. Their orientation to the object is the manifestation of the human reality, it is human activity and human suffering, for suffering, humanly considered, is a kind of self-enjoyment of man.
>
> *(Marx, 1975, pp. 229–300)*

The notion of "personality" is intrinsically linked with the notions of "need", "motive" and "interest". Specifically, "need" (and closely related to it "motive") is an extremely important concept and, according to Rubinstein, will become one of the research areas in the works of future Marxist psychologists. Virtually all contemporary psychology has either lost the notion of personality, claims Rubinstein in 1934, or frequently interprets it in Freudian (or post-Freudian) terms. Marxist interpretation of "personality" differs in many ways.

In order to clarify his standpoint, Rubinstein involves into a discussion of philosophical categories of "subject" and "object" that should be paralleled with "human being", "personality" or "inner world" and, on the other hand, "physical bodies" (or "objects"), "reality" or "external world". The principal point is, Rubinstein emphasizes following Marx, to think about "subject" and "object" not in opposition to each other, but as in inseparable unity. This is a good mental exercise and one can possibly accept this, but hardly understand the real meaning of this proposal. Indeed, a mechanism that would inseparably connect an object with a subject is needed. Rubinstein finds the mechanism of the link in Marx.

"Activity" (*deiatel'nost'* in Russian, *Tätigkeit* in German) is the missing link. Rubinstein borrows from Marx's analysis of industry as the inseparable unity of a worker, the work, the instruments (tools), the product of work (or labor) and the interrelations between them, then, he extends it to psychology at a higher level of generalization. Thus, activity unites a personality with the external world to the extent we can hardly separate them into the internal and the external. This methodological principle allows Rubinstein to overcome the traditional methodological problem of psychological science in its "introspectionist" versus "behaviorist" alternatives. Indeed, human actions reveal the mind and the mind guides the actions.

Then, like in industrial labor with its tools of productions and the industrial product, human actions require objects of action. The materials are transformed into goods in the process of labor. On the other hand, the actors themselves get transformed: they learn, acquire skills and automatisms, or even get more advanced in creative or intellectual sense, if they are lucky enough with the job. So, the transformation is mutual: not only the object gets transformed, but the subject also changes in the process of activity. Rubinstein alludes to Marx's *Capital* and proposes the idea that people change themselves, their own nature by virtue and in the process of changing their physical and social environment, the "external" nature. Overcoming the bounds of the nature – the physical, the biological and the social – as one might argue, is the real liberation, emancipation of human being ever possible and worth fighting for. Rubinstein quotes:

> Only through the objectively unfolded richness of man's essential being is the richness of subjective *human* sensibility (a musical ear, an eye for beauty of form – in short, *senses capable of human gratification, senses affirming them-selves as essential powers of man*) either cultivated or brought into being. For not only the five senses but also the so-called mental senses, the practical senses (will, love, etc.), in a word, *human* sense, the human nature of the senses, comes to be by virtue of *its* object, by virtue of *humanised* nature. . . . Thus, the objectification of the human essence, both in its theoretical and practical aspects, is required to make man's *sense human*, as well as to create the *human sense* corresponding to the entire wealth of human and natural substance.
>
> *(Marx, 1975, pp. 301–302)*

Interpreted in psychological terms, we can say that Rubinstein has just formu-lated the main law of human psychological development: personality develops not unless in transformative activity. Thus, Marxist psychology is necessarily a devel-opmental science of a personality. And it is here that another important concept of the system emerges: the "consciousness". The notions of the "consciousness" and "activity" form another inseparable unity in Marx's and, therefore, in Rubinstein's thinking. In order to clarify the link that binds the two, Rubinstein retreats to Marx's notion of the "ideal" as it is presented in his analysis of industrial produc-tion in *The Capital*. He reminds the reader that labor as a distinctly human form of activity is characterized by its two features:

First, the process of work ends in a result that was present in man already at the inception of the process, ideally (*ideal'no*): the real activity involves the ideal as its goal that makes this activity not direct but mediated. Then, second, the actor, the person, who performs this mediated activity not only changes the environment, but also realizes and materializes the consciously established goal that determines the method and character of the person's actions and volition (Rubinštejn, 1987, p. 118).

In other words, the kind of human activity that Rubinstein has in mind and discusses in this paper is essentially conscious: first, it is driven by consciousness and, on the other hand, it may transform consciousness in the process of activity or as its outcome. In order to avoid any confusion in the future and to better understand Rubinstein's psychological innovation and his distinctly Marxian interpretation of the concepts and terms, it seems most beneficial to coin a new psychological term, entirely in the spirit of this theoretical and methodological perspective: the blend of "activity – consciousness" as a psychological unit. An illustrative and observable manifestation of "activity – consciousness" in this sense is human language, more precisely, perhaps: "oral speech". Alternatively, one can think about the phenomenon of "conscious activity" or even better, "meaningful activity" that equally informs the observer about both the conscious and the operational aspects of human activity. The parallels between the "conscious", "consciousness", "meaning" and "sense-making" are entirely not incidental here: their linguistic interconnections in Russian and ways of rendering in English have already been productively discussed elsewhere (Yasnitsky & Van der Veer, 2016a).

Rubinstein points out that "activity" is never a characteristic of an isolated individual and supports this statement with another important quote from Marx: "Activity and enjoyment, both in their content and in their *mode of existence*, are *social: social* activity and *social* enjoyment" (Marx, 1975, p. 298). Then, he warns the reader not to get confused by potentially misleading the "social" in Marx and clarifies this specific interpretation:

> Social activity and social enjoyment exist by no means *only* in the form of some *directly* communal activity and directly *communal* enjoyment, although *communal* activity and *communal* enjoyment – i. e., activity and enjoyment which are manifested and affirmed in *actual* direct *association* with other men – will occur wherever such a *direct* expression of sociability stems from the true character of the activity's content and is appropriate to the nature of the enjoyment. But also when I am active *scientifically*, etc. – an activity which I can seldom perform in direct community with others – then my activity is *social*, because I perform it as a *man*. Not only is the material of my activity given to me as a social product (as is even the language in which the thinker is active): my *own* existence *is* social activity, and therefore that which I make of myself, I make of myself for society and with the consciousness of myself as a social being.
>
> *(Marx, 1975, p. 298)*

Thus, all human activity is necessarily social, therefore not individual and direct, but essentially collective (explicitly or implicitly) and mediated by social relations and products of such activity. Besides, as it follows from the quote, Rubinstein agrees with Marx that activity is not necessarily of practical nature (like, in case of industrial production), but can well also be intellectual or theoretical one, for instance, in science. Not surprisingly, the point on the social essence of activity is also valid for consciousness. According to Marx, consciousness as such is a social product and everything that relates to the psychic, mental and psychological sphere is necessarily socially determined. Hence, by virtue of being social, consciousness is historically concrete and ever changing in time, rather than abstract and universal.

The point on the historical nature of historical consciousness triggers a relatively lengthy discussion in Rubinstein's paper that seems to primarily address the concern of his peers, Soviet philosophers, very much preoccupied with the Marxist theory of historical materialism with its emphasis on the historical development of humankind as the reflection of historically changing socio-economic formations. Yet, this seems not to be of major relevance to 21st century psychology as such, which hardly shares the acute interest of Rubinstein's contemporaries in the radical reconstruction of human nature and the creation of the better, advanced, utopian and somewhat idealized "new man" of the future classless society of Communism. This line of argumentation leads Rubinstein to this conclusion:

> All the politically necessary changes we face under socialism – the reconstruc-
> tion of people's consciousness, and the overcoming of remnants of capitalism
> not only in economics but also in people's consciousness – find their theo-
> retical grounding in Marx' notion of how consciousness develops historically
> under the influence of transformatory social practice. In turn, itself primarily
> the product of historical development, consciousness is the precondition of
> this same historical development – its dependent but essential component.
>
> *(Rubinštejn, 1987, p. 122)*

This is one of those rare instances when there are some – albeit not sufficiently grounded as yet – reasons to doubt and question the utmost sincerity of these very words of Rubinstein.

Conclusion: psychology as a "genuine, comprehensive and *real* science"

The concluding section is among the smallest and the most superficial of all. Here, Rubinstein reiterates the claim of the system of psychological thinking contained in Marx's works, appeals to the need of critical application of Marx in psychology and regrets that his own paper is only a rough approximation of what this discipline could potentially gain from the wealth of Marx's ideas in their enrichment of the conceptions of consciousness and personality in their relation to human existence and development.

The final statement that concludes Rubinstein's paper goes as follows:

> A serious task now stands before Soviet psychology: to use concrete research
> work in order to actualize the potentialities, by accomplishing the unity of

both methodology and the factual material, both in theory and in practice, to strengthen its methodological position and conscious service to the construction of a classless society which is under way in the USSR, where we students of Marx and Lenin are carrying on what was central for the whole life of Marx.

(Rubinštejn, 1987, p. 128)

This looks like a clear statement of political loyalty and the Soviet psychologists' eagerness to conform to the rules of the Communist Party-state. True, that is the kind of statement it is. And yet, there is something else Rubinstein wisely does in the final part of his paper published in the penultimate issue of the last psychological journal in the country at the time of the Soviet political leadership's clear distrust of the psychologists of different kinds and their activities of various sorts. At the very end of his programmatic paper he enters another important Marxian quote that hinted at that place in Marx's "Economic and Political Manuscripts of 1844", where he equated the history of human industry and its actual existence with an "*open book* of man's essential powers, the perceptibly existing human *psychology*": "das *aufgeschlagne* Buch der *menschlichen Wesenskräfte*, die sinnlich vorliegende menschliche *Psychologie*", in Marx's own phrasing, the word "psychology" emphasized in the original. Yet, here "psychology" only means the psychic (as contrasted with physical, physiological or socio-cultural) aspect of human being. Yet further, Rubinstein brings about the final part of the quote, following Marx and stating affirmatively that only by taking into account the complexities of the entire social make-up of human existence from the perspective of industrial relations in the spirit of Marx's teaching, or somewhat metaphorically and closer to the very text of Karl Marx, a psychology, for which this book becomes open, can "become a genuine, comprehensive and *real* science" (in the original German, "zur wirklichen inhaltvollen und *reellen* Wissenschaft werden", yet again, the emphasis is the author's). In this context, "psychology" clearly stands not for the inner mental world of a human being, but for a name of a scholarly discipline that, according to Marx, is quite legitimate and possible, albeit mandatorily on a solid foundation of his, materialist thinking. Rubinstein not only repeated this claim in his paper, but also confirmed the Soviet psychologists' readiness and eagerness to do the job and zealously follow the path.

This was a very strong political "take-home message". It was efficiently communicated and, not the last, very well received, it appears.

The aftermath of the publication: *paradise regained* . . . or *paradise lost?*

As mentioned, the issue of the journal that followed the one with Rubinstein's publication of 1934 was the last one. The journal closed down. Psychology lost its last specialized periodical publication outlet. That was definitely a bad sign to the professional community from those who made decisions on scientific policy in the Soviet Union. In 1935 the number of psychological publications in the Soviet Union kept slightly rising, but considerably dropped in 1936. Also in 1936, on July 4, the Central Committee of the Communist Party of the Soviet Union issued a well-known Decree of Union "On Pedological Perversions in the System of Narkomproses" that banned the entire discipline of "pedology" (i.e., the integrative science of the child) and related mass movement. In addition, this very official document prohibited the use of the method of testing in the country, as strange and incomprehensible as it might appear to some of the contemporary readers raised in the context of industrially developed countries of the West. This episode in the history of the USSR is somewhat controversial and seems to have two general interpretations.

According to the first interpretation, this episode is a quintessential example of the brutal intrusion of power (the regime of the Communist Party) into the internal affairs of academia and the beginning of the "dark ages" for the entire field of psychology (and, generally, science) in the Soviet Union for the subsequent two decades, until the death of Joseph Stalin in 1953, at least. This interpretation had some popularity in Western historiography in the 20th century and is quite popular in contemporary post-Communist Russian Federation where it is well known under the label of the "oppressed science" (alternatively, the "repressed science"). According to the alternative interpretation, the image propagated by the "oppressed science" is one-sided, naïve and historically incorrect. In fact, as demonstrated by numerous studies in the history of Soviet science, its representatives and the entire social institute of theoretical and applied research – even despite the brutalities, political purges and tragedies in the biographies of a few individual scholars caused by the regime's decisions and activities – proliferated and prospered. Introductory reading on this counter-intuitive finding can be found in the contemporary classics on the history of Soviet science such as (Kojevnikov, 2004; Krementsov, 1997). The history of Soviet psychology truly corroborates this interpretation.

Unlike bad news, good news travels slow. The good news was that – largely owing to the intellectual effort of Sergei Rubinstein demonstrated in and propagated by his truly pioneering article of 1934 and the two university textbooks of 1935 and 1940 – Soviet psychology eventually found and gradually mastered its own Marxist language that was apparently approved by the leading official Marxist philosophers in their function of the supervisors of the entire Soviet academia. We have no definitive documents or official declarations to this effect. Yet, the sequence of events that followed the turbulence of the mid-1930s speaks for itself. Consider just one example. In 1938 the first post-Decree of 1936 textbook on psychology was published, and it was followed by a number of other ones that came out in the late 1930s–early 1940s. These publications took place not only in Moscow, the capital of the state, but also in Kiev and Tbilisi, the capitals of Soviet republics (the Ukrainian and the Georgian SSR), in the languages of the national minorities within the USSR. This is an unambiguous indicator of the dramatically improved status of psychology as officially recognized and, even more importantly, supported by the regime academic discipline throughout the entire country within its "system of Narkomproses" (i.e. *Narkomats* of Enlightenment, somewhat equivalent to the Ministries of Education and Cultural Affairs) of the Soviet Republics. A series of other events and processes corroborate and confirm this conclusion (Yasnitsky, 2015a). Therefore, if only there was any "Golden Age" in the history of Soviet psychology it would not start until 1936 – even though this year is also well known as the beginning of the "Great Purges" (alias, the "Great Terror") of 1936–1938 in the Soviet Union. The culmination of the disciplinary establishment of psychology in the USSR took place a decade later with a truly glorious decision of the leadership of the state and the party: in 1946 psychology was officially pronounced a public school subject and triumphantly entered educational curricula throughout the entire country along with other, long and well-established academic subjects. Finally, the career of Sergei Rubinstein until the beginning of the Cold War period is perhaps the best illustration of the real meaning of the "Golden Age" of Soviet science.

Yet, this story would be not quite complete without mentioning another historical episode. This episode took place in 1969, nine years after Rubinstein's death. Aleksei N. Leontiev and the closest members of his circle – some would refer to it as a "clan" – gathered at Aleksandr Luria's Moscow apartment in order to discuss the current issues in contemporary psychology and specifically the problems and the status of the "activity approach" (later known under the label of "activity theory"), which was the trademark of their own tradition in psychological research, allegedly with its roots in the works of Lev Vygotsky, their former associate, collaborator or teacher. Apart from Leontiev and Luria, Aleksandr Zaporozhets, Daniil El'konin and Piotr Gal'perin were present. The whole meeting and discussion was tape-recorded by Vladimir Zinchenko, their younger yet very promising and trusted colleague and the son of the late Piotr Zinchenko of Kharkiv (in Ukraine), yet another member of the geographically extended research group. The tapes were later transcribed and the texts of the discussion were published, even in the English translation.

Leontiev gave his "crown speech" as the undisputable leader of the "school" and the self-proclaimed official founder of Soviet Marxist psychology firmly based on allegedly his "activity approach". It was this very "approach", its advantages and drawbacks that was the main topic of discussion. All present but Luria and Zinchenko responded to the presentation with their talks, but of most interest to us in this context is the critical performance of Gal'perin. He gave an historical overview of the whole line of development of this intellectual tradition starting with Vygotsky (whose pioneering work he praised as innovative and consistent, although at the same time cited as incomplete and unfinished) until the later studies of Leontiev and his associates of the 1930s through 1960s. Let us skip the numerous exciting and intriguing details for now. Somewhere half-way through his presentation Gal'perin – well known among those in audience and beyond for his sharp mind, ever critical intellectual stance and unbiased judgment – introduced an explosive argument that, according to Vladimir Zinchenko's later memoirs (Zinchenko, 2003), had an effect of an atomic bomb for the entire theoretical construction of Leontiev's and cost the speaker Leontiev's good disposition ever since then. Gal'perin's direct speech is in order:

> Everything has its time. There was a time when these studies did something very important. They were the first to demonstrate new facts; but the point was that they stopped with these facts, whereas it was necessary to go further and decipher this activity substantively, and this was not done. A number of studies of the role of the nature of the broader activity of which a specific psychological activity is a part (for example, an investigation of will, which was also done under the leadership of Aleksei Nikolaevich [Leontiev] and showed that, if a child is playing, he tolerates voluntary assignments, but if he is not playing, he does not tolerate them): revealed a cardinal fact. There is an activity that is called play activity, and there is an activity that is called learning activity. In some cases some things go better in play activity, and in others, the opposite is true: learning activity is better.
>
> *(Galperin, 1995, p. 23)*

In this sequence Gal'perin refers to the famous interrelated studies that Leontiev's students Manuilenko and Istomina did in the mid-1940s in Moscow immediately after WWII (Istomina, 1948; Manuilenko, 1948). Of the two, Istomina's research is particularly notable for the stir it made across the state border of the USSR. Published in English translation (Istomina, 1975, 1978), this study virtually immediately made the author a scientific celebrity and became arguably one of the best known experimental psychological studies ever produced in the Soviet Union in the fields of developmental psychology and psychology of memory. Indeed, this publication provoked a controversy and triggered roughly a dozen of Western replication studies. Yet, the reason for controversy remained hidden from the eyes of Western scholars. Gal'perin elaborates on his arguments to Leontiev and suggests a few hints on the mystery of the controversy about Istomina's research in the West:

> But why does this happen? What is the mechanism of the fact that a child, say, begins to withstand all enticements in play, to which he must oppose his will? How does this happen? What occurs here? What is at work here? None of this was studied. But, strictly speaking, this would include what is called the transition to meaningful activity, and to study of the latter. And, since this was not done, we slipped into a theory of facts, i.e., what happened was that this factor, that factor and that factor acquired significance. The only thing that remained of the entire rich content of intention was the utterly barren fact that such and such a factor was important. The nature of mental activity itself remained as unknown as before and hence, despite all the talk about

the meaningful activity of the subject, to explain these mental processes we ended up turning to physiological processes. Is it not characteristic that all the investigations being carried out today under the direction of Aleksei Nikolaevich are oriented toward study of physiological processes: in perception, in emotions, studies of stress, etc.? The reason is that it is assumed that there are external conditions and there are mental processes. The mechanism of these mental processes is conceived as before in purely physiological terms. All of this is a deciphering of what I said then, that the concrete content of object-related activity, its operational side, was missing. Only now I should add, it was missing not only from theory: it was missing from experiments as well, because in experiments efforts were made to secure the external form of an object-related activity in which mental processes took place in one way or another.

(Galperin, 1995, pp. 23–24)

And now the speaker is ready to pronounce his final judgment. It does not quite look like an acquittal:

But this external object-related activity, especially a child's meaningful activity, say, learning or at play, did not become an object of study. It was not a direct object of study, and hence its relation to the corresponding mental activity was a relation of a condition summarily assumed. And no matter how hard it is to acknowledge it, the objective situation is that we can think anything we want about ourselves, but essentially we did not change the old psychology. We introduced new factors, we derived new facts, but we did not introduce new developments of these facts. Now it is time to ponder what we are going to do from here on in. If we continue this line of investigation, which lasted through the fifties and all of the sixties, we shall, in the end, come back to where we have already been, i.e., to a totally eviscerated concept of activity that commits no one to anything at all.

(Galperin, 1995, p. 24)

And then, as if those in the audience did not understand where all this leads and what kind of conclusion the speaker most directly drives at, Gal'perin refers to Rubinstein and, by doing so, he performs a *coup de grâce*, merciful killing or a control shot directly into Leontiev's head – whichever phrasing of the metaphor one prefers:

So you get the same situation that Sergei Leonidovich [Rubinstein] proclaimed: on the one hand, consciousness, and on the other, activity. How can one conceive of this? Its most illustrious formula is "the unity of consciousness and activity." There is consciousness, and there is activity, and there is their unity as something desirable. Strictly speaking, the implication is that here there is no unity.

(Galperin, 1995, p. 30)

What has just happened, one might ask? Well, this is very simple: Gal'perin has just pronounced (and quite correctly so!) Aleksei N. Leontiev – the Dean, the Member of Academies, the President and Vice-President, the Soviet psychologist, the Marxist philosopher, etc. etc. and, most importantly, the alleged co-founder of "cultural-historical psychology", the leading Soviet Marxist theoretician in psychology and the founder of the dominant "scientific school" of "activity theory" – a mere behaviorist.

This last episode serves as a perfect illustration of virtually the entire history of Soviet psychology. Rubinstein indeed "was, until his death in 1960, the most influential writer on psychological theory in the Soviet Union" (Payne, 1968, p. 2). Soviet psychological research developed under the slogans of Marxist theory and published with numerous quotes from the founders of Marxism-Leninism. Rubinstein always remained the figure of great authority even in the worst times in his scholarly career during the early Cold War. The ideas that he somewhat briefly sketched in his paper of 1934 were further developed in his books (1935, 1940, 1946) and were openly accessible to all scholars and students throughout the Soviet Union. By unanimous consensus of virtually all leading Soviet psychologists and their followers "activity" was declared the main object of psychological research and countless pronouncements to this effect can be found in Soviet publications in psychology. Furthermore, Rubinstein's ideas on activity, consciousness and personality were seemingly picked up and realized in Aleksei N. Leontiev's "own" declaratively Marxist activity theory that remained a dominant intellectual trend in the Soviet Union for quite a while. Even now Leontiev is considered as one of the leading Marxist psychologists in the world, at least by many of those international scholars who are familiar with his work. And yet, as it follows from the materials of internal discussions within the narrowest circle of top-rank members of Leontiev's circle, the whole enterprise boils down to an array of abstract quasi-philosophical Marxist pronouncements in published works of a theoretical and empirical nature, on the one hand, and a range of experimental empirical studies totally devoid of the Marxist research method indicated in Rubinstein's programmatic writings. True, the consciousness and activity fell apart. Even worse, ideology (in the sense of cultural norms and social values) was totally ignored and forgotten in psychological research in the Soviet Union. What was left instead can be best described in terms of a quasi-Marxist behaviorist psychology.

And this is perhaps the most disappointing and tragic discovery ever made by an historian of Soviet psychology.

References

Bauer, R. A. (1952). *The new man in Soviet psychology.* Cambridge, MA: Harvard University Press.

Dmitrieva, N. A. (2007). *Russkoe neokantianstvo: 'Marburg' v Rossii. Istoriko-filosofskie ocherki [Russian Neo-Kantianism: 'Marburg' in Russia. Historical-philosophical essays].* Moscow: Rosspen.

Dmitrieva, N. A. (2016a). Novye shtrikhi k portretam filosofov. Dva pis'ma E. Kassirera k S.L. Rubinsteinu [New Details to the Philosophers' Portraits. Two Letters of E. Cassirer to S. Rubinstein]. *Voprosy Filosofii, 2,* 127–136.

Dmitrieva, N. A. (2016b). S.L. Rubinshtein kak chitatel' 'Fenomenologii dukha' Gegelia'' [Sergei Rubnstein as reader of Hegel's 'Phenomenology of spirit']. *Problemy Sovremennogo Obrazovaniia, 4,* 9–19.

Dmitrieva, N. A., & Levchenko, V. V. (2015). Iz Marburga v Odessu: Materialy k nauchnoi biografii S.L. Rubinshteina [From Marburg to Odessa: Materials to S.L. Rubinstein's scientific biography]. *Kantovskii Sbornik, 51*(1), 55–71.

Galperin, P. I. (1995). Problems in the psychology of activity. *Journal of Russian and East European Psychology, 33*(4), 18–31.

García, L. N. (2019). On Vygotsky's international celebration, or how to critically appropriate authors from the past. In A. Yasnitsky (Ed.), *Questioning Vygotsky's legacy: Scientific psychology or heroic cult* (pp. 167–189). London and New York: Routledge.

Graham, L. (1972). *Science and philosophy in the Soviet Union.* New York: Alfred A. Knopf.

Istomina, Z. M. (1948). Razvitie proizvol'noi pamiati u detei v doshkol'nom vozraste [Development of voluntary memory in preschoolers]. In A. N. Leontiev & A. V. Zaporozhets (Eds.), *Voprosy psikhologii rebenka doshkol'nogo vozrasta* (pp. 65–80). Moscow: APN RSFSR.

Istomina, Z. M. (1975). The development of voluntary memory in preschool-age children. *Soviet Psychology, 13*(4), 5–64.

Istomina, Z. M. (1978). The development of voluntary memory in preschool-age children. In M. Cole (Ed.), *Soviet developmental psychology: An anthology* (pp. 100–159). White Plains, NY: M. E. Sharpe.

Joravsky, D. (1961). *Soviet Marxism and natural science: 1917–1932.* London: Routledge and Kegan Paul.

Kojevnikov, A. B. (2004). *Stalin's great science. The times and adventures of Soviet physicists.* London: Imperial College Press.

Kornilov, K. N. (1930). Psychology in the light of dialectic materialism. In C. Murchison (Ed.), *Psychologies of 1930* (pp. 243–278). Worcester, MA: Clark University press.

Krementsov, N. (1997). *Stalinist science.* Princeton: Princeton University Press.

Levchenko, V. V. (2010). *Istoriia Odes'kogo instytutu narodnoii osvity (1920–1930): Pozytyvnyi dosvid nevdalogo eksperymentu [The history of Odessa institute of public education: Positive experience of a failed experiment].* Odesa: TES.

Levchenko, V. V. (2012). Sergei Leonidovich Rubinshtein: Grani intellektualnoi biografii odesskogo perioda (1910–1920-e gg.) [Sergei Rubinstein: Some aspects of his intellectual biography of his Odessa period (1910s–1920s)]. *Visnyk Odes'kogo Natsional'nogo Universitetu, 17*(2), 109–124.

Lomov, B. F. (Ed.). (1989). *Sergei Leonidovich Rubinshtein: Ocherki, vospominaniia, materialy. K 100-letiiu so dnia rozhdeniia [Sergei Leonidovich Rubinstein: Essays, memoirs, materials. To his 100th annivesrary].* Moscow: Nauka.

Manuilenko, Z. V. (1948). Razvitie proizvol'nogo povedeniia u detei [Development of voluntary behaviour in children]. *Izvestiya Akademii Pedagogicheskikh Nauk RSFSR, 14,* 89–123.

Marx, K. (1975). Economic and philosophic manuscripts of 1844. In K. Marx & F. Engels (Eds.), *Marx & Engels collected works: Vol. 3. Marx and Engels: 1843–1844* (pp. 229–346). London: Lawrence & Wishart.

Murchison, C. (1930). *Psychologies of 1930.* Worcester, MA: Clark University Press.

Parkhomenko, O. G., Ronzin, D. V., & Stepanov, A. A. (1989). S.L. Rubinshtein v pedagogicheskom institute im. A.I. Gertsena [S.L. Rubinstein in A.I. Herzen Pedagogical

Institute]. In B. F. Lomov (Ed.), *Sergei Leonidovich Rubinshtein: Ocherki, vospominaniia, materialy. K 100-letiiu so dnia rozhdeniia* (pp. 146–158). Moscow: Nauka.

Pasternak, B. L. (2005). *Polnoe sobranie sochinenii s prilozheniiami [The Complete Works with Appendices]*. Moscow: Slovo.

Payne, T. R. (1968). *S. L. Rubinštejn and the philosophical foundations of Soviet psychology*. Dordrecht: Riedel Publishing Company.

Piaget, J. (1956). Some impressions of a visit to Soviet psychologists. *The American Psychologist, 11*(7), 343–345.

Romenets, V. A. (1989). O nauchnoi, pedagogicheskoi i obschestvennoi deiatel'nosti S.L. Rubinshteina na Ukraine [On S.L. Rubinstein's scientific, pedagogical, and social activity in Ukraine]. In B. F. Lomov (Ed.), *Sergei Leonidovich Rubinshtein: Ocherki, vospominaniia, materialy. K 100-letiiu so dnia rozhdeniia* (pp. 103–113). Moscow: Nauka.

Rubinshtein, S. L. (1922). Printsipy tvorcheskoi samodeiatel'nosti (K filosofskim osnovam sovremennoi pedagogiki) [The principles of creative self-activity (To the philosophical foundations of contemporary pedagogy)]. *Uchenye Zapiski Vysshei Shkoly g. Odessy, 2*, 148–154.

Rubinshtein, S. L. (1934). Problemy psikhologii v trudakh Karla Marksa [The problems of psychology in the oeuvres of Karl Marx]. *Sovetskaia Psikhotekhnika, 7*(1), 3–20.

Rubinshtein, S. L. (1935). *Osnovy psikhologii. Posobie dlia vysshikh pedagogicheskikh uchebnykh zavedenii [Foundations of psychology. A textbook for higher pedagogical educational establishments]*. Moscow: Uchpedgiz.

Rubinshtein, S. L. (1940). *Osnovy obshchei psikhologii [Foundations of general psychology]*. Moscow: Gosudarstvennoe uchebno-pedagogicheskoe izdatel'stvo Narkomprosa RSFSR.

Rubinshtein, S. L. (1946). *Osnovy obshchei psikhologii [Foundations of general psychology]*. Moscow: Gosudarstvennoe uchebno-pedagogicheskoe izdatel'stvo Ministerstva prosveshcheniia RSFSR.

Rubinshtein, S. L. (1957). *Bytie i soznanie. O meste psikhicheskogo vo vseobschei vzaimosviazi iavlenii material'nogo mira [Being and consciousness. On the place of the psychic in the universal interrelation of the phenomena of the material world]*. Moscow: Izdatel'stvo Akademii nauk SSSR.

Rubinshtein, S. L. (1959). *Printsipy i puti razvitiia psikhologii [The principles and the ways of the development of psychology]*. Moscow: Izdatel'stvo Akademii nauk SSSR.

Rubinshtein, S. L. (1973a). Chelovek i mir [The human and the world]. In S. L. Rubinshtein (Ed.), *Problemy obschei psikhologii [The problems of general psychology]* (pp. 255–385). Moscow: Pedagogika.

Rubinshtein, S. L. (1973b). Problemy psikhologii v trudakh Karla Marksa [The problems of psychology in the works of Karl Marx]. In S. L. Rubinshtein (Ed.), *Problemy obschei psikhologii [The problems of general psychology]* (pp. 19–46). Moscow: Pedagogika.

Rubinstein, S. (1914). *Eine Studie zum Problem der Methode: I. Absoluter Rationalismus (Hegel)*. Marburg.

Rubinstein, S. (1981). Probleme der Psychologie in den Arbeiten von Karl Marx. In M. Stadler (Ed.), *Probleme der algemeinen Psychologie* (pp. 11–32). Darmstadt: Steinkopff.

Rubinštejn, S. (1987). Problems of psychology in the works of Karl Marx. *Studies in Soviet Thought, 33*(2), 111–130.

Sieg, U. (1994). *Aufstieg und Niedergang des Marburger Neukantianismus. Die Geschichte einer philosophischen Schulgemeinschaft*. Würzburg: Königshausen & Neumann.

Slavskaia, A. N. (2015). *Osnovy psikhologii S.L. Rubinshteina. Filosofskoe obosnovanie razvitiia [Foundations of S.L. Rubinstein's psychology. Philosophical grounds of development]*. Moscow: Institut psikhologii RAN.

Todes, D. P., & Krementsov, N. (2010). Dialectical materialism and Soviet science in the 1920s and 1930s. In W. Leatherbarrow & D. Offord (Eds.), *A history of Russian thought* (pp. 340–367). Cambridge: Cambridge University Press.

Toomela, A., & Valsiner, J. (2010). *Methodological thinking in psychology: 60 years gone astray?* Charlotte, NC: Information Age Publishing, Inc.

Yasnitsky, A. (2015a). Distsiplinarnoe stanovlenie russkoi psikhologii pervoi poloviny XX veka [Disciplinary formation of Russian psychology of the first half of 20th century]. In A. N. Dmitriev & I. M. Savel'eva (Eds.), *Nauki o cheloveke: Istoriia distsiplin* (pp. 299–329). Moscow: Izdatel'skii Dom NIU VShE.

Yasnitsky, A. (2015b). Stalinskaia model' nauki: Istoriia i sovremennost' rossiiskoi psikhologii [Stalin model of science: The history and the state of the art of contemporary Russian psychology]. *PEM: Psychology. Educology. Medicine, 3–4,* 407–422.

Yasnitsky, A. (2016). The archetype of Soviet psychology: From Stalinism of the 1930s to the 'Stalinist science' of our days. In A. Yasnitsky & R. Van der Veer (Eds.), *Revisionist revolution in Vygotsky studies* (pp. 3–26). London and New York: Routledge.

Yasnitsky, A., & Van der Veer, R. (2016a). 'Lost in translation': Talking about sense, meaning, and consciousness. In A. Yasnitsky & R. Van der Veer (Eds.), *Revisionist revolution in Vygotsky studies* (pp. 229–239). London and New York: Routledge.

Yasnitsky, A., & Van der Veer, R. (Eds.). (2016b). *Revisionist revolution in Vygotsky studies.* London and New York: Routledge.

Yasnitsky, A., Van der Veer, R., Aguilar, E., & García, L. N. (Eds.). (2016). *Vygotski revisitado: Una historia crítica de su contexto y legado.* Buenos Aires: Miño y Dávila Editores.

Zazzo, R. (1982). Necrologie. Alexis Leontiev. *L'année Psychologique, 82*(2), 537–544.

Zazzo, R. (1989). Vygotski (1896–1934). *Enfance, 42*(1–2), 3–9.

Zinchenko, V. P. (2003). 'Da, ochen protivorechivaia figura . . .' ["Very controversial person, indeed . . ."]. *Zhurnal Prakticheskogo Psikhologa, 1–2,* 162–179.

PART II
Practice

3

SOVIET PSYCHOHYGIENE, OUTPATIENT PSYCHIATRY AND INTERNATIONAL KNOWLEDGE EXCHANGES

Grégory Dufaud

The Soviet Union inherited its tsarist predecessor's system of institutions for psychiatric care centred upon hospitals. Following the 1917 revolution, however, a new emphasis was placed upon psychiatric care in the community, about which we will use the expression: 'outpatient psychiatry'.[1] Measures in favour of this policy were first of all taken in Moscow – an important industrial centre and the new capital since March 1918 – which was the main beneficiary of these decisions and served as both laboratory and model. Towards the end of the nineteenth century, outpatient psychiatry had already been introduced through the creation of 'family colonies' in Moscow, Yekaterinoslav and close to Nizhny Novgorod: the chronically ill were placed with peasant families, who put them to work and were compensated. For the proponents of outpatient psychiatry, the 'family colonization' of patients was nothing more than a stop-gap measure whose goal, based upon the dual exploitation of the peasantry and the mentally ill, was more to relieve overcrowded hospitals than to help the patients.[2] But in the late 1910s and early 1920s, the aim of the newly founded outpatient services was above all social prophylaxis.

In fact, on one hand, psychiatrists worked according to a renewed approach to psychological disorders which considered social factors as decisive. When referring to a 'social psychiatry', contemporary observers were not only taking into account

---

1 Concerning 'deinstitutionalized psychiatry' or 'psychiatric care in the community', the Soviet Union used several competing terms in the 1920s and '30s: 'psychiatry outside the hospital' (*vnebol'nichnaia psikhiatriia* or *vnebol'nichnaia psikhiatricheskaia pomoshch*), 'psychiatric assistance' (*psikhiatricheskaia pomoshch*) and 'mental hygiene' (*psikhogigiena*). These terms experienced a semantic evolution similar to that of 'psychiatric care', which by the early 1930s began to be used to refer to psychiatric policy in general.

2 Julie V. Brown, 'The Professionalization of Russian Psychiatry: 1857–1911', doctoral dissertation, University of Pennsylvania, 1981, p. 332.

the environment but also the goal of considering society as a whole. On the other hand, the Bolsheviks argued in favour of a conception of medicine that intervened in every sphere of life and sought to carry out a vast programme of public health. Several disciplines closely linked to psychiatry were thus institutionalized, among them 'psychotechnics' and 'paedology': the former, developed by Isaak Shpilrein and Solomon Gellershtein, was conceived as an applied form of psychology; the latter, popularized by Lev Vigotsky, Pavel Blonsky and Aron Zalkind, was seen as the science of children's development.[3]

The importance of outpatient psychiatry remained limited during the New Economic Policy (NEP) period, which partially restored a market economy in order to save the regime from the disaster it faced as a result of the civil war. The People's Commissariat for Health wanted above all to increase the number of psychiatric hospitals and improve medical work. When Stalin took power, he began to accelerate the country's transformation and to emphasize class war. The NEP was abandoned, and the socialist offensive began. In order to care for those who were likely to develop nervous and psychological disorders as a result of the general tumult, outpatient psychiatry was made a priority in 1929. This prioritization was, however, short-lived, ending in 1931.

The recognition of psychological vulnerability

In the 1880s, the theory of 'degeneration' was very widespread among psychiatrists. It was formulated by the French alienist Bénédict-Augustin Morel, who conferred upon heredity a new function for both body and mind: mental illnesses were understood as the result of a combination of hereditary predisposition with physical and social causes.[4] During the first congress of psychiatrists in 1887, Ivan Sikorski underlined the great importance of heredity from both a practical and theoretical point of view. Yet the general consensus regarding the role of heredity nevertheless concealed differences of opinion between psychiatrists seeking to uncover the origin of mental illnesses and to broaden the range of aetiological hypotheses. Indeed, they ended up casting doubt upon the theory of degeneration itself. Not all of them subsequently abandoned the latter, but some developed a psycho-psychological model that weakened the hereditary theory in favour of social causes. In this sense, psychiatry contributed to the general upheaval of knowledge that took place in Russia at the time concerning the link between individual and society.

3 Lewis H. Siegelbaum, 'Okhrana Truda. Industrial Hygiene, Psychotechnics, and Industrialization in the USSR', in Susan Gross Solomon, John F. Hutchinson (dir.), op. cit., pp. 224–245; Isabelle Gouarné, 'La VIIe Conférence de psychotechnique (Moscow, Septembre 1931). Les conditions d'émergence du philosoviétisme dans l'univers de la psychologie scientifique française de l'entre-deux-guerres', in Cahiers d'histoire. Revue d'histoire critique, 102 (2007) Sciences et politique, pp. 65–87; Alexandre Etkind, 'L'essor et l'échec du mouvement "Paidologique". De la psychanalyse au "Nouvel homme de masse"', in Cahiers du Monde russe et soviétique, n° 4, 1992, pp. 387–418.
4 Jean-Christophe Coffin, La transmission de la folie, 1850-1914, Paris, L'Harmattan, 2003.

Beyond psychology, the emergence of this model was made possible by nervism and subsequently hypnotism. Nervism was conceived in the 1870s by Sergei Botkin of the Imperial Academy of Medicine and Surgery. Ivan Pavlov was without doubt his most famous pupil. Botkin defended a global approach to a human body whose equilibrium he saw as precarious as a result of the influence of external and internal elements. According to him, the nervous system serves an intermediary function between the body and its environment – and even ensures the body's very integrity.[5] Hypnotism, on the other hand, established itself as a medical theory in the 1890s, promoting the theory that the brain contains interrelated psychological centres. Even before the introduction of psychoanalysis in Russia, various psychiatrists put forward the idea of an 'unconscious' that influences the actions of individuals. Nervism and hypnotism inspired psychiatrists to believe in a dual component – somatic and psychological – of nervous and mental illnesses.

Various psychiatrists studied the role and influence of social issues in the appearance and evolution of pathologies. Unlike other European countries where psychiatrists studied them when considering the effects of industrialization, psychiatrists in Russia focused instead upon the effects of the 1904–1905 war with Japan and the subsequent revolution of 1905. The war with Japan was ground-breaking in the sense that, according to psychiatrist Pavel Iakobi, it had 'the unfortunate consequence of inaugurating the new psychological – and psychopathological – conditions of modern warfare'.[6] For the first time in the history of conflict, doctors set up dedicated psychiatric units with which they were able to study the reactions of individuals exposed to prolonged disturbances. This led them to define the hypothesis of psychological trauma based upon the discovery of a link between conflict and the development of mental and nervous disorders. Their investigation of a psychological state of collapse was continued by psychiatrists during the revolution of 1905. Leonid Prozorov thus argued that predisposition is not a determining factor for people suffering from psychological or nervous disorders following imprisonment. The idea of a 'traumatic event' was extended, and that of an 'extreme event' was introduced.

Psychiatrists therefore argued that social conditions can destabilize anyone and that they can lead to nervous or mental pathologies. Contrary to the theory of degeneration, they attributed a dynamic role to a person's surroundings. Reactions to this new theory differed widely, ranging from rejection to acceptance, and most psychiatrists combined the idea of a psychological trauma with that of a fragile or damaged nervous system.[7] The importance given to the social factor was a major

---

5 Corneliu E. Giurgea (with Marie Bronchart), *L'héritage de Pavlov. Un demi-siècle après sa mort*, Brussels, Pierre Mardaga, 1986, p. 27.

6 Paul Jacoby, 'Les victimes oubliées de la guerre moderne', in *Archives d'anthropologie criminelle*, no 19, 1904, p. 488. Quoted by Jacqueline L. Friedlander, 'Psychiatrists and Crisis in Russia, 1880–1917', doctoral dissertation, University of California-Berkeley, 2007, p. 205.

7 Jacqueline L. Friedlander, 'Psychiatrists and Crisis in Russia, 1880–1917', *op. cit.*, pp. 118–249.

change that restored psychiatrists' confidence in their therapeutic capabilities and heralded a future that was much more open compared to that promised by the theory of degeneration.

The model of Henri Phipps' clinic

With the recognition of the psychological vulnerability of the individual, psychiatrists developed structures for the personal treatment of patients during the earliest stages, specifically targeting alcoholism and associated disorders. Thus, in 1913, Lev Rozenshtein established a unit (for only a few months until the outbreak of the First World War forced it to close) to receive and treat alcoholics in working-class neighbourhoods of Moscow. Rozenshtein began his studies in Odessa, where he was convicted for his political activities. He continued his studies at Moscow University, where he received his diploma in 1908. Practicing at a psychiatric clinic near the university, Rozenshtein joined a number of his colleagues in protest over the government's policy on university autonomy and resigned in 1911. Subsequently, he worked at the Preobrazhenskii asylum, and then at Kanatchikova Dacha. A fierce supporter of extending the role of psychiatrists beyond the walls of the asylum, he was inspired by Adolf Meyer, a key figure of American psychiatry and a promoter of mental hygiene. We do not know exactly when Rozenshtein discovered Meyer's work, but we do know that he was present when the latter explained at the XVIIth International Medical Congress held in London in 1913 what aims a psychiatric clinic should pursue. After Germany, Austria and France, England was indeed the last stage of Rozenshtein's European trip (a Russian medical tradition).

A Swiss psychiatrist trained in Zurich, Meyer immigrated in 1892 to the United States, where he worked in numerous institutions before becoming the first Psychiatrist-in-Chief at the Johns Hopkins Hospital in 1910. Inventor of the dynamic psychiatry that refuses the opposition between the body and the mind, it focuses on sensory-motor response of the individual, seen as a mixture of anatomical, neural, mental and behavioural elements. For him, mental illness was the result of a long process of destabilization that began to manifest itself as small difficulties in day-to-day life. To prevent illnesses from developing into severe or chronic forms, Meyer asserted that psychiatrists should intervene in the early stages of illness, which is why he called for the reform of psychiatry.[8] It was precisely with this goal in mind that Meyer promoted mental hygiene, allying himself with Clifford Beers who, in his autobiography, wrote an account of his experience in psychiatric hospitals and described his recovery. Created in New York in 1909, the National

---

8 Susan D. Lamb, *Pathologist of the Mind. Adolf Meyer and the Origins of American Psychiatry*, Baltimore, The John Hopkins University Press, 2014, pp. 21, 88–98.

Committee for Mental Hygiene met with great success, leading to the creation of analogous institutions in 17 states across the United States by 1918.[9]

In his London speech, Meyer declared that the psychiatric clinic should authorize early case management for the mentally ill, if not in their own homes, then at least close to their place of residence. This intervention, Meyer specified, should take place before the patient was committed to an institution. Meyer also emphasized that preventative work should go hand in hand with considerable social work, to be carried out in collaboration with the hospital. Finally, Meyer stated that psychiatric clinics should study illness and aid in the training of future psychiatrists. In other words, psychiatric clinics should meet the needs of patients, physicians, of research and teaching, and of society. In order to fulfill their mission, they must contain all the necessary equipment and be organized in such a way as to separate patients out according to their pathologies. As an example, Meyer pointed to the institution he directed, having overseen its creation as Psychiatrist-in-Chief at the Johns Hopkins Hospital: the Henry Phipps Psychiatric Clinic, inaugurated in May 1913. This clinic included open units, a social service and a research department with three laboratories.[10] Through the psychiatric clinic, Meyer sought to provide care comparable to that provided in surgery, which had been profoundly transformed by the use of anesthetics and of antiseptic methods.[11] To succeed in integrating psychiatry into the general model of medical epistemology was among the greatest ambitions of psychiatrists.

The extension of psychiatry to society

In the immediate aftermath of the revolution in Russia, Semashko stated that the work of doctors was particularly valuable as it directly affected people's lives and contributed to the construction of socialism.[12] He prioritized prevention, and dispensaries were to be the primary tool, satisfying the demand for care of the sick and providing information on the state of health of the population.[13] The first measure toward developing outpatient psychiatry was the division of Moscow into

9 Hans Pols, '"Beyond the Clinical Frontiers". The Americain Mental Hygiene Movement, 1910–1945', in Volker Roelcke, Paul J. Weindling, Louise Westwood (eds.), *International Relations in Psychiatry: Britain, Germany, and the United States to World War II*, Rochester, University of Rochester Press, 2010, pp. 111–133.

10 Adolf Meyer, 'The Aims of a Psychiatric Clinic', in Eunice E. Winters (ed.), *The Collected Papers of Adolf Meyer*, Baltimore, The Johns Hopkins University Press, 1950–1952, vol. 2, pp. 191–202.

11 Susan D. Lamb, *Pathologist of the Mind, op. cit.*, pp. 99–129; 'Social, Motivational, and Symptomatic Diversity: An Analysis of the Patient Population of the Phipps Psychiatric Clinic at Johns Hopkins Hospital, 1913–1917', in *Canadian Bulletin of Medical History/Bulletin canadien d'histoire de la médecine*, n° 2, 2012, p. 246.

12 Nikolai Semashko, *Osnovy sovetskoi meditsiny*, Kharkov, Vseukrainskoe Gosurdarstvennoe Izdatel'stvo, 1920, p. 3.

13 Tricia Starks, *The Body Soviet. Propaganda, Hygiene and the Revolutionary State*, Madison, University of Wisconsin Press, 2008, pp. 49–51.

eight "sectors" (*raiony*) in 1919. Replacing the four sectors that existed in the prewar period, each of the capital's new districts was provided with a health clinic (*dispanser*). The "dispensarization" (*dispanserizatsia*) aimed at avoiding placement of patients in facilities that did not meet their needs and limiting overcrowding in hospitals. The psychiatrist in each sector was responsible for caring for the sick in their homes, providing follow-up for individuals who were returned to society by the hospitals, and having people admitted to a hospital if their condition required it.[14] Starting in 1923 at the initiative of a psychiatrist in Baumanskii *raion*, Izrail' Berger, the sector became the site of a policy to raise awareness about mental illness. After a few months, a commission was formed under the auspices of the Department of Health of the local Soviet to carry out inspections, protect patients, and defend their rights. This model was adopted by other sectors when Moscow officials decided to extend the awareness-raising policy to the entire city.[15] In order to oversee the outpatient psychiatry in the Russian Soviet Federative Socialist Republic (RSFSR), Rozenshtein obtained the creation of the State Health Center of Neurology and Psychiatry which, located within the National Institute of Neurology and Psychiatry in Moscow, opened in June 1924. When the National Institute was closed down, the State Health Center became an autonomous institution. Bringing together practice and research, it was made up of three units: outpatient services, a laboratory, and an office for on-site assistance and counsel.[16]

Outpatient psychiatry wanted to act as a break away from the asylum, which operated according to a specific concept of the individual and society. The tradition of asylums was based upon the premise that, deep down, every lunatic maintains an element of reason. It sought to rediscover the latter by removing patients from their pathogenic environments and isolating them in an orderly and regulated place which presented itself as an ideal form of society. Patients were completely dependent upon the psychiatrist, whose authority was absolute, by virtue of his specific knowledge. If the psychiatrist's responsibility was to find a form of treatment adapted to each patient's needs, his function went further: he must enforce the asylum's rules and maintain its orderly character, notably through its omnipresent wardens.[17] Outpatient psychiatry not only rejected the principle of isolation as

---

14 State Archives of the Russian Federation (GARF) f. a-482, inv. 3, d. 130, f. 12; Vladimir Grombakh, 'Moskovskaia psikhiatricheskaia organizatsiia', in *Zhurnal nevropatologii i psikhiatri imeni S. S. Korsakova*, n° 1, 1925, p. 108.

15 Izrail' Berger, 'O psikhosanitarnom prosveshchenii', in Aleksandr Miskinov, Leonid Prozorov, Lev Rozenshtein (eds), *Sovetskaia meditsina v bor'be za zdorov'ie nervy. Trudy 1 vsesoiuznogo soveshchaniia po psikhiatrii i nevrologii i gosudarstvennogo nevro-psikhiatricheskogo dispansera*, Ul'ianovsk, Izdanie Ul'ianovskogo Kombinata PPP, 1926, pp. 75–76.

16 G. Ia. Tartakovskii, 'Otchet po rabote Moskovskogo Gosudarstvennogo Nevro-Psikhiatritcheskogo Dispansera', in Aleksandr Miskinov, Leonid Prozorov, Lev Rozenshtein (eds.), *Sovetskaia meditsina v bor'be za zdorovye nervy, op. cit.*, p. 38.

17 Michel Foucault, *Histoire de la folie à l'âge classique*, Paris, Gallimard, 1972; *Le pouvoir psychiatrique. Cours au Collège de France, 1973–1974*, Paris, Gallimard, Seuil, 2003; Robert Castel, *L'ordre psychiatrique. L'âge d'or de l'aliénisme*, Paris, Éditions de Minuit, 1976.

an essential condition of treating madness, but also redefined the role of psychiatrists. It privileged the link between the patient and his social environment while rendering him more autonomous with regard to the institution. Maintaining the patient within the network of his ordinary, day-to-day relationships was considered more efficacious than confining him within hospital walls. Preoccupied by the environment in which patients lived, the psychiatrist delegated his authority in order to work directly with the population at large, in collaboration with various social actors, with a view to ensuring the equilibrium of the social environment. The resolutions of the second congress of neurology and psychiatry thus required that neurologists and psychiatrists maintain 'a closer link with daily life, their participation in the organization of work and lifestyles with the introduction of layers of workers through organizations'.[18] Thanks to outpatient psychiatry, doctors henceforth present themselves as social workers whose ambit is extended to all of society. Their goal is to control the latter in order to reduce, if not eradicate, the causes of nervous and psychological disorders.

This ambition leads them to intervene in the workplace, rivalling the neurologists who are already very active in this field. Semashko eloquently sang the praises of their respective competences:

> We speak of the regeneration of our antediluvian, barbarous lifestyle. In this regard, it is very important to carefully listen to neurologists. We speak of the good education of the younger generation. What better teacher (now known as a paedologist) could there be than the neurologist and the psychiatrist![19]

The intrusion of psychiatry in the field of neurology resulted in the redefinition of the concepts of neurasthenia and nervousness as borderline states with social origins rather than organic ones. Psychiatrists drew upon three large-scale studies of telephone operators, teachers and workers. The study of workers was carried out among the 300 employees of a knitting factory. Berger and his colleague sought to measure the phenomenon of nervousness, which they claimed had never really been studied as a social pathology. The study did indeed reveal the scale of the problem. Workers in good health constituted 22.3% of the total, whereas workers who were ill presented symptoms ranging from important (17.7%) to medium (22%) and weak (38%): 34.3% were neurasthenic, 15.9% hysterical, 15.1% psychopaths and 8.3% suffered from arteriosclerosis. Berger and his colleague argued that the causes of nervousness were not so much to be found in the organization of production as in the working conditions themselves. In order to improve the latter, they recommended that preventative measures be

18 'Resoliutsii 2-go Vserossiiskogo Soveshchaniia po voprosam psikhiatrii i nevrologii. Po voprosam Nevro-psikhicheskoi Gigieny i Profilaktiki', in Aleksandr Miskinov, Leonid Prozorov (eds.), *II-oe Vserossiiskoe soveshchanie po voprosam psikhiatrii i nevrologii*, Moscow, 1924, p. 59.

19 Nikolai Semashko, 'O zadachakh obshchestvennoi nevrologii i psikhiatrii', in *Sotsial'naia gigiena*, n° 3–4, 1924, p. 94.

strengthened, that ambulatory and consultative medical services be opened, and reiterated the importance of a rest period.[20]

The outpatient system at work

Moscow was home to a system of psychiatric healthcare unparalleled in the Soviet Union, and indeed in Europe, but was hampered by a lack of resources. The State Dispensary of neurology and psychiatry seems to enjoy more favourable conditions – there is no evidence of any complaints in the archives – thanks to which it is able to carry out a wide range of activities. In 1926, doctors and nurses received tens of thousands of patients and delivered an ever greater number of courses of treatment. The Dispensary carried out sanitary inspections in the factories and centres for alcoholics. Advanced training courses were also provided that emphasized prophylaxis, psychotherapy and 'dispensarization': in 1926, the vast majority of those enrolled in these courses were sent to work in provincial health departments. The Dispensary also included a commission tasked with fighting epilepsy.[21]

In the sectors, the situation fed the grievances of psychiatrists, who during meetings of the health departments of local soviets complained of the conditions imposed upon their work and which prevent them from properly fulfilling their mission. They had nowhere to receive patients, or at most only a temporary place. In Krasnaya Presnya, psychiatrists received patients in their own homes; the latter disturbed them day and night and sometimes refused to leave, annoying the other residents if not actually ruining the premises.[22] The definitive allocation of functional work places was a priority for practitioners, whose other demands included an increase in the number of consultations in order to reduce their workload and enable the too numerous patients to be treated properly.[23]

Overwhelmed, psychiatrists struggled to work on several fronts in mediocre material conditions.[24] Consultations took up most of their time. Every day (or almost), they received patients for hours on end. During 1925, in the Bauman sector, practically 20 people a day came for a consultation, of whom 194 were sent to hospital at the doctor's request.[25] Besides the consultations, psychiatrists also regularly called upon patients at home: in the Krasnaya Presnya sector, for example, weekly checks were carried out once a month by female warders (*nadziratel'nitsy*).[26]

20 Izrail' Berger, I. D. Dobronravov, 'O psikhigigienicheskoi dispanserizatsii (materialy po psikhogigienicheskoi dispanserizatsii rabochikh Trikotazhnoi chulochno-viazal'noi fabriki im. Baumana)', in *Zhurnal nevropatologii i psikhiatrii imeni S. S. Korsakova*, n° 2, 1925, pp. 49–72.

21 Leonid Prozorov, 'Nastoiashchee polozhenie dela psikhiatricheskoi pomoshchi v RSFSR', in Aleksandr Miskinov, Leonid Prozorov, Lev Rozenshtein (eds.), *Sovetskaia meditsina v bor'be za zdorovye nervy*, *op. cit.*, pp. 216–218; *Zhurnal nevropatologii i psikhiatrii imeni S. S. Korsakova*, n° 2, 1927, p. 236.

22 Central State Archives of the Moscow Region (TsGAMO) f. 2129, inv. 1, d. 252, f. 17.

23 TsGAMO f. 2129, inv. 1, d. 254, f. 55v.

24 TsGAMO f. 2129, inv. 1, d. 252, f. 17.

25 TsGAMO f. 219, inv. 1, d. 250, f. 31.

26 TsGAMO f. 2129, inv. 1, d. 252, f. 17v.

But psychiatrists were also required to attend in an emergency or at the request of a general practitioner. In Bauman, the psychiatrist's presence was requested 517 times in 1925 (without his intervention always being really necessary, as most cases were not linked to psychiatry). Last but not least, psychiatrists were also called upon to serve as expert witnesses during court cases, during which their competencies were required for matters concerning personal responsibility and, when necessary, the placing of persons under tutelage. In 1925, the Bauman psychiatrist was summoned 71 times by the court and the magistrate.[27]

Only a handful of sectors were able to set up mental hygiene commissions. By the end of 1926, barely five such commissions were more or less struggling along, working with practically no teaching materials.[28] In Bauman and Zamoskvorechye, they were particularly dynamic, organizing over 100 interventions and inspections a year in Bauman. Indeed, health department delegates considered their staff to be responsible and involved. However, in the Krasnaya Presnya, Khamovniki and Rogozhko-Simon sectors, their work was considered to be unsatisfactory. Several reasons for this were given. In all three sectors, there was a lack of staff and particularly trained staff. In Krasnaya Presnya, the team was not sufficiently united, whereas in Khamovniki and Rogozhko-Simon, the psychiatrists, working alone, are too busy to oversee the commission's work. As a result, all too rare inspections were not properly carried out, and the assistance provided by the Dispensary hardly permitted any improvement to be made.[29]

Yet despite these material difficulties, outpatient psychiatry was a reality in Moscow. Most hospital admissions were the result of requests issued by sectoral services. Outside the capital, however, the situation was more delicate. It was considered satisfactory in the Moscow region, in 12 of whose 17 districts open consultations were held by around 20 doctors, not all of whom were neurologists or psychiatrists. However, further out in the provinces, outpatient psychiatry was practically nonexistent. Leningrad and Rostov-on-Don were divided into sectors and dispensaries of neurology and psychiatry were set up in 11 towns, all located in European Russia: in addition to Leningrad and Rostov-on-Don, these were Vyatka, Voronezh, Ufa, Bryansk, Orel, Penza, Tambov, Tver and Nizhny Novgorod. But it was recognized that 'many of these establishments have barely begun to work'.[30] In reality, they only existed on paper, and those responsible for them could hardly claim any great activity – except perhaps in Vyatka, where the sanitary situation in factories was monitored.[31] For the supporters of outpatient psychiatry, Russia's provinces

27 TsGAMO f. 2129, inv. 1, d. 250, f. 31.
28 Izrail' Berger, 'O psikhosanitarnom prosveshchenii', *op. cit.*, p. 153.
29 TsGAMO f. 2129, inv. 1, d. 238, f. 44.
30 Leonid Prozorov, 'Nastoiashchee polozhenie dela psikhiatritcheskoi pomoshchi v RSFSR', in *Sovetskaia meditsina v bor'be za zdorovye nervy, op. cit.*, pp. 216–218.
31 L. K. Gromozova, 'Otchet o rabote Viatskogo Nevro-Psikhiatricheskogo Dispansera', in Aleksandr Miskinov, Leonid Prozorov, Lev Rozenshtein (eds.), *Sovetskaia meditsina v bor'be za zdorovye nervy, op. cit.*, pp. 147–148.

and countryside were thus crucially important if they were indeed to succeed in caring for 'the colossal masses of the mentally ill and borderline cases living among the people'.[32]

The priority given to outpatient psychiatry

As a result of the socialist offensive, outpatient psychiatry saw its status enhanced. Starting in the spring of 1928, with power concentrated at the top of the Soviet Union, Stalin imposed collectivization, rapid industrialization and an intensified class struggle. A draft decree of the Central Executive Committee and of the Council of People's Commissars spoke of the damage that socialist construction would *ipso facto* cause to the nervous and mental health of the population. The archives contain nothing on the conditions in which this document was drafted. One should however note that it intervened after several alerts were triggered in 1927. On one hand, a survey by the department of moral statistics underlined the scale of suicides in the country, and therefore the fragile state of the population.[33] On the other, psychiatrists noted that the people had never been so nervous. In this regard, Grombakh pointed to a number of factors: the 'economic situation', 'destitution', 'overwork', 'fighting to maintain one's place', 'unemployment or the fear thereof' and 'the need for more housing'.[34] The draft decree states:

> Socialist construction, in step with the country's industrialization, must, by the brutal raising of the cultural level of the masses, by the rapid rhythm of this development, inevitably increase the number of those suffering from nervous disorders and of ailments close to mental illnesses, for this construction involves groups of people who, carried by a great wave of enthusiasm and sparing themselves no effort, are simply unsuited to such intense, stressful and constantly changing levels of work.[35]

In order to prevent the onset of nervous and mental disorders, a Council of People's Commissars order of April, 1929, required that priority in matters of public health policy would from then on go to outpatient psychiatry rather than to psychiatric hospitalization.[36] The reform was to be carried out by the Institute for Prophylaxis in Neurology and Psychiatry, the former State Health Center of

32 Leonid Prozorov, 'Nastoiashchee polozhenie dela psikhiatricheskoi pomoshchi v RSFSR', *Sovet-skaia meditsina v bor'be za zdorovye nervy, op. cit.*, p. 216.

33 Published in 1927, the study considers suicides between 1922 and 1925. Kenneth Pinnow, *Lost to the Collective. Suicide and the Promise of Soviet Socialism, 1921–1929*, Ithaca, Cornell University Press, 2010, pp. 159–167.

34 TsGAMO f. 2129, inv. 1, d. 330, f. 384.

35 GARF f. 393, inv. 74, d. 126, ff. 4, 6.

36 'Postanovlenie soveta narodnykh komissarov RSFSR o meropriiatiiakh po ulutshcheniiu dela psikhiatritcheskoi pomoshchi v RSFSR [08.04.1929]', in *Zhurnal nevropatologii i psikhiatrii imeni S. S. Korsakova*, n° 3, 1930, pp. 110–112.

Neurology and Psychiatry, which had been renamed one year earlier. This pivotal shift in psychiatry can be attributed to the initiative of doctors who had managed to make a persuasive case for the importance of outpatient psychiatry in constructing the new society thanks to a series of shifts towards new matters for enquiry, ranging from the influence of political convulsions upon mental health to that of work and social conditions. The significance of these shifts was, however, solely due to the fact that a number of persons passed on the conclusions of studies carried out among patients up a chain that rose all the way to high-ranking soviet dignitaries.

However, this translation was dependent upon the transformation of the political landscape. The socialist offensive was based upon the idea that willpower can achieve anything, and that every person must devote himself fully to the cause. This individual effort on behalf of society as a whole required a sense of collective responsibility among all concerned. The socialist offensive must not only result in the country's economic transformation, but must also enable the individual to become a social being, one adapted to the environment whose construction he has contributed to: the process that the offensive seeks to initiate must transform individuals and society simultaneously. Indeed, the socialist offensive aspires to 'create a person who foresees great freedom by placing himself entirely at the disposal of society and who feels embarrassed to abandon the latter without permission'.[37] But the promise it represents can sometimes not become a reality. The diaries studied by Jochen Hellbeck reveal that many people felt a gap between their 'will' and the 'ideology'.[38] Psychiatry was to deal with those incapable of reducing this gap. But such a goal is likely to lead to the indexation of forms of pathological behaviour with the capacity of individuals to devote themselves to the construction of socialism.

The pre-eminence given to outpatient psychiatry bears witness to the fear among political leaders that the social world might remain beyond their control due to the efforts required of individuals for the country's industrialization. This fear, although updated in the circumstances, was, however, not at all characteristic of the late 1920s: the historiography of the New Economic Policy has shown that decisions made at the time were more usually dictated by doubts than by utopian ambitions.[39] This can be explained by the aporia intrinsic to the revolutionary project, whose ambition was to build something new from that which pre-existed it – but both the individual and his social environment have turned out to be

37 Vladimir Velichkin, 'Pravo na smert', in *Sovetskii vrach*, n° 17–18, 1930, p. 766. Quoted by Kenneth Pinnow, *Lost to the Collective, op. cit.*, p. 233.
38 Jochen Hellbeck, *Revolution on my Mind. Writing a Diary Under Stalin*, Cambridge, Harvard University Press, 2009, pp. 67–73.
39 Sheila Fitzpatrick, 'The Bolshevik's Dilemma: Class, Culture, and Politics in Early Soviet Years', in *Slavic Review*, 47, n° 4, 1988, pp. 599–613; Eric Naiman, *Sex in Public: The Incarnation of Early Soviet Ideology*, Princeton, Princeton University Press, 1997; Anne E. Gorsuch, *Youth in Revolutionary Russia: Enthusiasts, Bohemians, Delinquents*, Bloomington, Indiana University Press, 2000; Golfo Alexopoulos, *Stalin's Outcasts: Aliens, Citizens, and the Soviet State, 1926–1936*, Ithaca, Cornell University Press, 2002.

to reorganize the environment along more rational lines.[46] In his speech, Zalkind laid out the principles that, he claimed, governed socialist education: its collective nature, which fostered engagement on behalf of the common good; the necessity of engaging children in activities that encouraged a sense of responsibility or altruism; and the separation of education from religion, since the latter would be harmful to psychological development. According to him, a good education must thus combine hygiene, physical development and control of the social environment.[47]

As evidenced by the long exchange with the audience, Rozenshtein's and Zalkind's presentations evoked lively interest.[48] For Williams, Rozenshtein and Zalkind had proven that reorganizing society could resolve the problems targeted in mental hygiene. In order to alleviate the consequences of the Great Depression in the United States, Williams called for deep social transformations, following the examples set by Mary van Kleeck, a researcher in social science, the social worker John A. Kingsbury and the medical historian Henry Sigerist. Williams argued that capitalism, through the behaviours it induced and the values it carried, caused mental disorders for which psychiatry could only provide temporary relief. In several respects, he carried forward the line of analysis formerly pursued by Russian psychiatrists, who had attributed the proliferation of mental disorders in Russia to economic and political conditions. According to Williams, outpatient psychiatry was effective in the Soviet Union, because it was structural and society-wide in scope, by contrast with the United States where the approach was individualized. Williams was nonetheless unable to convince his colleagues, and only a handful of psychiatrists concurred with his analysis. They met a better reception among social workers, who faced the Depression's social impact on a daily basis. Thirty of these social workers joined him in 1936, when Williams organized a trip to the Soviet Union in 1936, which he had already visited three times since he resigned from the National Committee on Mental Hygiene in 1930.[49]

Interest in Soviet psychiatry was not limited to the United States. After the Congress in Washington, news spread that Soviet psychiatrists had made interesting advances and, in Europe, psychiatrists sought out more information. Like Williams, many of them were sympathetic to the Soviet regime, but their interest was certainly not solely political in nature. To obtain further information, European practitioners turned to the USSR's All-Union Society for Cultural Relations with Foreign Countries (VOKS). Founded in 1925, VOKS was originally structured

---

46 Lev Rozenshtein, 'The Development of Mental Hygiene in the Soviet Union', in Frankwood E. Williams (ed.), *Proceedings of the First International Congress on Mental*, New York, The International Committee for Mental Hygiene, 1932, pp. 145–148.

47 Aron Zalkind, 'The Fundamentals and the Practice of Mental Hygiene in Adolescence and Youth in Soviet Russia', Ibid., pp. 148–150.

48 'Questions and Answers', Ibid., pp. 151–161.

49 Hans Pols, 'Divergences in American Psychiatry During the Depression: Somatic Psychiatry, Community Mental Hygiene, and Social Reconstruction', in *Journal of the History of the Behavorial Sciences*, n° 4, 2001, pp. 381–384.

according to specialization, but was then reorganized according to geographical regions.[50] Writing from Genoa, Ettore Rieti addressed VOKS in January 1933: responding to changes to the Italian law on assistance to the mentally ill, he had begun collecting information on legislation and institutions in existence in various countries.[51] The same year, Spanish psychiatrists, too, requested materials. To meet these repeated requests, VOKS had articles translated, including one by Prozorov. In addition to translations, it sent along publications on public hygiene and copies of articles that appeared in German.[52]

Between insufficient support and rabid criticism

Be it from a medical or social point of view, outpatient psychiatry never played the role it was meant to. Rozenshtein gave two reasons for this during a meeting held at the People's Commissariat for Health in December 1931. According to him, the authorities did not pay enough attention to the field, nor did they realize its importance for public health. This was compounded by the opposition of various actors and doctors who argued that outpatient psychiatry acted as a brake upon the socialist offensive, in the sense that it discouraged individuals from sacrificing themselves to their work. Given the lack of support, establishments simply worked as well as they could, and problems and failures were considered to be a 'necessary evil'. For Rozenshtein, the government's decisions did not lead to significant change from the pre-existing situation. He considered this as detrimental to all of Soviet medicine, undermining as it did the foundations laid by Semashko.[53] At the time, outpatient psychiatry, without being actually called into question by the People's Commissariat for Health, was simply no longer a priority: following a series of recommendations made by the People's Commissariat of the Workers' and Peasants' Inspectorate (RKI), whose purpose it was to oversee the running of the state, the People's Commissariat for Health redirected its efforts towards hospitals.[54] This U-turn was one of the consequences of the abrupt changes that the People's Commissariat underwent, accused as it was of not properly implementing the principles

50 On VOKS and cultural diplomacy, see Michael David-Fox, *Showcasing the Great Experiment: Cultural Diplomacy and Western Visitors to the Soviet Union, 1921–1941*, New York, Oxford University Press, 2012; Sophie Coeuré, Rachel Mazuy (eds.), *Cousu de fil rouge. Voyages des intellectuels français en Union soviétique*, Paris, CNRS Éditions, 2012; Isabelle Gouarné, *L'introduction du marxisme en France. Philosoviétisme et sciences humaines, 1920–1939*, Rennes, Presses universitaires de Rennes, 2013; Jean-François Fayet, *VOKS Le laboratoire helvétique. Histoire de la diplomatie culturelle soviétique durant l'entre-deux-guerres*, Chêne-Bourg, Georg Éditeur, 2014.

51 GARF f. 5283, inv. 7, d. 627, f. 4.

52 GARF f. 5283, inv. 7, d. 627, ff. 2, 4; GARF f. 5283, inv. 7, d. 715, f. 1.

53 GARF f. a-482, inv. 24, d. 3, f. 303. For criticism of mental hygiene, see David Joravsky, *Russian Psychology, op. cit.*, p. 339.

54 'Postanovlenie kollegii NK RKI RSFSR o sostoianii psikhiatricheskikh bol'nits i postanovke psikhiatricheskogo dela v respublike [26 oktiabria 1931]', in *Zdravookhranenie v gody vosstanovleniia i sotsialisticheskoi rekonstruktsii narodnogo khoziaistva SSSR 1925–1940. Sbornik dokumentov i materialov*, Moscow, Meditsina, 1973, pp. 174–176.

of class warfare. The symbol of its reorganization was the dismissal of Semashko in favour of Mikhail Vladimirski, likewise a doctor and an Old Bolshevik.

Vladimirski redefines the main priorities of public health policy according to what Christopher Burton called the 'industrial principle'.[55] Henceforth, the sanitary system should no longer aim to be universal in scope, and must distinguish between different socio-professional groups according to the degree of their involvement in the construction of socialism. At the same time, the system of 'social protection' (*sotsial'noe obespetchenie*) itself becomes more restrictive, and begins to function as an instrument of political, social and economic discrimination.[56] Forced industrialization leads to a greater stratification of a society that privileges workers – and particularly the most qualified among them.[57] In the sanitary sector, the 'industrial principle' dictated that the Dispensary, based as it is upon territorial divisions, cannot meet the challenges of the socialist offensive: health services were distributed among dispensaries, and can only be accessed according to one's place of residence. Keen to abandon this territorial form of organization, the People's Commissariat for Health declared factory clinics to be the new basic healthcare unit, and assigned them the goal of improving workers' living conditions and modernizing the workplace. The ambition of reforming social mores through social hygiene and prevention is explicitly abandoned, sacrificed to the new productivist goals.[58]

★ ★ ★

Following the revolution, Soviet proponents of outpatient psychiatry, inspired by experiments conducted in the United States and Western Europe, undertook to win over the authorities, adapting medical elements in order to render them compatible with the new political priorities. Their approach transformed psychiatrists into actors that intervened directly in the lives of individuals in order to protect their nervous and mental health. The institutions established in Moscow and, to a lesser degree, in other Russian towns enabled psychiatrists to extend their work to hitherto untouched populations. Despite operational difficulties, these institutions formed a unique healthcare network that sparks interest abroad. But the decree of 1929 was a hollow victory for outpatient psychiatry. The socialist offensive that enabled it also prevented it from establishing itself in the long run, as the nomination of its proponents to influential positions was later followed by the dismissal of their supporters and allies at the highest levels of the state. Without the latter, they were reduced to inaction.

55 Christopher Burton, 'Medical Welfare During Late Stalinism: A Study of Doctors and the Soviet Health System', doctoral dissertation, University of Chicago, 2000, pp. 34–37.

56 Dorena Caroli, *Histoire de la protection sociale en Union soviétique (1917–1939)*, Paris, L'Harmattan, 2010, chapter 4, pp. 139–221.

57 See also Elena Osokina, *Our Daily Bread: Socialist Distribution and the Art of Survival in Stalin's Russia, 1927–1941*, Armonk, Sharpe, 2000.

58 Christopher Burton, 'Medical Welfare During Late Stalinism', *op. cit.*, pp. 35–36.

4

PEDOLOGY AS OCCUPATION IN THE EARLY SOVIET UNION

Andy Byford

Pedology as occupation

Pedology – in Russian *pedologiia* (педология), the 'science of the child' – was a multidisciplinary field focused on forging a scientific approach to the management of child biopsychosocial development. Pedology experienced remarkable institutional expansion in the Soviet Union during the 1920s in the context of the Bolsheviks' efforts to build a new, universal and progressive system of education, healthcare and child welfare (Fradkin, 1991; Balashov, 2012; Byford, 2020). By the end of the New Economic Policy era (NEP, 1921–28), pedology was enshrined as a 'Soviet science' at the service of the state in all policy domains relevant to the nurture of future generations of Soviet citizens. However, not long after, at the start of the 1930s, as Stalin began to impose ever-greater political control over both the Party and the state, pedology became, together with the rest of the Soviet scientific field, a target of stringent political disciplining. Then, a bit further down the line, in 1936, it was – somewhat suddenly and not entirely expectedly – denounced by the Party's Central Committee in stark terms as, in fact, an 'anti-Soviet pseudoscience', and its entire institutional infrastructure was dismantled for good (Ewing, 2001; Kurek, 2004).

One of the key challenges faced by those researching early-Soviet pedology is how to answer the most basic of questions: what precisely was 'pedology'? One way of conceptualizing it is as a *signifier for a framework of mobilizations of a particular body of scientific and professional work*. What this lens allows us to see is, first, that, in Russia, 'pedology' served as a prominent signifier for a framework of relevant mobilizations in one quite specific historical period – principally from the early 1920s until 1936, but not thereafter. It is true that the term 'pedology' had been in use already in pre-revolutionary Russia and that it was even then deployed in mobilizations of Russia's bourgeoning child study movement (Byford, 2008b, p. 64, 74–75; Byford, 2020, pp. 100–101). However, at this time, during the 1900s–1910s, 'pedology' featured as merely one of several partially overlapping signifiers circulating in the field (to include 'pedagogical psychology' and 'experimental pedagogy', for example) and it was by no means the most successful in mobilizational terms; it became increasingly conspicuous only during the early 1920s, and by the end of that decade, truly dominant (Byford, 2020, pp. 151–154, 185–211).

The second important consequence of conceptualizing 'pedology' as a signifier for a framework of mobilization is that it helps us see that this term refers, in fact, to a number of different mobilizations taking place at the same time. One very specific mobilization that one can follow across the 1920s took place around 'pedology' as a signifier for what was supposed to become a new scientific discipline (Byford, 2020, pp. 185–200). During the first half of the 1920s, pedology in the Soviet Union expanded mostly as a loose umbrella framework that successfully drew researchers to it precisely because they did not need to concern themselves too much about whether pedology was a discipline in its own right, what exactly its epistemological structure might be and how precisely their own work fitted in it. However, in the second half of the 1920s, as the Soviet state started to harness this field more systematically into its operations, especially in order to boost its ambitious, yet flagging, educational reforms, there was a notable shift towards transforming pedology from an inherently plural enterprise into a singular science with a more cohesive epistemology, better integrated institutional organization and more explicit political direction (Piskoppel' & Shchedrovitskii, 1991; Shvartsman & Kuznetsova, 1994; Etkind, 1997, pp. 259–285; Piskoppel', 2006; Balashov, 2012).

This is not, however, the mobilization that I shall be focusing on in the discussion that follows. What I will analyze instead is the mobilization that took place – still under the banner of 'pedology' – around a particular occupational role and related body of occupational work. More precisely, what I am interested in here is the constitution, in the early Soviet era, of 'the pedologist' (*pedolog*), as someone carrying out 'pedological work' (*pedologicheskaia rabota*), eventually in the context of the 'pedology service' (*pedologicheskaia sluzhba*) (Baranov, 1991; Tseniuga, 2010; Byford, 2020, pp. 218–244). What I have in mind is not simply the 'applied' dimension of the wider project of pedology to be differentiated from some 'pure' science of the child. In Western European developments of pedology before the First World War, there had, indeed, been explicit attempts to distinguish between a general science of child development that would be termed 'pedology' and a practical-professional branch of this science that some dubbed 'pedotechnics' (Hofstetter & Schneuwly, 2013). I am not looking to replicate this division here. Rather, what I am differentiating are distinct *mobilizations*, which took place under the same banner and were, of course, intertwined, but which are nonetheless important to distinguish. At the same time, I am not interested in charting the history of a given occupation – that of 'the pedologist' – merely in its own right. What 'the pedologist' was, how and why it emerged as an occupation, what in the end happened to it and why, is crucial to the story that I am going to tell. However, the true aim of this chapter is to demonstrate the critical and distinctive, yet so far neglected, role that specifically occupational, as opposed to scientific, mobilization played in the history of Soviet pedology.

The proto-pedologists (1900s–1910s)

The roots of pedology as an occupation are to be found before the revolution. The idea of a 'science of the child' had arisen in Russia well before the Bolsheviks took power. A vibrant movement devoted to the study of child development, involving psychologists, doctors, educators and parents, had mobilized quite effectively in the Russian empire over the last couple of decades of autocratic rule, though mostly through professional and civic initiative and with only partial and often ambivalent state support (Nikol'skaia, 1995; Byford, 2020, pp. 41–146). There is no space here to describe the history of Russia's pre-revolutionary child study in any detail, but what is essential to highlight, for the purposes of the argument that follows, is that, during the 1900s–1910s, some of the liveliest debates in this field revolved around the question of what occupations should embody and enact the new expertise that was being generated with the rise of scientific research into child biopsycho-social development, especially within the education system (Byford, 2006, 2008a, 2008b). And yet, the crucial characteristic of the late tsarist period was that, in the end, no brand-new occupational role was created. In other words, there was no successful constitution of a 'pedologist', as happened a bit later, in the early Soviet era. However, what we do see is the forging of roles that one can describe as 'proto-pedological' insofar as these served as foundations on which the occupation of the Soviet pedologist was subsequently built.

One of these 'proto-pedologists' from the late tsarist era was the school doctor. This was a recognized medical role in late imperial Russia, increasingly regulated by the state, but poorly remunerated and far from prestigious within the wider medical profession. For this reason, there were some concerted activist efforts during the last couple of decades of the empire to turn this role into something more than just a doctor servicing schools (Byford, 2006). However, this campaign never amounted to transforming the school doctor into something other than a doctor first and foremost. This was mostly because no new role, however expert, could compete with the status of a medical professional. Indeed, it was essential to school-doctor activists to maintain the prestige of medical qualifications as those defining of the school-doctor role, even while looking to boost it with additional functions and expertise. The result was the strategy of simply adding extra specialist training (in school hygiene, child psychiatry, psychometrics, anthropometrics and physical education) to the school doctor's existing general medical qualifications, while simultaneously promoting the superiority of science-based medical expertise over and above the practice-based expertise of schoolteachers. This, however, meant that the new and enhanced concept of the school doctor never went beyond that of a 'doctor in education', yet it at the same time explicitly and self-consciously entailed a form of jurisdictional trespassing, which was by and large resisted by teachers.

The second 'proto-pedologist' under construction in the late tsarist period was what one might call 'the enhanced pedagogue'. Since the middle of the nineteenth century, the professionalization of educators in Russia included a concerted campaign to boost the status of pedagogy as an academic discipline underpinning teaching as occupational practice (Byford, 2008b). This involved not just looking to improve pedagogy's standing in purely institutional terms, but also to fundamentally transform higher pedagogical training by placing at its centre a systematic initiation into the psychology and physiology of child development (Byford, 2020: 46–52, 83–105). However, this campaign to make pedagogy more 'scientific' introduced some uncertainty about what kinds of new occupational tasks, alongside traditional ones associated with teaching itself, teachers were entitled to perform. For example, a big question mark was placed over whether ordinary teachers should be carrying out psychological investigations on their pupils, using some of the latest psychological methods, such as mental tests, even if they did this for purely practical-pedagogical purposes (Sokolov, 1956; Byford, 2008a). This issue became highly controversial during the 1900s–1910s: while the application of experimental psychology to problems of education was promoted widely and successfully among Russian teachers throughout the 1900s, by the 1910s most academic psychologists became wary of ordinary teachers dabbling independently and amateurishly in the specialist methods of psychological research, notably psychometrics. They consequently argued that even though teacher training should continue to include a scientifically grounded introduction to such methods, as professionals, teachers had to limit their work and responsibilities to education itself (Byford, 2008b, 2014).

At the same time, however, the leaders of Russia's child study movement of this era, not least those coming from psychology, were keen to endow a smaller body of already experienced educators with more advanced, properly scientific, expertise, which would allow these individuals to claim a new type of authority and to carry out a set of functions that ordinary teachers would be neither qualified nor able to perform – from systematically studying schoolchildren with the help of the latest techniques of experimental psychology to offering scientifically informed guidance on how to rationally manage the education process (Byford, 2008b). Such a figure came very close to what would have been called a 'pedologist' later on. However, the institutions that provided this type of training in the tsarist era – namely, the St Petersburg-based Pedagogical Academy and Psycho-Neurological Institute – were both very new, 'alternative', non-state establishments, without powers to constitute new occupational roles in the empire's education system. In fact, the qualifications that these institutions were awarding were not recognized by the tsarist state as offering anything more than a simple boost to their holders' existing regular teaching qualifications. Moreover, the priority of those who ran this innovative training was less the creation of a new kind of practitioner within the education system and more the generation of a cohort of young researchers equipped to study child development, socialization and education using the latest scientific methods. The consequence of this was that those who went through this training ended up in limbo between the fields of education and science, for there was no role that matched their newly acquired expertise either within the education system or in the established university structure.

Pedology's niche (1920s)

After the October Revolution, the Bolsheviks embarked on building a radically new state education system that would cater equitably for the entirety of the child population of the former empire (Holmes, 1991). One of the key characteristics of this new system was the dissociation of education as such, or, more precisely, of teaching as occupational work, from the practice of measuring children's development (Mikhailychev et al., 2005a, 2005b). Traditionally, the development of children in the context of schooling would have been measured through various forms of evaluation and assessment carried out by the teachers themselves as part of their regular educational tasks. However, partly out of the spirit of progressive reformism and partly out of sheer necessity (given that large percentages of children for whom the new system was being built had not previously had access to systematic schooling and were starting from a very low educational base), the Bolsheviks abolished school marks and exams as meaningless and counterproductive, discriminatory and repressive.

However, this did not entail the abolition of either the notion of 'development' or, indeed, of the need to measure it – quite the contrary (Byford, 2020, pp. 224–229). First, the notion of 'development' (*razvitie*) was explicitly expanded and its meaning now stretched well beyond the accumulation of knowledge (*obrazovanie*), the acquisition of skills (*obuchenie*) and the formation of character (*vospitanie*). 'Development' was expected to comprehensively cover all aspects of a person's being – physical, to include both bodily growth and general health; psychological, to include the development of both functional cognition and a balanced personality; and social, to include moral, civic and even ideological development. Second, the Bolsheviks, as builders of what was supposed to become the most advanced of modern societies (and who were, in fact, trying to construct it at breakneck speed, amidst a constant threat of counterrevolution, and in competition with adversaries on the global stage), could hardly afford to neglect the systematic monitoring of the developmental progress of future generations.

It was precisely in this niche associated with overseeing and measuring all-round development in the child population at large that pedology arose as a body of occupational work. The precise position of this niche was ambiguous, however. On the one hand, it was envisaged as an inherent part of the new education system, insofar as it was expected to replace a pre-existing functional component (the traditional school assessments, exams and reports). On the other, this niche greatly exceeded the education system as such. Indeed, what pedological work measured and monitored was children's comprehensive biopsychosocial development. This included: regular medical checks; anthropometric assessments; psychometric evaluations; the testing of general literacy and numeracy; the monitoring of the 'health' of the wider social environment in which the child was being raised, including family, school and neighbourhood; plus following up on the child's moral and political formation. As a result, this niche was not an easy one to demarcate and define, either institutionally or professionally (Byford, 2020, pp. 151–154). In the early 1920s, given that the new education system was still in the process of being forged in piecemeal and largely experimental fashion, pedology's occupational niche arose in a rather disorganized way across multiple services and distinct institutional networks managed by different commissariats, especially those of healthcare (Narkomzdrav) and education (Narkompros). The consequence of this was that the niche was professionally heterogeneous and the attribute 'pedological' could be attributed to the work of professionals with different qualifications, the most obvious distinction being drawn between the 'doctor-pedologist' (*vrach-pedolog*) and the 'pedologist-pedagogue' (*pedolog-pedagog*).

Furthermore, while this niche cohered around the education system, pedological work was initially positioned largely outside the schools themselves, in hubs removed from the day-to-day pedagogical work of teachers. The most significant part of the early pedological servicing of schools, especially in the peripheries, was done through 'prophylactic clinics' (*profilakticheskie ambulatorii*) run by Narkomzdrav (Byford, 2016a, pp. 78–86). These were units staffed by doctors who monitored the health and psychophysical development of the local schoolchild population. In larger cities, the pedological servicing of schools was run from research labs affiliated to regional educational administrations, where psychologists with psychometric expertise played a significant role. These centres oversaw mass testing in schools and operated assessment clinics, offering consultations to parents, schools and kindergartens (Byford, 2020, pp. 230–238).

However, it would be wrong to conceptualize pedological work as situated completely outside the school gates. Indeed, systematic larger-scale monitoring had to be done in the schools and kindergartens themselves, which meant that significant parts of pedological work were delegated to regular educators who were not trained pedologists. For example, a key practice of staff looking after children in kindergartens became the keeping of detailed diaries on children's behaviour based on programmes of observation designed by leading academic authorities in the field (Kirschenbaum, 2001, pp. 114). In schools, the administering of mass tests was again, out of necessity, regularly entrusted to ordinary teachers (Kadnevskii, 2004). In both cases, though, the reliability of the data collected in this way was under question, not least since in these early years the training of educators working in Soviet kindergartens and schools was hardly standardized.

It is also important to note that, as a domain of occupational work, pedology grew in the Soviet 1920s in parallel and largely intertwined with another, similarly new, occupation – defectology – which likewise crystallized across and in-between the professional territories of education and medicine (Zamskii, 1995; Byford, 2017, 2018). Pedology and defectology overlapped especially in their diagnostic responsibilities – namely, the task of identifying deviations from 'normal' development. The key distinction between the two was that pedology serviced the regular school and focused on facilitating 'normal' development, whereas defectology's territory were 'pathologies' of development, to be 'corrected' in special institutions of care and education. Defectology had surged in importance in the early 1920s in the context of the Bolshevik government's efforts to deal with the traumatic effects of war, famine and mass displacement on the child population in the immediate aftermath of the revolution (Byford, 2016b, 2020, pp. 154–164). By contrast, the rise of pedology's niche was tied to the Bolsheviks' construction of the new progressive education system (Byford, 2020, pp. 164–170). The relationship between pedology and defectology during the 1920s was an evolving one and depended on the relative importance of their respective occupational niches. While defectology's niche was dominant at the start of the decade, pedology's came to prevail towards its end.

Instituting the pedologist in the Soviet education system (1928–31)

It was mostly from the mid-1920s, at the point when Narkompros's new progressive curricula started to be implemented more widely and systematically across the school network, that one sees a greater push to professionalize the occupational role of the pedologist. At first, this was carried out mostly through manuals outlining the methodologies, protocols and tests that were to become the toolkit of pedologists working in the education, healthcare and child welfare systems. However, this did not mean that there was a clear definition of the pedologist as a Soviet occupation. In practice, the background of those deemed qualified to carry out pedological work of one type or another remained open: the job continued be done by those with medical training as well as those who received suitable qualifications at a pedagogical institute, and this work was still being overseen and regulated by different commissariats.

However, in 1928, around the time of the First All-Union Pedology Congress in Moscow (the event that formally enshrined pedology as a 'Soviet science' at the service of the state), key figures at Narkompros, both political and academic, started to argue more vocally that it was essential to establish an occupationally more coherent pedology service, which would be tasked with providing comprehensive pedological support to Narkompros's school network (Byford, 2020, pp. 239–240). The Commissar of Enlightenment, Anatolii Lunacharskii, stressed that the function of the pedologist needed to be made distinct from that of the school doctor (Baranov, 1991, p. 103). In particular, he wanted to see the pedology service supporting schools become less dependent on Narkomzdrav and for there to be more specialists in pedology trained in relevant streams at the Narkompros-run pedagogical institutes. At around this same time, the prominent educational reformist, Pavel Blonskii, one of the authors of Narkompros's progressive new curricula and an active promoter of pedology in education, described pedological work as a serious and complex examination of a 'clinical' kind, yet which monitored and fostered not 'health' but 'development' (Byford, 2020, p. 238). Thus, while using medical paradigms to model pedological work, Blonskii explicitly distinguished the two domains in terms of their respective functions and goals.

A further push to constitute the school pedologist as a specialist occupational role in the education system came from the lobby campaigning for the expansion of mass testing in Soviet schools. One of the leaders of this lobby was, again, Blonskii (Kadnevskii, 2004; Leopoldoff, 2014; Byford, 2020, pp. 230–238). The First All-Union Pedology Congress had, in fact, revealed significant divisions among Soviet psychologists over the mass use of psychometrics in schools, and one of the key arguments against the practice was that tests were all too often being entrusted to untrained and unreliable run-of-the-mill teachers. Blonskii, who was originally very encouraging of the involvement of teachers in testing as a way of promoting this practice in education more generally, resolved at this point that the future of psychometrics in the Soviet education system depended on preparing qualified specialists who would, crucially, be permanently based in schools. This did not preclude such figures coming from the ranks of teachers, so long as they were appropriately trained and employed specifically as pedologists with a distinct set of occupational tasks, to include, notably, psychometrics (Byford, 2020, pp. 237–238).

However, although the Soviet government issued directives designed to stimulate the creation of a more systematic pedology service for its school network already from 1928, Narkompros was slow to implement them, failing to pour sufficient resources into the initiative. A report produced in 1931 highlighted that Narkomzdrav still seemed to be overseeing the lion's share of ground-level pedological work in the country, while the service run by Narkompros remained haphazard and understaffed (Byford, 2020, p. 240). Another reason for this was that the priority of pedology's academic leadership at this particular juncture was the mobilization of pedology as a science rather than an occupation. Indeed, 1928–30, the years that followed the First All-Union Pedology Congress, were a crucial period during which this otherwise fragmented and multidisciplinary field worked hard to form a more cohesively organized scientific enterprise. This did not mean that the leaders of pedology ignored the practical role that the state expected pedology to play in the education system. Far from it – they hoped to make pedology as science pervade Soviet education from top to bottom. However, they tended to conceptualize pedological work carried out locally as an inherent part of a *scientific* hierarchy: pedology units servicing schools were understood as 'ground-level cells' (*nizovye iacheiki*) that fed empirical data up the chain to pedology's scientific centre (the major research institutes based in Moscow) where general theories and recommendations would be formulated on the basis of systematic analysis and then

expertise, but decisions were a matter for the 'brigade' as a whole; this meant that the pedologist's recommendations could be diluted or even voted down.

Significantly, though, each school pedologist was at the same time in regular communication with the regional pedology centre. The latter might ask the school pedologist to take on certain tasks, such as gathering data for some general study or report; or conversely, the school pedologist could refer to the regional centre some especially problematic child that the school was unable to deal with on its own. Thus, even when intimately embedded in school life, the school pedologist was never simply and straightforwardly a school role, but simultaneously acted as part of a top-down service that operated autonomously from the schools themselves.

Moreover, the occupation-specific expertise of school pedologists was understood to be ultimately rooted in the authority of 'science' – specifically the science black-boxed as 'pedology' (Byford, 2020, pp. 219–224). While all Soviet teachers were expected to gain some grounding in pedology as part of their professional training, pedology as 'science' still seemed rather remote, specialist and technical to the run-of-the-mill educator. It is not that pedology was viewed as dissociated from the interests of practicing educators or the aims of education as such, but simply that the authority of pedology as a body of expertise was experienced as separate from the educators' own professional authority. This was why it was not uncommon for schools to see recommendations coming from the pedologists as interfering or misplaced, especially if they implied criticism of the teachers or the school management. However, the separate nature of pedology's authority, black-boxed as the view of 'science', could also be very useful to schools. For example, teachers and administrators would readily invoke it in situations where a case needed to be made for an underperforming pupil to be streamed into a separate class or for a particularly troublesome child to be moved to a different school.

With the start of the second five-year plan in 1932, the priority of all branches of the Soviet state, including Narkompros, was to enhance the efficiency with which targets were met and outputs delivered. One of Narkompros's key policies in this context became streaming by ability and the referral to 'special schools' of pupils who for one reason or another slowed down the pace of regular pedagogical work and the realization of standard school programmes (Byford, 2020, pp. 224–229). The idea of streaming had been developed and promoted already in the late 1920s (by figures such as Blonskii, for instance), but it was only in the 1930s that the measure started to be taken more seriously by Narkompros officials and school authorities as an effective tool for managing school discipline and improving overall outputs. School pedologists were placed right at the centre of this policy and its implementation became one of the core tasks of the pedology service.

Evaluations resulting in a pupil being moved to an auxiliary class or special school were complex and not solely the work of the pedologist: they also included contributions from teachers, the school doctor and school administrators (Byford, 2020, pp. 222–224). A certain proportion of children selected for referral were labelled 'difficult to educate' (*trudnovospituemye*); another group was those diagnosed with a mental health condition (*psikhonevrotiki*). For these two categories decisive were pedagogical and medical verdicts respectively. However, by far the largest percentage of referrals were those labelled 'mentally backward' (*umstvenno otstalye*). What was meant by this seemingly harsh term (another translation of *otstalost'* being 'retardation') was not exactly the more serious forms of congenital learning difficulties that would fall within the remit of defectology. Rather, the term entailed a lower than average cognitive performance that prevented the child from following the standard school programme at the required level and pace. Although all diagnoses and referrals were explicitly based on a range of assessments, crucial to the diagnosis of 'mental backwardness' was an 'objective' measure of a child's 'level' of cognitive development, which was established by means of tests. There was, however, a variety of tests used as part of such diagnostics, resulting in some ambiguity about what precisely constituted 'mental backwardness'. Crucially, though, even when tests measured general intelligence or specific mental functions, the output was understood as something that mapped onto the child's ability to realize normative educational goals (Byford, 2014, 2020, p. 232).

However, what was really important about tests was that as instruments that produced objective outputs, they came to embody the instrumental nature not just of pedological assessment more generally, but also of the pedology service as such, including the pedologist as an occupation and pedology as a body of science-based expertise. As an occupation, pedology thereby became an instrument to which particular decisions within the system could be delegated (Byford, 2020, pp. 223–224). Decision-making around the question of whether a child should be referred to a special school was neither automated nor automatic, nor was it all down to the pedologists. And yet, such decision-making was – of necessity, since otherwise it would be neither efficient nor replicable – enclosed in a series of black boxes, each fitted inside the other, starting with the test administered by a pedologist as autonomous expert-practitioner representing a bureaucratically-organized service and finishing with pedology as the science that had supposedly mastered the laws of child development and the techniques of its objective measurement.

One could argue that such comprehensive black-boxing of pedology as an instrument serving the education system was essential to pedology's continued existence in the Soviet Union after 1931–32 (Byford, 2020, p. 224). However, this black-boxing also contributed to the remarkable swiftness of pedology's downfall in 1936. Instrumentalized and black-boxed as pedology had become over the course of the 1930s, it was very difficult to defend once this instrument and its outputs came to be viewed as, in fact, highly problematic. Just as a particular process of decision-making had effectively been delegated to it, so the blame for the glitches that came out of this were pinned on that same instrument – not just the tests, but also those administering them, and, ultimately, on pedology as a body of scientific knowledge that endowed the service with legitimacy.

The downfall of pedology as the demise
of an occupation (1935–36)

Even though pedological work was in full swing during the early 1930s, the service was not immune to criticism (Ewing, 2001; Byford, 2020, p. 244). Yet the dispersed, local and routine nature of ground-level pedological work, which featured as merely a functional component of a more general system of operations through which schools were managed by Narkompros, protected the pedology service from more systematic and sustained political scrutiny. This did not, however, last forever. Crucial to the eventual downfall of pedology in the summer of 1936 was the suddenly much closer attention that pedological work started to receive from the very top of the Party in 1935.

Up until 1935, what pedologists did on a daily basis in schools had not been watched particularly closely by Party structures, not least since the highest echelons of the Party had not been expressing any great interest in pedology since the 1931–32 campaign to politically subordinate the field's academic leadership. However, over the course of 1935, a few politically sensitive incidents taking place in schools were brought to the attention of the Politburo prompting the Party to start to scrutinize much more closely what Narkompros was doing to keep control over the schoolchild population (on what follows see especially Rodin, 1998; Byford, 2020, pp. 244–248). A number of commissions, each headed by a leading Party figure, were formed to look into the matter at different educational levels, with Leningrad Party boss Andrei Zhdanov becoming responsible for high schools. Although pedology itself was not the focus of enquiry, the work of these commissions led their members to become much better acquainted with the work of the pedology service as a key instrument in Narkompros's approach to managing discipline and delivering educational targets. In this context, the commissions approved, in fact, the policy of removing disruptive pupils from the regular classroom, deeming this both necessary and effective. However, there were aspects of the work of the pedology service which raised alarm bells. For example, it was argued that pedologists must ensure that referrals did not display bias against children from working class or ethnic minority backgrounds. Of particular concern was also the pedologists' routine collection of detailed personal and medical information about the children's parents and families more generally. Zhdanov saw this as something highly sensitive from a political point of view and ordered that the practice be stopped.

The findings of these commissions did not in themselves threaten the pedology service. However, the key consequence of their work was that local Party structures were now suddenly on alert and began to observe the activities of ground-level pedologists much more closely than had been the case before, considering them to be of interest to Party bosses. At the start of 1936, the section for schools of the Leningrad-area Party committee alerted Zhdanov that local pedologists did not appear to be listening to the directives that he had issued only a few months earlier. Zhdanov's attention was drawn to extensive surveys that the Leningrad Pedology

Institute was at that time conducting among the families of schoolchildren in the Pskov district. Zhdanov was clearly annoyed: on 4 April 1936 he gave a speech at the meeting of the Leningrad Party bureau where he denounced pedologists for going around prying into people's private affairs, seeking out negative aspects of family life, and investigating not just the children but also their parents and grandparents, asking questions concerning class origins, while seemingly only looking for defects and anomalies in people's family histories. Zhdanov at first appeared to be targeting only the Leningrad Pedology Institute. However, by the sheer logic of campaigns designed to impose Party control across a particular domain of state operations, the errors of this Institute came to serve as merely an example of a much wider and deeper problem. The torch was suddenly shone very brightly on the pedology service more generally, as an instrument that Narkompros was relying on to manage the efficiencies of the education system. Zhdanov was at the forefront of this campaign of critical scrutiny and his vocal disapproval began to attract and concentrate various previously isolated complaints and grievances about pedological work.

Among the most problematic issues to emerge was the pedologists' role in referring so many children to special schools. Zhdanov condemned the readiness with which children were being taken out of regular classes, arguing that such a policy disincentivized teachers from trying to improve pupils' performance and behaviour using their own methods and techniques. Moreover, the speed at which schools for the underachieving and the misbehaving were mushrooming had produced some unintended effects. The overall percentage of those relegated (somewhere in the region of 2%) was not huge, especially if one's understanding of underachievement was relatively fluid. However, by grouping such children into larger cohorts, and especially when they formed entire schools, these populations suddenly appeared much bigger. Moreover, managing schools populated entirely with the underperforming and the disruptive was a challenge, not least since providing such schools with additional resources and expertise, as was recommended by leading pedologists who promoted this type of triage, was not, in fact, within the state's means. The whole matter was made worse by the way in which such children were labelled. Though individual cases varied, they were invariably categorized using terms that carried stigma, not just for the children, but also their families, and ultimately the state. Zhdanov complained about the impression that the mass nature of such referrals gave of Soviet society as supposedly experiencing 'degradation' (*degradatsiia*) and he blamed this on tests, describing them as pseudoscientific instruments that produced spurious diagnoses of 'backwardness'.

In June 1936 Zhdanov orchestrated a meeting with Leningrad teachers and pedologists billed 'The Audience of Teachers and Pedologists of Leningrad Schools with Comrade Zhdanov'. At this meeting he gave a speech titled 'On the Pedological Distortions in the Narkompros RSFSR' ('O pedologicheskikh izvrashcheniiakh v Narkomprose RSFSR') announcing that the question of the future of pedology had, thanks to his personal initiative, been placed on the agenda of the next meeting of the Politburo. Two days later, the Politburo discussed the agenda item tabled by Zhdanov and formed a commission made up of Komsomol leader A. V. Kosarev, Commissar of Education A. S. Bubnov, Commissar of Healthcare G. N. Kaminskii, and Zhdanov himself. Their task was to prepare a decree on the matter of pedology on behalf of the Party's Central Committee. This became the now infamous decree 'On the Pedological Distortions in the System of the Narkompros', issued on 4 July 1936. In it, the Party's Central Committee accused 'the so-called "pedologist"' of using pseudoscientific tests and questionnaires to justify the exclusion of large numbers of children, especially those from working class and minority backgrounds, from regular schooling, while apparently blaming poor performance and indiscipline in a deterministic way on innate pathologies and the family's social background.

Even though the decree denounced pedology wholesale as a 'reactionary pseudoscience', its core charges focused on the occupational work of ground-level pedologists. Indeed, what followed was first and foremost the rapid and comprehensive dismantlement of pedology's occupational network, starting with the mass redeployment of school pedologists to other posts available in the system (Ewing, 2001). This process began already on 7 July 1936, as Commissar Bubnov sent a telegram to all local educational administrations with the order to relieve every pedologist of their duties with immediate effect. Most pedologists were swiftly re-employed as teachers, while some were given posts in the educational administration. Those with medical degrees were turned into school doctors. By August 1936 over half the staff had been successfully allocated a new role. This is not to say that the summer was not a period of grave uncertainty for former pedologists who had every right to worry about becoming targets of more serious reprisals. In the wake of the Party decree, the press caricatured 'the pedologist' as an evil scientist sabotaging the Soviet education system. However, this was a caricature of a particular kind of occupational work, rather than of concrete individuals who held this job title. In other words, it was the role that needed to go, not the person fulfilling it. As a result, there were no mass repressions and punishments more typically included the loss of the right to claim the years spent in the post as part of one's pensionable employment.

The Party's anti-pedology decree also entailed the condemnation of and blanket ban on all the key instruments that pedologists used in their daily work, especially tests, questionnaires and family surveys. Schools were simultaneously ordered to remove from pupils' school files all biopsychosocial data that had been collected by the pedologists. However, the most important aspect of the dismantlement of pedology as an occupation was the denunciation of the policy of streaming and referrals, in which the pedology service had played such an instrumental role. This included not only putting the brakes on the practice, but reversing it, i.e. transferring children back from special schools to regular ones or, in some cases, simply re-categorizing an entire school from special to normal (Ewing, 2001).

However, it was not sufficient simply to abolish the post of pedologists, to ban the tools of their trade, and to dismantle the institutional structure of their operations. It was also essential to replace the very functions of pedological work – that of monitoring and managing all-round biopsychosocial development in the Soviet schoolchild population – by the work of another occupation. One of the key points made by the Party's decree was that the occupational work of pedologists had been in conflict with the occupational work of another profession – namely, teachers. More specifically, the work of pedologists was said to have been trespassing on what was supposed to be the rightful territory of professional educators, while apparently actively undermining their work as pedagogues. It was argued, for example, that the prioritization of referrals entailed a lack of trust in the teachers' pedagogical expertise, and that the privileging of tests as modes of evaluation implied a distrust of the teachers' own practices of measuring development. This was not a difficult argument to make given the return of formal school marks and standard, scholastic modes of assessment following the 1931 educational reform.

During the latter half of 1936, teachers were swiftly mobilized into the campaign of pedology's political denunciation. Throughout that school year they were expected to lambast the former pedology service from their own perspective, playing the part both of its victims and of witnesses to its harmful effects on Soviet children, parents and education more generally. More important, however, was that the occupational role of 'the teacher' was hereby being lined up to replace that of 'the pedologist'. This was framed as the 'reinstatement' of teachers in their rightful occupational role (Ewing, 2001). Teachers were now recast as the true heroes of the future successes of Soviet education, not least by being expected to take on full professional responsibility for the task of monitoring, managing and directing the development of future Soviet generations into productive, disciplined and patriotic citizens.

Conclusion

Crucial to the emergence of pedology as a domain of occupational work was the conceptualization of human ontogenetic development as something that was subject to systematic, rational management, but that exceeded the remit of every preexisting occupation focused on the nurture of the young in a given society. The occupational niche that came to be filled by pedology was tied to the territory occupied by educators broadly defined, but depended on the assumption that the education profession itself was not equipped with the necessary scientific knowledge and expertise to properly conceptualize, measure and foster 'development' in its full, all-round, biopsychosocial sense. In tsarist Russia, two 'proto-pedological' occupational forms – the school doctor and the 'enhanced pedagogue' – arose on the margins of the core territory of upbringing and education, but these assumed only supplementary positions in the field as holders of important parts of the missing expertise, without, however, successfully forming new occupational roles as such.

In the 1920s' Soviet Union, the ambition of the new power-holders to construct a progressive education system in which an expansive biopsychosocial definition of development trumped traditional, narrowly pedagogical conceptions of it, proved highly conducive to the institutionalization of a new territory of expertise that crystallized under the banner of 'pedology'. The latter was tied to the education system, but it at the same time formed an autonomous domain that in multiple ways exceeded the management of education strictly speaking. What is more, this field, as a field of science, assumed a hierarchically superior position over and above the education profession itself, thanks to explicit support that it received from those in positions of political power. Critical to this new field becoming also a territory of occupational work was the ambition of the new Bolshevik-run state for its system of upbringing and education to be directed towards fostering development precisely in the above broad sense, and also, for this development to be systematically monitored and managed across the country's schoolchild population as a whole. The conceptualization and measurement of the development of future Soviet citizens was consequently entrusted to pedology, which was to be proactively mobilized as a domain of both scientific and occupational work placed expressly at the service of the state.

The precise positioning of pedology in relation to the education system remained complex and ambiguous, though. For most of the 1920s, pedology as occupation was a professionally heterogeneous territory and the occupational functions and expertise of ground-level pedologists were not defined in a uniform way. Although there was a push in the latter half of the 1920s towards constructing the occupational role of the pedologist more explicitly as a function of managing child development specifically within the education system, significant parts of pedological work and expertise continued to be positioned outside the schools themselves. This was partly because large portions of such work were still being carried out by medical professionals, and partly because, in the late 1920s, the mobilization of pedology as a scientific enterprise trumped its development as an occupational role.

The year 1931 became, however, a critical turning point in the fate of pedology in the Soviet Union. On the one hand, following the Party-political disciplining of the field's highest echelons, the previously dominant development of pedology as a 'science' effectively ceased. On the other, the radical U-turn in Soviet educational policy fatally undermined pedology's occupational niche and led to pedology becoming reduced to an instrumentalized service that performed a set of pragmatic functions associated, among other things, with the policy of streaming and referrals deployed as a way of managing discipline and enhancing overall performance across the school network. This, moreover, inextricably implicated pedology as an occupation in a policy and practice that was by the mid-1930s starting to produce a series of problematic effects.

Pedological work was initially protected from view by its relatively routine, ground-level character. However, once it was noticed by the top of the Party it was rapidly seized upon as the element on which to pin what were perceived to be some serious administrative and political errors committed by Narkompros. Crucially, the impossibility of politically controlling such mass, highly dispersed ground-level occupational work led to the radical measure of pedology's comprehensive abolition by Party decree in the summer of 1936. Thus, despite the catchy headline of pedology's purge as a 'pseudo-*science*', it was the erasure of pedology's *occupational* role, work and instruments that encapsulates more accurately what was ultimately at stake in this infamous episode in the history of the early-Soviet human sciences.

References

Balashov, E. M. (2012). *Pedologiia v Rossii v pervoi tret'i XX veka*. St Petersburg: Nestor-Istoriia.

Baranov, V. F. (1991). Pedologicheskaia sluzhba v sovetskoi shkole 20–30-kh gg. *Voprosy psikhologii*, 4, 100–112.

Byford, A. (2006). Professional cross-dressing: Doctors in education in late imperial Russia (1881–1917). *The Russian Review*, 65(4), 586–616.

Byford, A. (2008a). Psychology at high school in late imperial Russia (1881–1917). *History of Education Quarterly*, 48(2), 265–297.

Byford, A. (2008b). Turning pedagogy into a science: Teachers and psychologists in late imperial Russia (1897–1917). *Osiris*, 23, 50–81.

Byford, A. (2014). The mental test as a boundary object in early-20th-century Russian child science. *History of the Human Sciences*, 27(4), 22–58.

Byford, A. (2016a). Imperial normativities and the sciences of the child: The politics of development in the USSR, 1920s-1930s. *Ab Imperio*, 2, 71–124.

Byford, A. (2016b). Trauma and pathology: Normative crises and the child population in late tsarist Russia and the early Soviet Union, 1904–1924. *Journal of the History of Childhood and Youth*, 9(3), 450–469.

Byford, A. (2017). The imperfect child in early twentieth-century Russia. *History of Education*, 46(5), 595–617.

Byford, A. (2018). *Lechebnaia pedagogika*: The concept and practice of therapy in Russian defectology, c. 1880–1936. *Medical History*, 62(1), 67–90.

Byford, A. (2020). *Science of the child in late imperial and early Soviet Russia*. Oxford: Oxford University Press.

Etkind, A. (1997). *Eros of the impossible: The history of psychoanalysis in Russia*. Boulder: Westview Press.

Ewing, E. T. (2001). Restoring teachers to their rights: Soviet education and the 1936 denunciation of pedology. *History of Education Quarterly*, 41(4), 471–493.

Fradkin, F. A. (1991). *Pedologiia: mify i deistvitel'nost'*. Moscow: Znanie.

Hofstetter, R., & Schneuwly, B. (2013). 'Ascension, embrasement et disparition d'une science. Le point de vue d'un observateur privilégié: Claparède et la pédologie au début du XXe siècle', in J. Friedrich, R. Hofstetter & B. Schneuwly (eds), *Une science du développement humain est-elle possible? Controverses du début du XXe siècle* (pp. 45–64). Rennes: Presses universitaires de Rennes.

Holmes, L. E. (1991). *The Kremlin and the schoolhouse: Reforming education in Soviet Russia, 1917–1931*. Bloomington: Indiana University Press.

Holmes, L. E. (1999). *Stalin's school: Moscow's model school No. 25, 1931–1937*. Pittsburgh: University of Pittsburgh Press.

Kadnevskii, V. M. (2004). *Istoriia testov: Monografiia*. Moscow: Narodnoe obrazovanie.

Kirschenbaum, L. A. (2001). *Small comrades: Revolutionizing childhood in Soviet Russia, 1917–1932*. New York and London: Routledge Falmer.

Krementsov, N. (1997). *Stalinist science*. Princeton: Princeton University Press.

Kurek, N. S. (2004). *Istoriia likvidatsii pedologii i psikhotekhniki*. St Petersburg: Aleteiia.

Leopoldoff, I. (2014). A psychology for pedagogy: Intelligence testing in USSR in the 1920s. *History of Psychology, 17*(1), 187–205.

Mikhailychev, E. A., Karpova, G. F., & Leonova, E. E. (2005a). Diagnostika i pedagogicheskaia korrektsiia v shkole 20-kh godov. *Pedagogicheskaia diagnostika, 5*, 3–6.

Mikhailychev, E. A., Karpova, G. F., & Leonova, E. E. (2005b). Pedagogicheskaia diagnostika v reshenii obrazovatel'nykh zadach Rossii pervoi poloviny XX veka. *Pedagogicheskaia diagnostika, 2*, 3–10, *3*, 3–9.

Nikol'skaia, A. A. (1995). *Vozrastnaia i pedagogicheskaia psikhologiia v dorevoliutsionnoi Rossii*. Dubna: Feniks.

Piskoppel', A. A. (2006). Pedologiia i psikhotekhnika: Istoricheskii opyt metodologicheskogo oformleniia i obosnovaniia kompleksnykh nauchno-tekhnicheskikh distiplin. *Medologiia i istoriia psikhologii, 1*(2), 47–56.

Piskoppel', A. A., & Shchedrovitskii, L. P. (1991). Mificheskoe i real'noe v sud'be sovetskoi pedologii. *Psikhologicheskii zhurhnal, 6*, 123–136.

Rodin, A. M. (1998). Iz istorii zapreta pedologii v SSSR. *Pedagogika, 4*, 92–98.

Shvartsman, P. I., & Kuznetsova, I. V. (1994). Pedologiia. In *Repressirovanaia nauka* (Vol. 2, pp. 121–139). St Petersburg: Nauka.

Sokolov, M. V. (1956). Kritika metoda testov na russkikh s"ezdakh po eksperimental'noi pedagogike (1910–1916). *Voprosy psikhologii, 6*, 16–28.

Stoiukhina, N. I. (2008). Pedologiia v Nizhnem Novgorode: Istoriko-Psikhologicheskoe issledovanie. In *Nauchnye idei F. A. Fradkina v kontekste sovremennykh issledovanii istorii i teorii vsemirnogo pedagogicheskogo protsessa* (pp. 210–215). Vladimir: Vladimirskii gos. gum. un.

Tseniuga, S. N. (2010). Pedologicheskaia sluzhba v uchebnykh zavedeniiakh Prieniseiskogo kraia (1920–1930 gg.). *Pedagogika, 4*, 79–84.

Umrikhin, V. V. (1991). "Nachalo kontsa" povedencheskoi psikhologii v SSSR. In M. G. Iaroshevskii (Ed.), *Represirovannaia nauka* (pp. 136–145). Leningrad: Nauka.

Zamskii, K. S. (1995). *Umstvenno otstalye deti: Istoriia ikh izucheniia, vospitaniia i obucheniia s drevnikh vremen do serediny XX veka*. Moscow: NPO Obrazovanie.

PART III
Dialogues

5

THE GOLDEN AGE OF SOVIET PSYCHOLOGY IN THE MIRROR OF CONTEMPORARY MARXIST PSYCHOLOGY IN BRAZIL

Gisele Toassa, Flávia da Silva Ferreira Asbahr and Marilene Proença Rebello de Souza

A quote from a classic Brazilian psychologist synthesizes the pathos of Marxism in our country. As in the Soviet Union, there has been a history of striving for liberty and progress facing the hardships of extreme inequality:

> What does social progress ultimately consist of? In the development of intelligence, by continually striving to make the best use of the resources of nature from which we derive livelihood, and in the sharpening of altruistic sentiments, which make life ever smoother, allowing greater cordiality among men, a perfect solidarity, a greater interest in common happiness, a growing horror of injustice and iniquity.
>
> *Bomfim (1903/2008, p. 25)*

This chapter presents a brief – and therefore necessarily personal – history of psychology and Marxism in Brazil. Our text relies on books, thesis and other historiographical materials, as well as an original research in the CNPQ's national directory of research groups. Our priority is the legacy of Lev Semionovich Vygotsky and his co-workers as the most popular authors in national Marxist psychology. In order to contextualize it, we resort to historiographical research on the political history of the country, pointing to the creation of the first popular Communist organizations and their developments in the Brazilian intellectual life, which, despite their wealth, were late in exerting an impact on psychology as a whole science and profession. The first initiatives to constitute a Marxist psychology arose only in the 1970s, bearing the hallmarks of the civil-military dictatorship and the subsequent process of redemocratization. As a way to follow the legacy of Vygotsky and his co-workers back to the 1970s–1980s to a sketch of their development to our days, we mention the researchers who first approached their psychology, as well as their main topics, their research groups and their institutions. Keeping in mind the diversity of the leftist spectrum in which this early approximation occurred, we also mention the first publishing of the most influential books by Vygotsky and his co-workers in Brazil.

Brazil and Marxism

Portugal has made Brazil an agro-exporting colony whose independence was not because of popular struggles, but an agreement established within the Portuguese Crown itself. Dom Pedro I, the ruling prince of the House of Braganza, declared independence for the Colony in 1822 (in a cunning blow to popular interests that transferred the metropolis' debts to the new independent country) and abdicated the throne in favor of his son, D. Pedro II in 1831, subsequently returning to Portugal. The abolition of slavery occurred only in 1888, and the Proclamation of the Republic in 1889 (Fausto & Fausto 2014).

Through a new *coup d'état*, this time by military and conservative means, the First Republic began, whose economic hegemony shifted from the state of Rio de Janeiro to that of São Paulo and Minas Gerais. The first, a major coffee producer; the second, a milk and dairy producer. Hence, the curious nickname attributed to the First Phase of the Republican era: "Coffee-with-Milk Republic". Though inspired by positivism, this Republic did very little for the modernization of the country, ending in 1930 with astronomical indices of illiteracy in the general population. The ruling elite kept the structure of the social classes virtually intact, dealing with European liberalism in the same way as the imperial government had. The equality and freedom of all before the law, supposed pillars of the republic, they were of no use in the face of the culture of favor, familism and authoritarianism that pervaded the relations between state, capital and labor (Martins, 2011). This basic conservatism took shape with the existence of eugenic policies, which took shape in the attempts to "whiten" the population through European immigration. While the masses of the *mestizo* population were destined for oblivion or state violence until the beginning of the twenty-first century, whites were reserved for wage labor in southern Brazil, in São Paulo's coffee farms and in the nascent industries of the same state.

It is important to remember that the extreme levels of social inequality in the country have generated many popular struggles and revolts since the seventeenth century, especially the formation of numerous *quilombos*, subsequently destroyed by the forces of order. The massacre of the village of Canudos (1896–1897) by the Republican Army became a milestone of these struggles. However, the camp was based on the messianism and autonomous religiosity of the rural population, without being influenced by the proletarian European struggles, essentially composed of urban workforce. Similarly, Brazil had creative interpreters, who were original forms of thinking in tune with the needs of the majority of the population. Manoel Bomfim, whom we recognize at the beginning of the text, besides being a doctor, educator, politician and social scientist, was also one of the pioneers of scientific psychology, founding the first laboratory in the history of Brazilian psychology in 1906, with the assistance of George Dumas and equipment imported from Paris and Leipzig (Antunes, 2016). However, its legacy goes virtually unnoticed in the field of psychology.

It was up to the Italian and Spanish immigrants, who became wage earners in the industries of São Paulo City, to form the first anarchist circles in Brazilian history, organizing the working class in the First Republic. Moraes Filho (2003) indicates that the name of Marx, father of "German materialism", had been mentioned in the Brazilian press since the year of the Paris Commune (1871), but not infrequently he is confused with Comte, Spencer and positivism. The first socialist circle dates from 1889, and the first publications are from the 1890s. A significant wave of strike manifestations took place between 1917 and 1919, with the founding of the Brazilian Communist Party (PCB) in 1922, in parallel with the creation of several other Communist parties in Latin America. Indeed, this was the foundational decade of Marxism in the subcontinent. However, Moraes Filho states, "it was only after 1930 that Marx's work really began to spread in Brazil, both in foreign languages and in translations, which multiplied" (p. 51, our transl.).

Like so many other national leaderships of the Communist parties, the PCB enthusiastically Stalinizes over the 1930s, a wave that ebbs from the Soviet thaw. However, Moraes Filho (2003) notes that the text "On the principles of Leninism" (1924) remained in use until at least the late 1960s, with Stalin hailed as an example of firmness even by the 1968 movements. Marxism-Leninism survived at least until 1975, when Venezuelan Ludovico Silva wrote an *Anti-Manual para uso de Marxistas, Marxólogos y Marxianos* (Netto, 2012). According to the same author, some leaders were scorched by the alignment with the Marxism of the III International, in a national context in which Trotskyism was politically insignificant in organizational terms, despite making noise at the ideological level.

Nevertheless, the revolution most celebrated by the Latin American left soon became the Cuban Revolution (1959), with its own trajectory of defiance of US imperialism (Barão, 2003). Cuba brought hope against US predatory action, which had replaced the British Empire by fomenting dependent capitalism, with monocultures of exploitation, cultural subservience and atrocious dictatorships in the subcontinent, unconditionally backed by local elites. The criticism of imperialism and the native ruling classes became the tonic of Marxism in Latin America, which gained increasing diversity throughout the twentieth century. According to Netto (2012), from the 1930s onwards, "autochthonous publishing activities centered on Marxist literature and featuring national productions" (p. 6) multiplied more vigorously after 1956. Between the 1930s and 1960s, the Brazilian author Caio Prado Jr. (1907–1990) published seminal books on the historical specificity of Brazil's insertion in the world economy, whose counterpoint fell to Gramscian Nelson Werneck Sodré (1911–1999). According to Netto, social movements, universities and research institutes intervened in Marxist elaboration.

Netto (2012) goes on to describe how, in the early 1960s, the Frankfurtians, G. Lukacs, Henri Lefebvre, Erich Fromm, Roger Garaudy, Jean-Paul Sartre, Louis Althusser, Bertold Brecht and Mikhail Bakhtin references in the Latin American debate. However, the most significant post-Stalinist contribution to Marxist thought and praxis would come with Liberation Theology, one of the main sources of Paulo Freire's pedagogy of emancipation (1921–1997), which in turn has repercussions in several subcontinent countries – inspiring the Liberation Psychology (*psicologia de la liberación*) of Martín-Baró (1943–1989). This pedagogy managed the Popular Circles of Culture and the publication of the book *Pedagogy of the Oppressed* in 1970 by Paulo Freire, among many others, inspiring some timid initiatives related to Marxist social psychology in Brazil in the same decade, despite being marked by the spontaneity of ideas and practices. Following the military coup of 1964, Institutional Act No. 5 (AI-5) of December 1968 heightened state violence, marking the 1970s as a decade of defeats to the left wing, from the Stalinists to the autonomists.

Torture and death had been trivialized in the basements of dictatorship. But from the middle of the decade, several facts contribute to the crisis of the military regime, which proposes a "slow, gradual and safe" opening in which the military themselves took control of the democratic transition (Chaui & Nogueira, 2007). Thus, establishing structural vices in the political system that is in serious trouble at its core to the present day, with the *coup* of 2016 and the recent election of Jair Bolsonaro – the captain of the dictatorship – in 2018. We now have to deal with how Marxist ideas developed in psychology.

Brazilian social psychology and Marxism: encounters

According to Antunes (1999), the history of psychology in Brazil can be divided into five periods: 1) Pre-Institutional (Colonial Period); 2) Institutional (nineteenth century); 3) Autonomization (1890–1930); 4) Consolidation (1930–1962); and 5) Professionalization (1962 onwards), and scientific psychology had gained decisive momentum since the third phase, with a predominance of French influence. The creation of the first laboratories and through specific chairs takes place from 1906, occurring in the Normal Schools and housing for people with mental problems, especially in the states of São Paulo and Rio de Janeiro, although there were also outstanding experiences in Minas Gerais, Bahia and Pernambuco. The first undergraduate course in psychology dates from 1953 at PUC-RJ, nine years before the profession was recognized in 1962 (Molón, 2001). Nevertheless, courses remained scarce and concentrated in the Southeast of the country. The first professional in psychology affiliated with the Communist Party of Brazil in the 1930s was the Jungian psychiatrist Nise da Silveira (1905–1999).

After the beginning of the Civil-Military Dictatorship (1964–1985), the regime started to regard Marx's studies – though never formally prohibited – with suspicion. According to Carone (2007), the 1968 AI-5 prohibited political activities and demonstrations, resulting in the compulsory retirement of several left-wing professors from public universities.

Even in a dangerous scenario, something of Marx was studied in some areas of psychology at federal universities in the mid-1970s, such as Federal da Paraiba in 1974 and social psychology at the Federal University of Minas Gerais, after curricular reforms (Jacó-Vilela, 2011). At the University of São Paulo, Ecléa Bosi (1936–2017) defended his doctorate in psychology in 1971, using Marxists such as A. Gramsci, T. W. Adorno and L. Goldmann, the inaugural text of a specifically Brazilian tradition in critical psychology. It was up to publisher Enio Silveira of the Civilização Brasileira publishing house to publish a good number of Marxist works in the 1960s, despite the publisher's persecution and financial difficulties in the 1970s.[1]

In that decade when some psychologists read Marxist works, Vygotsky began to make himself present. Although the authorship is not clear in Freitas (1994), it seems to have been up to Agnela da Silva Giusta (?–2013), then a master student, to bring copies of Vygotsky's works from Italy in 1975, including *The Psychological Development of the Child*. Justa would have done the first handcrafted translation of one of the chapters of this book, used from 1977 in the area of Learning Psychology of the Getulio Vargas Foundation Higher Institute for Advanced Studies in Education, Rio de Janeiro, RJ (Freitas, 1994; Fávero, 2003). The student became interested in Vygotsky from J. Piaget's commentary on Soviet psychology in a 1974 book, *Wisdom and Illusions of Philosophy*. Others interviewed by Freitas (1994) also report having read and/or purchased, in Brazil, editions imported from L. S. Vygotsky in 1977, also close to the emergence of M. Bakhtin's first readings in the field of Linguistics. As Freitas describes, the authors arrived quietly in Brazil and "they were lodged, after random encounters, in the homes of teachers of Psychology, Letters and Education" (p. 38), in an authoritarian scenario marked by the great use of the technique and behaviorism in the documents of educational public policy officials because of the MEC-USAID[2] agreement. With regard to Soviet psychology, the 1980s were marked by the protagonism of two São Paulo institutions: PUC-SP and Unicamp, respectively in social psychology and education, two of the vital universities for the survival of the left wing in the years of dictatorship.

Institutional milestones considered important by several commentators for the emergence of a critical social psychology were the Congress of the Inter-American Society of Psychology in Miami, 1976, followed by the First Meeting of Social Psychology at PUC-SP, in 1979, which was attended by 100 participants (Molón, 2001). The context was that of the "crisis of experimental social psychology" of the 1970s, based on the criticism of Latin American researchers to positivist Western psychology. Against this proposal, the group formed around Silvia Lane (1933–2006) at PUC-SP – the "São Paulo School of Social Psychology" – read Marx, Engels, Gramsci, Heller, Sartre, Ianni, R. Fausto (Carvalho, 2014, p. 101), besides Vygotsky, Luria, Leontiev, Politzer, Sève, Martin-Baró, Fals-Borda, P. Freire, Montero, Merani, among others.

The founding of the Brazilian Association of Social Psychology took place in 1980 (with Lane as the first president). In 1982, Lane and another professor of social psychology, Maria do Carmo Guedes, traveled around Latin America to learn about experiences in community psychology. During this trip, they established connections with psychologists from Venezuela, Colombia, Mexico, Ecuador, Peru and Cuba (Carvalho, 2014, pp. 99–101). According to Lane, the way out of the crisis in psychology, by way of Marxism in the mentioned countries, developed in a scenario marked by the following factors:

> a) cultural domination by US intellectual production; b) the willingness of researchers and professionals from these countries to seek new research methods and fundamentals, so action research is the alternative privileged methodological approach; c) and, in spite of many similarities concerning the historical-social problems encountered and also to the proposals formulated in response to such problems, teachers and students expressed the need to better promote the exchange between such experiences.
>
> *(Carvalho, 2014, p. 101)*

Jacó-Vilela et al. (2016) comment that, for this first generation of social psychologists, the relevance of working in favor of the popular strata was a central aspect, being "Catholics working in grassroots communities and affiliated with Liberation Theology; former auxiliaries and enthusiasts of Popular Education, by Paulo Freire; Marxists of varying orientations" (p. 533), although Lane reported to Coelho (2007) that she had already been a reader of Marx since her graduation in philosophy in the 1950s. According to Carvalho (2014), some of the first works in community psychology at PUC-SP date from the 1960s. The multiplicity of daily life became "of interest" to psychology, eventually unfolding in another field, school psychology, with the works of M. H. de S. Patto (1981, 1984, 1990; see Toassa, 2016), as we shall see later, solidly based on Marxism.

In general, it is clear that the political opening of the civil-military dictatorship in the 1980s was decisive for the formation and diffusion of a Marxist psychology in Brazil. Another important determination was the approach of psychologists to public policies, since the professional regulation that occurred in 1962 prioritized clinical care in private spaces, over practices in institutions (Hur, 2005).

Carvalho (2014) observes a heterogeneous, not rarely superficial, appropriation of historical-dialectical materialism at this first moment. In his work on ideology, A. da C. Ciampa, for example, used M. Harnecker's manual on historical materialism, not Marx and Engels or contemporary authors on ideologies. W. Codo would have shown a more consistent appropriation of Marx's concept of work, contributing significantly to the structuring of a Marxist work psychology in Brazil, which remains quite vigorous to this day. The author's readings were also in dialogue with behaviorism: for example, Codo (1984) defends psychology as a science of behavior and quotes Skinner to justify the universal tendency of humans to control their environment, which would also apply to his work. Moreover, the reasoning of the São Paulo School was never closed to non-Marxist references. As Carvalho shows:

> Agnes Heller's theory of social objectivation and Jürgen Habermas's theory of communicative action will be those around which the set of theoretical discussions of the São Paulo School of Social Psychology will take place in the 1990s and 2000s.
>
> *(p. 167)*

Thus, the São Paulo School showed a relationship of unity, but not identity, and Lane (Codo & Lane, 1984) formulated a project of fundamental categories for social psychology: consciousness, activity, identity, language, ideology, alienation and group process, with a view to social transformation in meeting the interests of the working class (Carvalho, 2014, p. 146), with calls for overcoming a class society and praxis, contrary to separation between researcher and research participants. The empirical research is usually present in the group's theses and dissertations. However, it is worth noting that there is also a strong presence of the critical theory of society in the field of psychology (as in part of Bosi's production, already commented), in research groups throughout the country that have no relation to the São Paulo School, not to mention other areas such as arts, education, philosophy and social sciences.

The most celebrated book of the São Paulo School (Lane & Codo, 1984) refers to Vygotsky and Leontiev precisely in the chapter on the design of the fundamental categories of the psyche, being the only *en passant* authors mentioned in Soviet psychology. In Lane's orientations theses and dissertations, Leontiev, Vygotsky and Luria emerge in the 1980s, but they are cited more often in the 1990s – with Leontiev, the opposite is true: it is more often cited in the 1980s (Sousa, 2008, p. 69). González-Rey (2007) recognizes the importance of Lane's treatment of work as a form of human activity, and notes that

> She begins her contact with Soviet psychology with a deeper mastery of Leontiev than Vygotsky, ends his work in close proximity to themes and challenges that derive from Vygotsky's theoretical positioning in his later works and which today bring us more challenges than certainties.
>
> *(p. 60, our transl.)*

The same author, following a consensus position among the commentators of the São Paulo School, notes Lane's shift toward studies on the processes of imagination, emotions and fantasy, categories that would have been left to the background by Leontiev's Activity Theory (González-Rey, 2007). Freitas (1994) notes that the group linked to Silvia Lane began with studies of the theory of activity by Rubinstein and Leontiev; the latter's studies would soon have also reached a university in Minas Gerais, although it is not specified. The category affectivity had been incorporated into the cast of the fundamental categories of the psyche in Lane and Codo (1984). In all scenarios, the importance of recognizing human nature is historical and social predominated.

However, in a context of still early readings of Soviet psychology, mediated by low quality editions, Carvalho rightly notes some superficiality of the readings of the São Paulo School on Soviet authors. Another aspect that had been noticed with some reservation is that Lane herself is more cited in her theses and dissertations than Marx and Engels themselves (Sousa, 2008). Between 1974 and 2006, only Lane directed 38 dissertations and 32 theses, in a context in which the Graduate Programs in Social Psychology were still scarce (Sousa, 2008). Her alumni hold important institutional positions to this day, celebrating a legacy largely dependent on the deceased author's enormous personal and professional charisma. Another aspect to consider is that, with a small advantage, foreign Marxist references predominate in the group's works (Sousa, 2008, p. 68), but there were many references to authors persecuted by the dictatorship that the PUC had embraced – such as Florestan Fernandes, Octavio Ianni, Jose Arthur Giannotti, Paul Singer and others. In these references, there is an absence: in both Sousa and Carvalho we are reminded of Paulo Freire's forgetfulness, although he also worked at PUC-SP. Apparently, the author's work was present in the early days of the foundation of community psychology, with strength in PUC-SP and PUCCAMP, being left in the background by Lane's group.

Internationally prestigious author with a doctorate from the Institute of General and Pedagogical Psychology of Moscow, Russia, the Cuban Fernando González-Rey (1949–2019) had an extensive knowledge in the field of Soviet Marxist psychology. In addition to cooperating with the São Paulo School since the 1980s, while still residing in Cuba, he became a visiting professor at UNICAMP in 1997, then at institutions in the Midwest and South, such as Campinas (SP), Goiania (GO), Passo Fundo (RS) and Brasília (DF), having established residence in the latter city. We owe to González-Rey the spread of the legacy of important Soviets, such as S. L. Rubinstein and – especially – L. Bozhovich, until then a complete unknown in Brazil. His historically informed reading of Soviet psychology persisted even after the author migrated from Marxism to Complexity Theory, a transit pointed out by Santos (in press). His wide capacity for collaboration is reflected in the formation of various groups linked to his "theory of subjectivity".

After the collapse of the USSR, Carvalho notes that there was the "abandonment or transformation of important foundations and categories of historical-dialectical materialism, such as the structure and dynamics of classes (and of class struggle), the centrality of work and the perspective of overcoming capitalism" (Carvalho, 2014, p. 147), with a greater approximation of the São Paulo School to the "neo-Marxists" Heller and Habermas.

Although presenting much less historiography registers, other centers of knowledge production/reference authors were already gaining ground: consolidating a production made since the 1980s in the Department of Psychology of the Federal

University of Rio Grande do Norte (UFRN), in 1995, the Marxism and Education research base was created, designed and led by Professor Oswaldo Yamamoto (Jacó-Vilela, 2011). The production of this group, strong and centered on the relationship between social psychology and public policy focused on vulnerable populations and social movements, remains centered on Marxism to this day. With many authors who rely on the contributions of Soviet psychology, active in undergraduate and postgraduate, such a group, along with others located in the states of São Paulo and Parana, shows strong signs of internationalization.[3] To this end, the formation of a coalition led by the Workers' Party in the Federal Government during the period of 2003–2016 was fundamental, and sought to affirm Brazil's economic and political leadership in South America. In the area of education, the Party significantly increased the number from federal universities and institutes, as well as research funding in the country.

Psychology, Marxism and education (1970–1990)

Although the presence of Marxism in social psychology has been strong, the relative "gigantism" of the area of education – as well as the greatest left wing force in this area field – became fertile for the spread of Marxist psychology; in particular, the Soviet branch. According to Freitas (1994), along with Vygotsky came Rubinstein, Leontiev and Luria, apparently, initially studied at UNICAMP.[4] However, Vygotsky in fact, attracted the most general interest of the researchers.

Freitas (1994) highlights Claudia Lemos's pioneering spirit in Vygotsky and Bakhtin's studies at IEL-UNICAMP. Freitas notes that the Brazilian group was also a mean for the diffusion of the authors in other universities of São Paulo, Minas Gerais and Rio de Janeiro. Studies by the Soviet authors also began in the University of São Paulo Neurology with the group of L. Menna-Barreto, who, together with professors from the Faculty of Education of the same University, headed the organization of the anthology *Language, Development and Learning* (Leontiev et al., 1988). Freitas also reports the passage of interest of various researchers to Soviet psychologists without necessarily having political activism or preference for Marxism.[5]

Ana Luiza Bustamante Smolka and Marta Kohl de Oliveira (who, respectively, became professors of UNICAMP and USP) had contact with Vygotsky, as an author immersed in the context of constructivism and cognitivism, still in the USA of the 1970s. They returned to the USA in the late 1980s, when the works of Wertsch, Bruner and Cole were already popularizing. For the diffusion of Vygotsky, the publication of the books *Mind in Society* (1984) and *Thought and Language* (1987) in Brazil, in indirect translations of English, played a fundamental role.

Vygotsky became a fashion author in the early 1990s, moving from academic studies to insertion into educational policies: in-service teacher training, curriculum frameworks, municipal, state and even federal level projects. Freitas (1994) argues that the spread of Vygotsky and Bakhtin in education came because of redemocratization and the political climate conducive to reflection on Brazilian social, political and economic contexts. There was a growing perception that Piaget or Skinner did not offer adequate theoretical and methodological support, losing themselves in a crisis of psychology similar to the dualism between objectivism and subjectivism portrayed by Vygotsky in his time. According to one of the testimonies given to Freitas (1994), the literacy work with poor children based on Piaget or the Argentine author Emilia Ferreiro (1937–) did not have the desired effects. Because of this, the most politicized teachers resorted to the studies of anthropology, discourse and culture – for example, Smolka's (1987/2012) classic study of literacy classes, strongly based on Luria and the idea of literacy as a discursive process.

In the process of Brazilian redemocratization, which began in the mid-1980s, after 21 years of military dictatorship, there was a search, especially in the field of educational policies, for leftist theoretical references that could address the serious problems of Brazilian educational institutions: access to formal education had not yet been universalized, the percentage of dropout and failure in school was very high, and the number of functional illiterates also stood out (Ferraro & Ross, 2017). In this perspective, from 1985 onwards, left and center-left governments were elected to state and municipal administrations in different regions of the country, although there have always been major difficulties in maintaining and growing them ever since.

In processes of reformulation of curriculum proposals and educational projects of states and municipalities, Vygotsky emerges as a reference author. His concepts, such as a zone of proximal development and higher psychological functions, begin to appear in educational documents.

In this text, we highlight the curriculum proposals of the states of Santa Catarina and Parana, in the southern region. In Santa Catarina, 1984, there is a first major strike of teachers of the public school system after the military dictatorship, and the process of expanding popular participation in discussions about state education is discussed. At the end of this decade begins the preparation of a Curriculum Proposal, promulgated in 1991, which will seek in Gramsci and Vygotsky their political and theoretical foundations. At that time, Vygotsky appears to be a "socio-interactionist" (Hentz & Herter, 2001), but his Marxist foundations are already included in the curriculum proposal:

> This philosophical framework is expressly recorded in the 1991 document, in which its authors adopt the conception of historical and dialectical materialism as a reference for all work, including those that followed in later years. From the pedagogical point of view, the theoretical option assumed in the proposal was the historical-cultural approach. The choice for this philosophical and pedagogical perspective is also registered in the documents published in 1998 and 2005.
>
> *(Thiesen, 2007, p. 43)*

It is worth mentioning that the elaboration of the proposal had the collaboration of UFSC teachers, who were also beginning their studies on the Soviet school.[6]

In Parana, a similar process occurred, but instead of being grounded in a theory of psychology, the state secretary of education sought in the work of Demerval Saviani (1943–), an important philosopher of Marxist education, to contribute to the elaboration of his curricular proposal, the *Basic Curriculum for the Paraná State Public School*.[7] Saviani, together with his research group, developed, from the 1980s, the foundations of historical-critical pedagogy, the pedagogical theory of Marxist epistemological foundation (Saviani, 1995).

At the national level, Vygotsky, Luria and Leontiev appear as a reference, along with Piaget and Ausubel, in the *National Curriculum Parameters* (PCNs), promulgated in 1998. PCNs are a set of texts containing the national curriculum guidelines prepared by the Federal Government during the first mandate of Fernando Henrique Cardoso (1994–1998). It is noteworthy that the Soviet authors are mentioned in a paragraph in the document, only when the concept of learning of the PCNs, articulated with the constructivist conception, is presented, as we see in an excerpt from the document itself:

> In general terms, the frame of reference is delimited by what can be called "cognitive approaches" in the broad sense. These include the genetic theory of Jean Piaget and his collaborators at the Geneva School, both with regard to the conception of change processes and the classical structural formulations of operative development and recent elaborations on cognitive strategies and procedures, problem solving; activity theory, in the formulations of Vygotsky, Luria and Leontiev and collaborators, in particular as regards the way of understanding the relations between learning and development and the importance given to interpersonal relationship process; the extension of theses in the field of cultural psychology, such as those stated in the works of M. Cole and collaborators, which integrates the concepts of development, learning, culture and education; and Ausubel's theory of significant verbal learning and its unfolding into other theories. The central core of the integration of all these contributions refers to the recognition of the importance of constructive mental activity in the processes of knowledge acquisition. Hence the term constructivism, calling this convergence.
>
> *(Brasil, 1998, p. 71)*

Vygotsky's works in the Parameter references are *Mind in Society* and the abridged version of *Thought and Language*, respectively, published in 1984 and 1987.

Returning to the academic field and to the pedagogue A. L. B. Smolka, from the association of this teacher, among other colleagues of the Faculty of Education, with the Spanish philosopher and psychologist Angel Pino Sirgado (1933–2013), the Thought and Language Research Group (GPPL) was officially constituted in 1987. Graduated from the Catholic University of Louvain and hired by UNICAMP since 1977, this was the second time Pino had resided in Brazil: while still a priest, he had worked with the Catholic Youth in the 1950s, and coordinated and organized some of the first grassroots ecclesial communities, organizations based on Liberation Theology – leftist Catholic thinking.

> Pino explored broad themes, such as the social nature of human development; semiotic mediation; the processes of meaning; affectivity; the imaginary creation. He devoted special attention to the living conditions of childhood; the rights of children and adolescents; to the promising vision of an aesthetic education.
>
> *(Smolka et al., 2015, p. 329)*

Sirgado's solid and diverse background – a connoisseur of Marx and Bakhtin – made him a reference in Vygotsky studies, with which he made contact in the 1980s. In 1991, he organized the dossier *Thought and Language: Studies from the Perspective of Psychology*, published in the CEDES Notebooks. The material focused on the importance of mediation, the role of work in the constitution of humankind, among other topics. The GPPL formed links with PUC-SP and educated many researchers who came to work in the South of the country, including the Federal University of Santa Catarina.

Another of the 24 persons interviewed by Freitas, all of them pioneers of studies of Soviet psychology in Brazil, also reported researching Leontiev, Bakhtin, Wallon and Rubinstein. The influence of the latter, however, was hardly felt in the Brazilian educational commentary, being scarcely mentioned until our days.

Sarmento (2006) tells us about Vygotsky's initial *boom* in Brazil in research on theses and dissertations defended during the years of 1986–2001, which took him as a reference. The author located 366 dissertations and theses that referred to the author, distributed by 46 Brazilian universities, mostly from the Southeast, Midwest and South. Of the set, 299 used Vygotsky as a complement and 69, in fact, were based on his work. As for the areas, 267 works were defended in the field of education and psychology, areas that concentrated 56 of those based on Vygotsky's work.

In summary, Sarmento concludes that PUC-SP, UNICAMP, USP and UFSC Postgraduate Programs (in descending order) were the initial diffusion poles of Vygotsky's approach in Brazil, totaling 47% of the total number of works that referred to the author and 64.3% of the 56 dissertations and theses based on him defended in the period, with wide advantage in the area of education – whose number of programs was also much more expressive than those of psychology. Education and psychology comprise 81.1% of the works defended; four journals in these areas concentrate 45% of the published articles.[8]

Concerning the content, Sarmento (2006) observed a repetition of the themes investigated, especially with regard to the development-learning relationship and the processes of teacher-student interaction, or students among themselves. There was a wide range of subjects and contexts, from kindergarten to high school, and many works were not merely in the field of psychology as the foundation of education, but sought to think directly about the implementation of processes and pedagogical practices in the field of studies on teacher's training, curriculum and teaching methodology. The following table summarizes the themes identified in the investigative corpus:

Theme 1: Biography of Vygotsky
Theme 2: Context of the emergence of theory
Theme 3: Denomination of Theory
Theme 4: Authorship
Theme 5: Higher psychological functions
Theme 6: Language orality, writing and drawing
Theme 7: Internalization and the constitution of the human being
Theme 8: Human development design and development lines
Theme 9: Levels and development zone and the learning process
Theme 10: Toy's role in child development
Theme 11: Social interaction and its interfaces in the educational context
Theme 12: Implications of the Historical-Cultural Theory in the school context
Source: Sarmento (2006, p. 55)

Most of the theses and dissertations report field research, with a small number of bibliographic studies. Sarmento disagrees with Duarte (2001) regarding Vygotsky's misunderstandings of interpretation, finding more "consensus" than "dissent" about it. According to the author, the divergences related especially to the naming and authorship of the theoretical contributions attributed to Vygotsky and his collaborators, based on works translated by authors such as H. Daniels, G. Blanck, R. van der Veer and J. Valsiner and L. C. Moll. According to Sarmento, in general, the works referred to Vygotsky's Marxist bases. However, other authors of education were not satisfied with these mentions. Vygotsky grew to the point where it was disputed in the academic arena in its links with public policy.

School psychology and the search for a critical conception of science

Another important field in which Vygotsky's theory has evidence in Brazil is school psychology. Even before the arrival of Vygotsky's works in Brazilian lands, we highlight the approach of the area with Marxist and Marxian ideas, in a movement of searching for references to overcome the biologizing and individualizing hegemonic explanations about school failure, prevalent until the '80s. In this field, we highlight the works of Maria Helena de Souza Patto, professor at the Institute of Psychology of the University of São Paulo (IPUSP), especially the works *Psicologia e ideologia* (1981) and *A produção do Fracasso Escolar: histórias de submissão e rebeldia* (1990)[9], respectively her doctoral and associate professor thesis (Toassa, 2016).

In these works, Patto, using the theoretical framework of historical materialism and authors such as Marx, Gramsci, Althusser, Heller, Kosik, among other foreign and Brazilian Marxists, makes a profound analysis of how psychology is constituted as an ideological science, which corresponds to positivist ideals of science. For the author, hegemonic explanations about school failure focus exclusively on the child, especially the poor child, public school student, the causes for "not learning". Among hegemonic conceptions of learning disabilities, Patto mentions racial theories, differential psychology, psychometrics and the theory of cultural deprivation. According to the researcher, they are ahistorical conceptions that take as natural what is social, as social what is political, as cause what is consequence, and as abstraction what is concrete reality of mankind (Patto, 1997).

From the radical criticism of these conceptions, Patto proposes an epistemological turn in the understanding of the "learning difficulties" that are now analyzed from his institutional and political production as school failure (Toassa, 2016). Thus, the author denounces the production of failure resulting from the precarious working conditions of education professionals, the humiliation and prejudice practices present at school, the education policies that generate obstacles to educational practices, among other factors.

Patto's critique is a turning point for Brazilian school psychology that will need to review its studies and conceptions. The author brings dialectical historical materialism as a central method to the analysis of school failure, but resorts much more to authors of sociology and education, producing a sociological analysis of the phenomenon, which partly rejects the theories of psychology.

It is in the '90s that a generation of school psychologists, some of them guided by Patto, will reconcile with psychology, seeking to reconstruct this field from the movement of criticism of the relations between psychology and education. At this time, anthologies organized by Machado and Souza (1997) and Tanamachi et al. (2000) are published. These and other works published throughout the 1990s and early 2000s sought to build new theoretical and methodological foundations for psychology at school in a critical perspective.

Historical-cultural psychology appears as one of the theoretical possibilities for the constitution of critical school psychology, and Vygotsky, Luria, Leontiev, Davidov, Bozhovich, Elkonin, Galperin, among others, as reference in the works of the field. We highlight their studies on the relations between development and learning, thought and language, experiences, conscience, mediation, social environment and role of school activity, with a predominance of a social perspective defending the valorization of education as a process of democratization of school knowledge, as debated by Saviani's historical-critical pedagogy. We can also frequently notice the significance of contributions of the dialectical materialist method in School Psychology.

Currently, cultural-historical psychology is one of the predominant references in school psychology, as we can see in the works presented in events of the area, for example, in the National Congresses of School Psychology (CONPE), organized by the Brazilian Association of School and Educational Psychology (ABRAPEE), and in the publications of the main journal of the area, the *Brazilian Journal of School and Educational Psychology*, also produced by ABRAPEE.

A controversy: what is the social nature and what are the implications of the Marxism of Vygotsky and his collaborators?

As we have commented historically, Marxism has been much stronger in education than in psychology. Already something dispersed in the national territory at the beginning of the twenty-first century Vygotsky had become important enough to be disputed: what was the meaning of the Marxist foundations of his work? Given these fundamentals, what would be the possibilities of developing it today? Have his former students – known or unknown in Brazil – been part of this work after his death? What did Vygotsky really write, given the obvious translation problems presented in popular editions in Brazil? What relationship did the readings done so far have with the history of Brazilian education?

In the wake of these concerns, an article by educator Newton Duarte (1996a), professor at the Araraquara campus of the Paulista State University (UNESP), began a major controversy developed in his book *Vygotsky e o "aprender a aprender": crítica às apropriações neoliberais e pós-modernas da teoria Vygotskyana* (Duarte, 2001). Duarte bases his argument on three points: criticism of a constructivist or neo-liberal appropriation of Vygotsky's work; defense of a Marxist base of Vygotsky's work; and critique of the distancing between Vygotsky and Leontiev and Activity Theory (Bovo, Kunzler & Toassa, 2019).[10]

Linked intellectually to Saviani's thinking, Duarte's work develops a critique of neoliberal interpretations of Vygotsky and the supporters of the New School appropriations in Brazilian education.[11] His reflections are based on the perception that the spread of the ideas of the New School, by John Dewey (1859–1952) and other authors, would have contributed to distort the perception of the Marxist character of Vygotsky's work, inserting it in the neoliberal context of the pro-posals aimed at teaching the population how to "learn to learn", exempting the state from promoting a quality public education, as is remarkable in the history of Brazil. Our national system of primary education was effective only in the 1950s; the public education of children and adolescents presents, until our days, a marked precariousness.

Duarte (2001) points out how the dissemination of Piaget's ideas in Brazilian education ended up being used in order to justify the devaluation of teaching work – since the Swiss author attributes centrality to the process of balance that permeates the relationship between subject and object during the course of the study development process. As other authors have already noted, the role of the educator – historically undervalued in Brazil – is in the background. Moreover, for Duarte, Piaget would have a biological point of view, contrary to Vygotsky's Marxist theoretical orientation. These aspects made the associations between the authors quite strange, although common, as also pointed out by Sarmento (2006) and found in important educational documents, such as the National Curriculum Parameters mentioned above.

Duarte (2001) makes a clear differentiation between Vygotsky and authors called Interactionist or Constructivists, such as Piaget, presenting as argument Vygotsky's own critique of the latter, and the biologicist character of the Piaget's perspective in opposition to the historicity of psychism in Vygotsky's work and his followers. Their argument culminates in the affirmation of the Marxist precepts that underlie the conception of Vygotsky and his school, adulterated by the United States publishers in order to "purify" it from their Marxist precepts. Several editions have been undermined with regard to Vygotsky's Marxism, which Duarte thought was continued by Leontiev and other components of the "Vygotsky's School", and whose continuity was not so evident, precisely by the mutilation of Vygotsky's work.

According to research by Bovo et al. (2019), the author criticizes associations of Marxism to psychologies alien to such a perspective (Duarte, 1996a, 199 6b, 1998, 2001, 2002, 2004). Duarte also criticizes the attempt of some scholars, such as van der Veer, to separate Activity Theory from Historical-Cultural Psychology (Duarte, 2001), endorsing, internationally, the perspective of authors of a Marxist psychology such as M. Elhammouni and M. Golder, also contributing to the process of internationalization of a Marxist reflection on the concrete nature of the subject in relation to a culture based on flexible capitalism, in which school education tends to become progressively in the background as an indispensable process for cultural formation of critical citizens. In the national context, Duarte criticized several authors mentioned in this chapter, such as Kohl de Oliveira, Smolka and Freitas, among many others.

Despite these important reflections, however, Duarte (1996a, 1996b, 2001) ends up endorsing the Vygotsky School's hagiographic perspective, which holds that the author composed a trio with Leontiev and Luria to develop historical-cultural psychology. However, the "revisionist revolution" in the history of psychology, headed by Anton Yasnitsky (with the help of collaborators from different countries), has been showing the fragility of this historiographical thesis, based much more on oral than documentary tradition. Although Vygotsky's American editions may indeed have taken the author's mention of the classics of Marxism, it is necessary to understand the difficulties of diffusing his thinking within the Soviet Union itself, as well as Leontiev's somewhat secondary role in structuring Vygotsky's psychology. The lack of more systematic historical studies led Duarte (2001) to consider Vasili

Davidov as author of the Vygotsky Circle, when the research of such author is later than the group and he had never mingled with Vygotsky (Bovo et al., 2019). In the last few years, however, other commentators have presented, with more historical foundation, some conceptual dissonances between Vygotsky and Leontiev (such as Martins, 2013; Toassa, 2016), in addition to Vygotsky's reading as the author of his own Marxist materialism, which cannot be reduced to the readings of "Marxism-Leninism" that guided Leontiev's work from the mid-1930s (Toassa, 2015).

However, it should be noted that Duarte has had a strong presence in postgraduate studies, and particularly in the training of professors in the area of education at public universities in São Paulo and Parana, many of which are in line with his perspective (case of many professors in the State University of Maringa, UEM), from the Historical-Cultural Psychology and Education group. It is also worthwhile to notice that a favorable working environment was created with the contributions of Soviet educators and psychologists besides Vygotsky, with emphasis on other groups not directly related to Duarte, such as those headed by João Carlos Libâneo (PUC-Goiás), Manoel Oriosvaldo de Moura (USP) and Andréa Maturano Longarezi (UFU).

Historical-cultural psychology in the current context: a look at Brazilian research groups

Even in a disputed scenario, it is suggested that the influence of historical-cultural psychology has grown in the national scenario, especially in the field of academic research. For example, between 2018 and 2019, a survey was conducted[12] for the research groups registered in the directory of the National Council for Scientific and Technological Development (CNPq) that formally indicated Vygotsky's theory[13] as guiding their work, and 115 groups were located, spread over practically all Brazilian states, as we will see in the following. It is noteworthy that a similar survey had been carried out in 2010 and, at that time, 53 groups had been located, showing a growth of over 100% of groups in just eight years.

The collected data allowed the construction of a panorama about the dissemination of historical-cultural theory in Brazil today. From the description of 115 groups the following information was extracted: terms used to name the historical-cultural theory; areas of knowledge to which groups are linked; geographical distribution of groups; nature of the institution to which the group belongs; year of formation of the groups. In a second moment, we sought to map which are the main themes of study and research of the groups.

First of all, we noticed the variety of terms, highlighting a greater presence of the expressions "Historical-Cultural Theory", with 51 groups; "Historical-Cultural Psychology", with 27 groups and "Socio-Historical Psychology", adding up to 10 groups. Note the semantic dispersion in the naming of Vygotsky's theory in Brazil, with about 15 terms referring to the theory.

In their description, the groups appear linked to the large areas of knowledge proposed by CNPq.[14] Regarding these areas of knowledge, it was verified what was the great area and the specific area of concentration of the listed groups. There is a predominant distribution in the great area of human sciences, in the specific areas of education, which concentrates the majority of the research groups mapped (58.26%), covering 67 groups, and in the psychology area, which corresponds to 32.17%. with 37 groups. The remaining areas of knowledge represent a small proportion. These data demonstrate that Vygotsky's theory in Brazil remains linked especially to the field of education, serving as a subsidy to educational policies and research.

Another interesting segment of data obtained in the survey is that the groups are distributed throughout the country, from North to South. Most are located in the Southeast (38.2%) and South (20.87%), confirming the regional inequality of the research development in the country. The Northeast region (17.39%) is the third in number of research groups, followed by the Midwest (17%) and the North (10%). The states with the largest number of groups were São Paulo (34 groups) and Parana (13 groups), and no groups were located in Alagoas, in the Northeast, and in two Northern States, Acre and Amapa.

A survey was made, in order to know what was the nature of the institution in which the groups were linked: public (municipal, state and federal institutions); and private, including private confessional institutions. The data show the role of Public Universities as the central place for research and knowledge production in the country, as 88.8% of the groups are in Public Universities, distributed in Federal (50.43) and State Universities (38.26%).

The CNPq's group directory also gives us access to the year of group creation. The first was created in 1992 (Thought and Language Research Group)[15], followed by the creation of two more groups in 1997 alone and four more groups in 1999. From 1999[16] onwards, new groups are created each year, especially 2012, with the registration of 16 new groups.

Regarding the themes studied by the groups, it was analyzed what the group wrote in "Repercussions of the group" and "Lines of Research" and sought to categorize the main research themes of the groups that fall into the areas of knowledge "Psychology" and "Education".

The topics studied by groups linked to psychology were: a) human development (16 groups); b) psychological phenomena and processes (13 groups); c) formation of the psyche in its relationship with schooling processes, in a total of 12 groups; d) education, highlighting here subjects studied by groups linked to psychology as an area of knowledge, also with 12 groups; e) work processes (11 groups); f) public policy analysis (10 groups); g) school and educational psychology, seven groups; h) epistemological, methodological and HISTORICAL studies of historical-cultural psychology (seven groups); i) health-disease processes, with seven groups, working with different dimensions of health; j) violence, also with seven groups; l) inclusion and special needs (five groups); m) studies on sexuality, with four groups; n) human rights, with three groups; o) social psychology: two groups, one that uses the term in its name and another as a line of research;[17] p) aesthetic dimension and historical-cultural theory, also with two groups;

q) other topics: racial identity (one group), activity clinic (two groups) and neu-ropsychology (one group).

It appears that the themes linked to education, directly and indirectly, are pre-dominant in the groups of psychology that are linked to PHC, but sexuality and gender, violence and human rights begin to appear in the second survey.

Groups linked to the "education" knowledge area develop research on and at all levels of education, from early childhood education to higher education, and on different educational modalities such as formal, non-formal, informal and distance education. The main research topics are:

1 Teacher training, including terms such as activity/teaching and educational work: 31 groups.
2 Didactics and teaching methodology, including terms such as school prac-tices, pedagogical practices, pedagogical activities, pedagogical workshops: 24 groups.
3 Literacy, including groups that explicitly brought mathematics literacy: five groups.
4 Art and aesthetics: four groups.
5 Themes related to inclusive education, special education and disability issues: nine groups.
6 Teaching of specific curricular areas, such as mathematics, cartographic geog-raphy, physics, sciences, physical education, foreign language and botanic: 19 groups, with greater concentration in the area of mathematics teaching.
7 Culture, cultural diversity and family: 10 groups.
8 Curriculum and educational organization: six groups.
9 Human and psychic development, including themes such as mental actions, creativity, cognition and conduct: 17 groups.
10 Ideology; language and discursive practices: 11 groups.
11 Public Policies in Education (planning, development and evaluation); Public Education Network: 14 groups.
12 Teaching and learning processes; educational processes; cognition; appropria-tion of knowledge: 29 groups.
13 Studies on sexuality and gender: two groups.
14 School failure, school complaint and medicalization of education: two groups.
15 Specific themes that appeared in only one group: peasant education; indig-enous education; community schools; ethnography in the classroom; precon-ception; cheers; museums and zoos.

The highlights are the "teacher training", "didactics and teaching methodology" and "teaching and learning processes", all with more than 20 groups, demonstrat-ing the predominance of Vygotsky's contributions about development and learning in the Brazilian groups. Contemporary themes, whose discussion has proved urgent in school education, such as sexuality and gender, prejudice and racial issues in school, still appear incipiently.

Final considerations

The history of the reception, diffusion and production of Marxist psychology, and its Soviet variants in Brazil, as studied by García (2016), occurred belatedly in relation to, for example, Argentina, where it had gained momentum from the 1950s and 1960s. Among the local determinations for the late development of these relations between Marxism and psychology, we should highlight the beginning of the civil-military dictatorship in 1964 (early in relation to the other Latin American nations). State violence intensified towards the end of the same decade, significantly worsening the conditions for the development of leftist thinking. However, cultural reasons specific to the field of psychology must have played a relevant role: as we pointed out, the profession of psychologist was recognized only in 1962, focusing on clinical practice in private spaces, in a liberal fashion. This characteristic, coupled with the scarcity of psychology training courses, as well as their concentration in the Southeast, may justify the relative national and international delay in the development of psychology and Marxism relations in Brazil.

An important aspect, as explained at the beginning of this chapter, is that, in the decade of legalization of the profession (1960s), there were already solid Marxist studies in other human sciences, focusing on the specificities of Brazilian social, economic and political development. It was also during this decade that Paulo Freire emerged as an exponent of Marxist-based pedagogy, followed by several other authors and social movements. Still with a small number of postgraduate programs in the 1970s, Brazilian psychology interested in dialoguing with Marxism imported Soviet references of its own, in addition to working with Marx and Engels themselves, Frankfurt School, Budapest School – and in scale that we could not evaluate in this text by the scarcity of historical references, also with texts of Marxist authors like H. Wallon and L. Sève. A cycle of cooperation with other Latin American countries has also begun, aiming at establishing a new *praxis* capable of understanding the specificities of this land and its people.

Some Brazilian teachers who came into contact with works of Soviet psychologists and published them in Brazil (Freitas, 1994) did so initially by hand, working in study groups that were slow to work with Portuguese-language translations of Vygotsky, which were only made from the 1980s, gaining momentum in the late 1990s/early 2000s. Nonetheless, translations of *Collected Works* to Spanish language are still widely used nowadays, as the texts included there have not been translated – or at least not in quality – to Portuguese. We note, therefore, that there were three entry points for Soviet psychology in Brazil: through other Latin American countries (notably Cuba); from United States; and from Europe, with the work of Spaniards in Brazil (at university or in advisory to educational legislation). For this reason, to this day Vygotsky's reading as a "socio-interactionist" or "socio-constructivist" author is quite strong, with no major concern with pointing out his Marxist roots or developing a critical psychology. Note that the list of topics exposed by Sarmento (2001) remains current, with the use of low quality translations to our days.

A very curious aspect of Vygotsky's presence in our country, however, was that the author was late in arriving, but it was acquiring such importance that we can state that Brazil has become one of the most "Vygotskyan" countries in the world. As Sarmento (2006) also shows, hundreds of theses and dissertations already referred to the author over the years 1986–2001. But for the late "Vygotsky's boom", it was crucial to incorporate references to the author in at least one of the national educational legislation documents, as well as some states of the federation, exerting a "ripple effect" on state and municipal documents, in teacher training courses, etc. Vygotsky is gradually being studied in the most diverse fields of education, becoming part of the university curriculum for teacher education. At the same time, it occupies space not only in social psychology, but also in school psychology. Publications and even journals specializing in CHAT's contributions multiply.

The new intellectual and political scenario in which the author's work was arranged produces an important clash about the denomination of his theory and its theoretical-philosophical roots, two aspects that, for a long time, aroused doubts in the national context. Although the incorporation of Soviet psychologists was already developed within leftist groups, Duarte's work (2001) marked a new identity space, that of those interested in making a Marxist reading of Vygotsky's work and associates – a relatively diverse space that includes, in turn, a range of relationships with other Marxist theorists, and even with the work of Spinoza, an author rooted in the philosophical field. In this ambience, several other Soviet authors began to occupy space in the educational scenario, which was expressed by the holding of events, the creation of new research groups and the realization of new translations of texts by Vygotsky and his Circle. The themes studied, the groups, as well as the historical and theoretical studies that seek to present themselves on the international scene have multiplied.

Understanding the specificities of the Brazilian and Latin American context – and, why not, the rest of the postcolonial world – contributing to solve the many social problems that exist here, to dialogue more effectively with local authors, announces itself as one of the paths to progress by which Manoel Bomfim had already advocated in the early twentieth century. Marxist psychologists in general, and Vygotsky in particular, are presented as the basis for interpreting this complex universe, which, as Bomfim (2008) stated, sometimes imitates the European and the North American without restrictions, and sometimes now seeks their own paths, more attuned to a cultural *mestizaje*.

Notes

1 http://observatoriodaimprensa.com.br/armazem-literario/_ed825_sou_brasileiro_democrata_e_editor/
2 Ministry of Education and Culture (MEC) e a United States Agency for Internacional Development (USAID), in Carvalho (2014).

3 It is also worth remembering that UFRN will host the ISCAR / 2021 meeting, headed by professors linked to the Yamamoto group, and with the participation of several research groups throughout Brazil.

4 In presenting such a process, Freitas considers Rubinstein as closer to Leontiev and Luria's "mechanistic materialism" than to Vygotsky. The author notes that the former had studied in a UNICAMP group in the 1980s; we do not know, however, any evidence that Rubinstein had ever become popular in Brazil.

5 Generally speaking, studies about Luria's theory persist in neurology and related fields to this day.

6 To learn more about the Santa Catarina Curriculum Proposal, see Coan and Almeida (2015) and Hentz and Herter (2001).

7 See Noda and Galuch (2018) for details on Parana's educational policies.

8 They are: Carlos Chagas Foundation Research Notebooks, Education & Society, Psychology in Study, Psychology: Theory and Research (Sarmento, 2006, p. 49).

9 This is the year of the first edition of this work, which in 2015 was already in its fourth edition.

10 Prior to these works, Duarte's doctoral thesis (1993) focused on the foundations of a Marxist theory of individuality, based on Marx & Engels, Agnes Heller, and A. N. Leontiev, showing alignment with the contributions of this latter author.

11 Cunha (2005) describes the "New School of Education" in Brazil, in many ways inspired by Dewey's ideas.

12 This is the research entitled "Historical-Cultural Psychology in Brazilian research: survey of research groups registered in the CNPq directory", whose general objective is to investigate the insertion of Historical-Cultural Psychology or Historical-Cultural Theory within the scope of scientific research in Brazil. The research is funded by the Fundação de Amparo à Pesquisa de São Paulo (Fapesp) and coordinated by Flávia da Silva Ferreira Asbahr (UNESP-Bauru), Marilene Proença Rebello de Souza (IPUSP) and Sonia Mari Shima Barroco (UEM). Grant number: FAPESP: 2017/ 219365.

13 The keywords used to locate the groups were: Historical-Cultural Theory; Historical-Cultural Psychology; Socio-Historical Psychology (o); Vygotsky School; Vygotsky School; Vygotski School; Activity theory; Soviet psychology; Socio-Cultural Theory; Socio-Historical Theory (o); historical-cultural approach; historical-cultural perspective; psychology and Marxism; subjectivity theory; socio-historical approach. The election of these keywords is justified by their use by the Soviet authors themselves or by the current consensual use of Brazilian researchers in the field.

14 The table with CNPq's knowledge areas can be found at www.cnpq.br/documents/ 10157/186158/TabeladeAreasdoConhecimento.pdf, accessed on March 9, 2019.

15 This is the Thought and Language Research Group, mentioned earlier, at the Faculty of Education of UNICAMP, initially by teachers Ana Luiza Bustamante Smolka, Angel Pino Sirgado, Luci Banks-Leite, Maria Cecilia Rafael de Góes and Afira Vianna Ripper. Information at: www.gppl.fe.unicamp.br/, accessed on March 25, 2019.

16 The groups mentioned are: Pedagogical Implications of the Historical-Cultural Theory, coordinated by Sueli Guadalupe de Lima Mendonça and Suely Amaral Melo, from UNESP-Marília (1997); Historical-Cultural Theory and Mathematical Education (1997), Psychological Aspects of the Socio-Historical Theoretical Focus/ GEPAPET- Socio-Historical (1999), -Group for Studies and Research in Social Psychology, Education and Health: contributions of Marxism (NEPPEM – 1999), Childhood, Family and Society (1999) and Theories of Education and Pedagogical Processes (1999).

17 It is striking to us that this important field of psychology has little repercussion among the groups that are linked to historical-cultural theory, and how the linkage of the theoretical approach with education has been predominant.

References

Antunes, M. A. M. (1999). *A psicologia no Brasil: leitura histórica sobre sua constituição.* São Paulo: EDUC.

Antunes, M. A. M. (2016). Pioneers of psychology on Brazilian education: Manoel bomfim, a radical thinker. In M. P. R. de Souza, G. Toassa, & K. C. S. F. Bautheney (Org.), *Psychology, society and education: Critical perspectives in Brazil* (pp. 51–67). New York: Nova Science Publishers.

Barão, C. A. (2003). A influência da revolução cubana sobre a esquerda brasileira nos anos 60. In J. Moraes, Q. de & D. A. Reis Filho (Ed.), *História do marxismo no Brasil* (Vol. I, pp. 259–316, Rev. 2nd ed.). Campinas, SP: Editora da UNICAMP.

Bomfim, M. (1903/2008). *A América Latina: males de origem.* São Paulo: Centro Edelstein.

Bovo, A. C. de L., Kunzler, A. P., & Toassa, G. (2019). Da "Escola" ao "Círculo" de Vigotski. *Memorandum: Memória e História em Psicologia, 36,* 1–23. doi:10.35699/1676-1669.2019.6842

Brasil. (1998). *Parâmetros Curriculares Nacionais: terceiro e quarto ciclos do ensino fundamental: introdução aos Parâmetros Curriculares Nacionais.* Secretaria de Educação Fundamental. – Brasília: MEC/SEF. Disponível em http://portal.mec.gov.br/seb/arquivos/pdf/introducao.pdf

Carone, I. (2007). O papel de Silvia Lane na mudança da Psicologia Social do Brasil. *Psicologia & Sociedade, 19*(2), 62–66. doi:10.1590/S0102-71822007000500020

Carvalho, B. P. (2014). *A Escola de São Paulo de Psicologia Social: uma análise histórica do seu desenvolvimento desde o materialismo histórico-dialético.* Tese (Ph.D. in Social Psychology), Pontifícia Universidade Católica de São Paulo, São Paulo.

Chaui, M., & Nogueira, M. A. (2007). O pensamento político e a redemocratização do Brasil. *Lua Nova, 71,* 173–228. Centro de Estudos de Cultura Contemporânea. São Paulo, Brasil.

Coan, I. B. F., & Almeida, M. (2015). de L. P. de. Histórico da proposta curricular de Santa Catarina. *Holos,* [s.l.], *6,* 251–276, dez. doi:10.15628/holos.2015.1738

Codo, W. (1984). Relações de trabalho e transformação social. In S. T. M. Lane & W. Codo (Eds.), *Psicologia social: o homem em movimento* (pp. 136–151). São Paulo: Brasiliense.

Coelho, M. H. de M. (2007). Sílvia por ela mesma. *Psicologia & Sociedade, 19*(spe2), 7–14. doi:10.1590/S0102-71822007000500003

Cunha, M. V. (2005). John Dewey, the other face of the Brazilian. New school. *Studies in Philosophy and Education, 24*(6), 455–470.

Duarte, N. (1993). *A individualidade para-si: contribuição a uma teoria histórico-social da formação do indivíduo.* Campinas, SP: Autores Associados.

Duarte, N. (1996a). A escola de Vygotsky e a educação escolar: algumas hipóteses para uma leitura pedagógica da psicologia histórico-cultural. *Psicologia USP, 7*(1–2), 17–50. doi.org/10.1590/S1678-51771996000100002

Duarte, N. (1996b). *Educação Escolar, Teoria do Cotidiano e Escola de Vygotsky.* Campinas, SP: Autores Associados.

Duarte, N. (1998). Concepções afirmativas e negativas sobre o ato de ensinar. *Cadernos Cedes, 44*(19), 85–106. dx.doi.org/10.1590/S0101-32621998000100008

Duarte, N. (2001). *Vygotsky e o "aprender a aprender": crítica às apropriações neoliberais e pós-modernas da teoria Vygotskyana.* Campinas, SP: Autores Associados.

Duarte, N. (2002). A teoria da atividade como uma abordagem para a pesquisa em educação. *Perspectiva, 21*(2), 279–301. Recuperado em 13 de fevereiro, 2018, de periodicos.ufsc.br/index.php/perspectiva/article/view/9646/8881

Duarte, N. (2004). Formação do indivíduo, consciência e alienação: o ser humano na psicologia de AN Leontiev. *Cadernos Cedes*, *24*(62), 44–63. dx.doi.org/10.1590/S0101-32622004000100004

Fausto, B., & Fausto, S. (2014). *A concise history of Brazil*. New York: Cambridge University Press.

Fávero, Maria de Lourdes de Albuquerque. (2003). O autoritarismo institucional e a extinção do IESAE. *Educação & Sociedade*, *24*(85), 1257–1275. https://dx.doi.org/10.1590/S0101-73302003000400008

Ferraro, A. R., & Ross, S. D. (2017). Diagnóstico da escolarização no Brasil na perspectiva da exclusão escolar. *Revista Brasileira de Educação*, *22*(71), 1–26. doi:10.1590/S1413-24782017227164

Freitas, M. T. A. (1994). *O Pensamento de Vygotsky e Bakhtin no Brasil*. Campinas, SP: Papirus.

García, L. N. (2016). Versiones tempranas de Vygotski: su recepción en la Argentina (1935–1974). In A. Yasnitsky, R. van der Veer, E. Aguilar, & L. N. García (Eds.), *Vygotski revisitado: una historia crítica de su contexto y legado*. Buenos Aires: Miño y Dávila Editores.

Hentz, P., & Herter, M. L. (2001). Propuesta curricular de Santa Catarina y psicología histórico-cultural. In. M. Golder (Ed.), *Vygotsky, psicólogo radical*. Buenos Aires: Ateneo Vygotskyano de la Argentina.

Hur, D. U. (2005). *Políticas da Psicologia de São Paulo: as entidades de classe durante o período do regime militar à redemocratização do país* (MA dissertation, Program of Social Psychology), Universidade de São Paulo.

Jacó-Vilela, A. M. (2011). *Dicionário Histórico de Instituições de Psicologia no Brasil*. Rio de Janeiro: Imago and Brasília, DF: Conselho Federal de Psicologia.

Jacó-Vilela, A. M., Degani-Carneiro, F., & Oliveira, D. de M. (2016). A formação da psicologia social como campo científico no Brasil. *Psicologia & Sociedade*, *28*(3), 526–536. http://dx.doi.org/10.1590/1807-03102016v28n3p526

Lane, S. T. M., & Codo, W. (Ed.). (1984). *Psicologia social: o homem em movimento*. São Paulo: Brasiliense.

Leontiev, A. N., Luria, A. R., & Vygotsky, L. S. (1988). *Linguagem, desenvolvimento e aprendizagem*. São Paulo: Ícone.

Machado, A. M., & Souza, M. P. R. (Ed.). (1997). *Psicologia Escolar: em busca de novos rumos*. São Paulo: Casa do Psicólogo.

Martins, J. B. (2013). Da relação Vygotsky e Leontiev – Alguns apontamentos a respeito da história da psicologia soviética. *Interamerican Journal of Psychology*, *47*(1), 43–51.

Martins, J. D. S. (2011). *A sociabilidade do homem simples: cotidiano e história na modernidade anômala*. São Paulo: Contexto.

Molón, S. I. (2001). A Psicologia Social abrapsiana: apontamentos históricos. *Interações*, *6*(12). 41–68.

Moraes Filho, E. de. (2003). A proto-história do marxismo no Brasil. In J. Q. de Moraes & D. A. Reis Filho (Ed.), *História do marxismo no Brasil* (Vol. I, p. 13–58, Rev. 2nd ed.). Campinas, SP: Editora da UNICAMP.

Netto, J. P. (2012). Nota sobre o marxismo na América Latina. *Novos Temas*, Salvador/São Paulo, *5*(6), 43–60.

Noda, M., & Galuch, M. T. B. (2018). Políticas públicas de educação no ensino básico do Estado do Paraná: da dívida social à formação para o mercado (1980–2000). *Revista HISTEDBR On-Line*, *18*(2), 545–569. https://doi.org/10.20396/rho.v18i2.8652356

Patto, M. H. S. (1981). (Org.) *Introdução à psicologia escolar* (2nd ed.). São Paulo: T.A. Queiroz.

Patto, M. H. S. (1984). *Psicologia e ideologia (uma introdução crítica à psicologia escolar)*. São Paulo: T.A. Queiroz.

Patto, M. H. S. (1990/2010) *A Produção do Fracasso escolar: histórias de submissão e rebeldia.* São Paulo: Casa do Psicólogo.

Patto, M. H. S. (1997). Para uma Crítica da Razão Psicométrica. *Psicologia USP, 8*(1), 47–62. https://dx.doi.org/10.1590/S0103-65641997000100004

Rey, F. L. G. (2007). Encontro da psicologia social brasileira com a psicologia soviética. *Psicologia & Sociedade, 19*(spe2), 57–61. https://dx.doi.org/10.1590/S0102-718 22007000500019

Santos, M. R. dos (in press). Seria a Teoria da Subjetividade uma vertente da Psicologia Histórico-Cultural? *Psicologia em Revista.*

Sarmento, D. F. (2006). *A teoria histórico-cultural de L. S. Vygotsky: uma análise da produção acadêmica e científica no período de 1986–2001.* Tese (Doutorado em Educação). Faculdade de Educação, Universidade Federal do Rio Grande do Sul.

Saviani, D. (1995). *Pedagogia histórico-crítica: primeiras aproximações.* Campinas: Autores Associados.

Smolka, A. L. B. (1987/2012). *A criança na fase inicial da escrita: a alfabetização como processo discursivo* (13th ed.). São Paulo: Cortez.

Smolka, A. L. B., Góes, M. C. R. de, & Laplane, A. L. F. de. (2015). Desenvolvimento Humano: história, natureza e cultura. *Cadernos CEDES, 35*(spe), 329–332. https://dx.doi.org/10.1590/CC0101-32622015V35ESPECIAL154113.

Sousa, E. A. D. (2008). *Sílvia Tatiane Maurer Lane: dissertações e teses orientadas no Programa de Estudos Pós-graduados em Psicologia Social na PUC-SP – uma contribuição aos estudos sobre a psicologia social no Brasil.* Tese (Doutorado em Psicologia da Educação), Pontifícia Universidade Católica de São Paulo, São Paulo, SP.

Tanamachi, E. de R., Souza, M. P. R., & Rocha, M. L. da. (2000). *Psicologia e educação: desafios teórico-práticos* (pp. 73–102). São Paulo: Casa do Psicólogo.

Thiesen, J. da S. (2007). Vinte Anos de Discussão e Implantação da Proposta Curricular de Santa Catarina na Rede de Ensino: desafios para um currículo de base histórico-cultural. *PerCursos, 8*(2), 41–54. Available at http://revistas.udesc.br/index.php/percursos/arti cle/view/1556. Accessed on September 1, 2019.

Toassa, G. (2015). Is there a "Vygotskian Materialism"? Ontological and epistemological concerns for a contemporary Marxist Psychology (Part I). *Dubna Psychological Journal, 3*, 46–57.

Toassa, G. (2016). Beyond the 'fractured discourse': Reflections on the subject and methodology of intervention in school psychology. In M. P. R. Souza, G. Toassa, & K. C. S. F. Bautheney (Ed.), *Psychology, society and education: Critical perspectives in Brazil* (pp. 113–130). New York: Nova Publishers.

Vygotsky, L. S. (1984). *A formação social da mente.* São Paulo: Martins Fontes.

Vygotsky, L. S. (1987). *Pensamento e linguagem.* São Paulo: Martins Fontes.

6

ALEXANDER LURIA: MARXIST PSYCHOLOGIST AND TRANSNATIONAL SCIENTIFIC BROKER

A personal account

Alexandre Métraux

Introduction

All Soviet psychologists were voluntarily self-proclaimed Marxists, by definition. This claim, however, can be questioned in relation to a few scholars and in the period of the 1920s only. Since then – that is, from the 1930s until the collapse of the Soviet Union in 1991 – this was a uniformly and officially held worldview and methodological position shared by everyone in Soviet psychology. Indeed, virtually any psychological book published in the USSR would open with invocations of the decisions of the Congresses of the Communist Party of the Soviet Union, outright claims of the authors' loyalty to the philosophy and methodology of Marxism, and the quotations from the forbares of Marxism-Leninism such as Karl Marx and Friedrich Engels, or from Vladimir Lenin and later Stalin, Breshnev, and so on. In case of scholarly journals, quite often a first couple of publications in each journal issue would be overtly dedicated to such claims and statements. This was a ritual, hardly ever questioned or contested.[1] One might, therefore, be somewhat puzzled by references to some scholars as "sincere Marxists" that one occasionally comes across in scholarly literature, in Russian language during the Soviet era and in Western publications alike. The idea of the emphasis that some Soviet scholars might qualify as "sincere Marxists" is thought-provoking and highly illustrative. Thus, rephrasing an all too well-known quote from Orwell's *Animal Farm* of 1945, one might say, "All Soviet psychologists were sincere Marxists, but some of them were more sincere than others". The sad irony of this statement is not in need of further comments.

---

1 On the idiosyncratic rituals of Soviet science see Krementsov, 1997; Yasnitsky, 2016.

Soviet Marxist psychology, in turn, was always declaratively focused on the person, personality (*lichnost*, in Russian) in his/her concrete social conditions of life and practical activity as peasant, teacher, child, neurological patient, etc. Paradoxically enough, along with numerous pronouncements of the primacy of personality in Soviet psychology of theoretical and speculative kind, one hardly encounters dense empirical studies on personality in thoroughly described and analyzed social settings done by Soviet scholars. Even in studies published in the Soviet Union under the banner of social psychology one encounters consistent omission of politically charged topics such as the material conditions of social life and activities in a politically tense climate, labor conditions, official and civil society institutions, administrative policies, incomes, worldview(s) and human values, and the like. This observation holds true of most histories of Soviet science, and in particular of Soviet psychology, that came out in the Soviet era – and even during the post-Soviet era. This chapter in a number of ways aims to fill this gap, at least, partially.

Thus, I would like to state this firsthand: this chapter is a personal account, based on my personal experiences of the latest four decades of my life, or so. Therefore, it is bound to deal with personality in some sense: my own personality. Furthermore, the story has something to do with personality, in a different sense: this is a story of my dealing with another personality, the renowned Russian scholar, the cultural, experimental, and neuro-psychologist, Alexander Luria. I do not approach Luria from the stance of academic research in the field of the history of science; my approach is dependent on very concrete contingencies, from which I then move to some (only some) general, abstract assertions concerning the life and work of a psychologist (and neuropsychologist) who aimed at making psychology concrete, i.e. a science that, quite in line with Marxist methodological requirement, moves from the abstract to the concrete. There is a curious opposition there: my approach was from the concrete to the abstract; Luria's approach was, officially at least, from the abstract to the concrete. And the little irony is: he started on a concrete level (i.e., psychoanalysis of the costume, methods of psychotechnics, etc.). Besides, an active advocate for a dialogue between people (specifically, international scholars worldwide), cultures, and scientific traditions, I have long acted as a scientific "broker" between a number of academic traditions by virtue of my translating, editing, and other scholarly activities, account of which can be found in one of my earlier papers.[2] In the manner characteristic of this chapter, my personal story is yet again curiously reflected in the story I am trying to tell. In this story its protagonist is also viewed not the least as an international scholar of global fame and as an actor of the 'transnational science,' who equally belonged in the local, highly idiosyncratic Soviet scientific culture and the global intellectual milieu. The somewhat paradoxical unity of the two, the compatibility of the incompatible, is, perhaps, the main theme of this story, after all.

---

2 On my 'encounter' with Vygotsky's life and works see Métraux, 2015.

The initiation to the life and work of Alexander Romanovich Luria (1902–1977) could have happened differently, but this is how it happened. On an early October morning of 1979, I met Gertrud Weiss Lewin in her residence. She knew why I would visit her – to find out which unpublished documents by Kurt Lewin (1890–1947), treasured in her residence, could be edited and published in the multi-volume edition of Lewin's works which was at that time in the process of being prepared. After an extended conversation, Gertrud Weiss Lewin decided to open the drawers where the Lewin-*Nachlass*[3] had been deposited.

Among the folders disposed in the drawers, there were pages written by Alexander Luria.

I do not remember when I came across Luria's name for the first time. In October 1979, the name brought to my mind the vague notion that it was the name of a Russian scholar who had had something to do with Soviet psychologist Lev Vygotsky (1896–1934).

When giving the eye to these pages, I caught a glimpse of other names: Vygotsky, yes, many times Vygotsky, and Köhler, Piaget, Katz, Boas, Zeigarnik, Koffka, Janet, Lashley, Goldstein, Gelb, and others.[4] These names appeared first to simply be names denoting persons in Luria's letters to Lewin.[5] Later I learned that most of them also denoted acquaintances with whom Luria would interact either on

---

3 That is, the collection of archival documents of Kurt Lewin, currently in the Archives of the History of American Psychology at the Drs. Nicholas and Dorothy Cummings Center for the History of Psychology, located at The University of Akron in Akron, OH.

4 Wolfgang Köhler headed the Institute of Psychology at the University of Berlin in Germany in the 1920s and early 1930s; Kurt Lewin, one of the most open-minded and productive psychologists of the time, was a member of Köhler's institute; both are regarded as Gestalt psychologists. Bluma Zeigarnik was a doctoral student of Lewin; she is known for the so-called *Zeigarnik effect* which implies that unfinished tasks are better remembered than complete ones; after having obtained her Ph.D. in Berlin, she returned to Soviet Moscow and was subsequently involved in various research projects there (see e.g. Zeigarnik, 1972). Kurt Koffka was also a German Gestalt psychologist who immigrated to the USA some years before he would have been forced to do so after 1933; he joined Luria's second psychological expedition to Central Asia in 1932. Kurt Goldstein was a highly esteemed neurologist (and neuropsychologist) working in Frankfurt on the Main and, later, in Berlin; he examined dozens of brain-injured subjects and may be seen as a theorist whose approach was similar to that of Luria. Adhémar Gelb was Goldstein's expert for psychological matter and his closest collaborator; both scholars are traditionally counted as being close to Gestalt psychology. Jean Piaget was a Swiss child psychologist working at Geneva University and, as well after 1945, as guest professor at Sorbonne University in Paris; he was widely read by Vygotsky, Luria, and other Soviet psychologists. Pierre Janet was a French near-polymath: first a philosopher, then a psychologist, and finally a physician, who taught at the Collège de France; a specialist of psychopathological conditions and successor of Jean-Marie Charcot as head of the psychological laboratory at the Salpêtrière in Paris. Karl Spencer Lashley was an American psychologist whose main research focused on the cortical basis of learning and discrimination. Franz Boas is known for his pioneering anthropological research which was based on the rejection of simple evolutionary ideas; he thereby recognized the relative independence of ethnic group within the frame of cultural diversity. For obvious reasons, most of the documents I was dealing with were dated between WWI and WWII, the *interbellum* period.

5 See Métraux, 2002.

international meetings such as academic congresses and/or in more or less extensive correspondence and/or as partners in research projects. This scholar thus became 'visible' to me *from the outset* against the background of a vast national and international network.

One of the outcomes of this 'discovery' of unlooked-for archival material was – this holds especially for Luria – that rather than moving from published monographs and articles to a later attempt at contextualizing the work of a scholar by way of chasing down documents in archives, I could move in reverse order: from freshly found unpublished sources that provided background or context information to the study of Luria's printed works.

Another coincidence needs to be mentioned. In the summer of 1980, I met Boris M. Velichkovsky at the XXIInd International Congress of Psychology in Leipzig. Instead of listening to one speaker after the next, we found a quiet corner and talked about Luria, with whom Velichkovsky had worked and on whom he had many recollections. We then started to collaborate on Luria.[6] I should also mention that frequent visits to the German Democratic Republic (GDR) offered occasions for meeting academics of that country. Some of these colleagues arranged one day an encounter with Elena Alexandrovna Luria in Berlin (GDR). She subsequently sent items of her father's archive, among them copies of Sigmund Freud's letters to Luria (see the following).

These circumstances may explain why my approach to Luria and to some few aspects of Soviet psychology has had a lasting effect: that of considering and often reconsidering the topics whose traces emerged from unpublished sources.

An objection lures against doing this kind of research on the history of Soviet psychology, viz. its avowedly idiosyncratic cherry-picking. Concerning my approach to Luria, it depends indeed (and *exceptionally*) upon cherry-picking. And yes, I do not deal here with many other aspects of Luria's life and work. Instead, I try to find out (i) what may be regarded as historically justifiable interpretation and (ii) what is further needed for reaching the level of a well-founded understanding of his role in the history of Soviet psychology.

I shall thus focus on (i) single events and deeds in Luria's life to be described and analyzed as far as necessary; and on (ii) needs for additional research that might lead to the revision of the now traditional conception of Luria's life and work.

Luria and psychoanalysis

In his memoirs, *The Making of Mind: A Personal Account of Soviet Psychology*, Luria recalls his strong interest in things psychoanalytic in his early career:

> I plunged into psychoanalytic research. To begin with, I established a small psychoanalytic circle. [. . .] I then sent news of the formation of this group

---

6 See Velichkovsky [Veličkovskij] & Métraux, 1981, 1986.

to Freud himself, and was both surprised and pleased when I received a letter in return addressed to me as "Dear Mr. President." Freud wrote how glad he was to learn that a psychoanalytic circle had been founded in such a remote eastern town of Russia.[7]

Luria must have assumed that this account was sufficiently ample and precise. A new look at the reports he would send to Vienna from Kazan on the psychoanalytic association he had initiated, however, does not fully corroborate the narrative in *The Making of Mind*. An anonymously published note in the 1922 autumn issue of the *Internationale Zeitschrift für Psychoanalyse* asserted that

> as we have been told, a "Psychoanalytic Association" has recently been founded in Kazan (Russia). This association is formed by a circle of psychologists, doctors, and educationists, and is closely connected with the Kazan Society for the Social Sciences. In the coming weeks, the association will hold some meetings on which reports will be made.[8]

Style and syntax of the note suggest that it did most probably not stem from Luria. It seems that Otto Rank, at that time in charge of secretarial duties for Freud's journal, wrote it. But Rank relied on information sent by Luria. In the first letter (dated July 3, 1922) to Luria, Freud thanked him for a "writing" (*Schrift*) on psychoanalysis and added that he was looking forward to receiving *further news* from the Kazan "circle":

> Highly esteemed colleague, I thankfully confirm receipt of your writing on psychoanalysis and will be delighted to get news that shows strong interest of your circle in psychoanalysis. Please, when writing to Professor Ermakov, tell him on my behalf that we fail to contact him by mail and that I have not yet received the second part of my lectures translated by Wulff. With many friendly regards to you and the members of the association, yours Freud.[9]

But another note, again anonymously published in the same journal, has probably been written by Luria or by some other member more or less fluent in German:

> The *Kazan Psychoanalystic Association* was organized [sic] in the Summer of 1922. Its interests are close to the theoretical problems of psychoanalysis, to its application to the humanities and the social sciences, and to therapy. Furthermore, the Kazan Society has recently established contacts with the

---

7 Luria, 1979, p. 24.
8 Anon, 1922a.
9 Sigmund Freud to Alexander Luria on July 3, 1922, transcribed and published for the first time in Métraux, 1993, p. 11.

Moscow association, which has been officially recognized as a local group during the last Congress.[10]

Available sources support the evidence that young Luria was by all means an energetic promoter of two groups in Kazan in 1922 and 1923. He acted as president of one of these societies (the social scientific one) and as secretary (or most likely also as head) of the psychoanalytic one. He produced a "writing" on a (probably psychoanalytically inspired) topic which, however, remains mysteriously unknown. He also wrote a monograph published in Kazan. And he gave several talks there: on September 7, 1922, on the state of psychoanalysis, on October 21 on the psychoanalysis of costumes, on December 10 on various Russian psychological trends, on February 18, 1923, on some principles of psychoanalysis and (on that same day) on a theatre play by Leonid Andreyev, on March 5 on psychoanalysis in the context of contemporary psychology, on March 18 on the analysis of pre-sleep phantasies, and, finally, on September 4 on psychoanalysis and Marxism.

If one's reading sticks to the sole narrative in *The Making of Mind*, one hardly would expect that Luria valued psychoanalysis as the framework for a promising psychological research program. Yet thanks to the reports sent to Vienna for publication in the *Internationale Zeitschrift für Psychoanalyse* (either anonymously or signed by their author), some previously unnoticed details of the history of Soviet psychology may be grasped. Luria was thus involved, too, in getting psychoanalytic ideas fuelled into the channels of scientific communication, as Freud's second letter (dated October 6, 1922) to "Dear Mr. President" shows: "I'm glad to read the letter you sent to Doctor Rank and herewith grant permission to translate my work *Massenpsychologie und Ich-Analyse* into Russian. With best wishes, yours sincerely, Freud."[11] Whether Luria had sent the request on his own or on someone else's behalf remains unsettled.

Hence, when joining Konstantin Kornilov's newly reformed Institute of Psychology in Moscow in late 1923, Luria was well prepared to contribute an essay on psychoanalysis for a collective publication of the scientific members of the institute on the *theoretical foundations* of psychology.[12] To be more precise: Kornilov invited Luria to submit one of two articles on psychoanalysis to the volume he was editing (the author of the other article was Boris Fri(e)dman, also a member of the Moscow institute). Note, too, that Mikhail Reisner's essay on social psychology and Marxism in the same volume also touched on psychoanalysis. This visibility of psychoanalysis is remarkable on two counts: (i) it attests to the continuity of the Russian reception of psychoanalysis into the post-revolutionary epoch, and (ii) it

10 Anon, 1922b.
11 Sigmund Freud to Alexander Luria on October 6, 1922, transcribed and published for the first time in Métraux, 1993, p. 11.
12 See Kornilov, 1925.

shows the closeness of psychoanalysis to materialist psychology *as defined* by various Soviet authors of the 1920s.

But unlike ideologically outspoken scholars, Luria was careful in his attempt to conceive psychoanalysis as a materialist approach to the study of human consciousness and conduct. Instead of claiming that it embodied a fully fledged theory of human mental states and processes, Luria, as he put it, "hope[d] to show that in studying individual behavior, the unconscious drives underlying it and their connections with organic states, psychoanalysis [. . .] [was] heading in the direction of a monistic theory of individual behavior."[13] And he added:

> In its view of mental activity as an energy process not different in principle from somatic processes, psychoanalysis provides us with a purely monistic, developed conception of this energy, stipulating that it may quite easily assume psychic forms or patently somatic forms.[14]

Note the wording "heading in the direction of" rather than "being," "mental activity as an energy process not different in principle" rather than without the clause "in principle," "stipulating that it may" rather than "showing" or "demonstrating that it easily assumes." This way of putting it saved sufficient freedom (or space) *for further investigations* beyond the strong metaphysical and/or ideological identification of '*physical=bodily=organic=(partly) mental states and processes*,' on the one hand, with '*mental=conscious-cum-unconscious states and processes*,' on the other hand. Even a monist psychology satisfying the criteria of sound materialism would still have to examine more rigorously than Freud and his followers had done the way in which individuals are physically *and* socially determined in their wishes, thoughts, and dreams, etc., by the energy of their drives.

Compare this with Vladimir A. Artemov's article on the problem of aptitude and Marxism, also published in Konilov's volume. In the summary, Artemov (who later became one of the leading Soviet psycholinguists and a renowned expert in experimental phonetics)[15] asserted,

> The psychic [*psikhika*] is nothing but a specific higher order property of organized matter, with respect to which the external, objective manifestations of that specific matter yield various sorts of movement: pantomime, facial expressions, bodily and linguistic reactions. We can therefore define psychology as the science of animal and human behavior.[16]

– behavior *qua* types of reactions, to be clear. Artemov added, without addressing the possibility of *intervening* individual conscious states and processes, that "we need

---

13 Luria, 1977, p. 19.
14 Ibid., p. 20.
15 Cf. Artemov, 1956.
16 Artemov, 1925, p. 111.

to study the behavior of man as an organism of the bio-social order."[17] Monism/ materialism in psychology as the hallmark of research done in Kornilov's institute therefore lent itself to rather divergent, if not opposed theoretical and/or ideological interpretations – divergences, to be sure, that were not brought to a halt during the Soviet regime.

Luria's approach to psychoanalysis soon came under heavy critical fire. A Soviet scholar frequently associated with the 'Bakhtin Circle,' Valentin N. Voloshinov derided the article as a clumsy attempt to construe Freudian psychoanalysis in terms of a materialist theory. In his book of 1927, *Freydizm* (Freudianism), Voloshinov argued mockingly that the notion of 'whole person,'[18] which Luria had defined as the key object of *psychoanalytic research*, was but a queer revival of the concept of human being set forth by Romantic philosophers such as Schelling, or even by Leibniz who conceived the monad as an entity capable of reflecting itself and the whole universe in its windowless interiority.[19] Targeting the *pseudo*-materialism of Luria's psychoanalytic approach, Voloshinov's attack rejected it in the end as an *alternative to pre-Marxist*, i.e. pre-materialist trends in psychology; it likewise rejected the terms in which Freud and his followers (including Luria) had defined the concept of whole person. This concept "does not include one single objective parameter by way of which this person could be inserted into the material reality of the surrounding nature."[20] Since human behavior is said to be caused by drives, but given that drives, on psychoanalytic view, originate in the *subjective* dimension of the person, psychoanalysis – again: as conceived by Luria as a follower of Freud – was doomed to fail as a non-subjective, i.e. objective, materialist, and truly monist science.[21]

When contributing to the volume edited by Kornilov, Luria, however, did not claim that psychoanalysis had already evolved into a well-confirmed psychological theory. His essay had in fact only *outlined* the psychoanalytic *approach* as a workable research program for the Soviet psychology to come. Voloshinov's purpose therefore was to subvert Freudian psychoanalysis *plus* its Lurian offspring, and to replace it by a genuinely Soviet, Marxist, and monist approach to human behavior and consciousness.

Some months later, another paper on key issues of Freudian psychoanalysis penned by Luria was published, who now put the focus on the impact of Ivan Pavlov's physiological theory of unconditioned and conditioned (or rather unconditional and conditional)[22] reflexes on the psychoanalytic research program. Considered from a historical point of view, Luria's endeavor was not too innovative, for

---

17 Ibid., p. 112.
18 On the semantically intricate concept of person (*lichnost*) (especially in Russian psychology and philosophy, and with reference to Ilyenkov, see Appendix 2), see Bakhurst, 1995.
19 Cf. Voloshinov, 1993, p. 100.
20 Ibid., p. 102.
21 Cf. Ibid., pp. 101–102.
22 For the Pavlovian terminology see the useful *Pavlov Lexikon* in Todes, 2014, pp. 732–738.

he had previously mentioned an article of similar scope in his paper for Kornilov's volume.[23] The essay on Pavlovism and Freudianism (to make things perhaps too simple by the use of catch-labels) remains noteworthy because it was written in German, and accepted by and published in a psychoanalytic journal.[24] Whereas Luria had previously relied on non-Russian ideas, conceptions, and terms in order to strengthen his efforts of re-founding a new, Soviet psychology, the article at stake evidently turned things upside down. The epistemological and ideological lead was now ascribed to a key trend of *Russian* physiology (in general) and psycho-physiology (in particular) – a trend *publicly* recognized to rest on materialist principles and methods, hence to be a model for doing *modern* psychological research in the USSR.

Whatever the consequences of Voloshinov's attack may have been for Luria,[25] the latter could nevertheless contribute some entries to the *Great Soviet Encyclopedia* (*GSE*) on psychological topics.[26] Soviet researchers such as Vygotsky, Alexei Leontiev, Boris Teplov, Yuri Kannabikh, and some other members of the 'new Soviet psychology' contributed specialized entries on psychology and psychiatry as well. Some of Luria's entries covered these topics: Alfred Adler (*GSE* 1:597–598), apperception (*GSE* 3:173), association in psychology (*GSE* 3:633–636), dynamic psychology (*GSE* 22:455–456), psychoanalysis (*GSE* 47:507–510), and Hermann Ebbinghaus (*GSE* 63: 136–139). Add to these entries the long one on psychology by Luria and Leontiev (*GSE* 47:510–548). Yet all author names, and most of the entries, disappeared from the second edition of the *GSE*.[27] If there was a place where psychologists such as Luria and his colleagues could reach social visibility, it was undoubtedly an encyclopedia for everybody like the *GSE*. Isn't it strange that these entries have not been considered more closely by historians of (Soviet) psychology?

What has remained of Luria's early interest in psychoanalysis, and what conclusions are to be drawn from a not all too far-reaching examination (as the present one) of his early academic life? If asked, most historians of psychology (and historically minded psychologists) who have been aware of Luria to begin with would answer: psychoanalysis simply vanished from his attention. Though signs of attention for psychoanalysis do not occur in the works published after 1935 or so (except in Luria's life-writing itself), the answer fails to reach its goal. It discards a *formal* feature in Luria's works. Take the two famous case histories which grew out his 'romantic science' endeavor (also see later in this chapter). They are endowed with the narrative quality characteristic of psychoanalytic case histories.

23 See Luria, 1977, p. 45, reference to Humphrey, 1920.
24 See Luria, 1926.
25 Or for Voloshinov himself and for some early Soviet psychoanalysts, a point still unsettled in the history of psychology and the social sciences.
26 For further data on topics of psychology (re)presented in the *Great Soviet Encyclopedia* see Scheerer, 1984.
27 See Hogg, 1998 for a survey of the history of the *GSE*.

They also remind one of the case histories contained in Luria's US-published solid volume *The Nature of Human Conflict* of 1932, which largely illustrated *how* to combine rigorous data collecting with descriptive concreteness.[28] By the way, a subtle re-orientation of his research program had happened while Luria was working on the topic of human conflicts from 1923 to 1930.[29] In his analyses on symptoms induced by conflicts, he was drawing in part from the studies undertaken at the psychiatric clinic Burghölzli in Zurich on the psychological diagnosis of evidence. In spite of owing in their approach to psychological experimentalism, the ultimate goal of the Burghölzli studies was psychoanalytic (in a broader, no longer strictly Freudian) sense.[30] But as *The Nature of Human Conflict* shows, the experimental orientation was clearly non-psychoanalytic, although the text presented case histories such as those Luria had encountered when dealing first in Kazan, then in Moscow with matters of psychoanalysis, and thus also with the forms of psychoanalytic narratives. Note that Luria had not yet turned to medicine for good when working on the monograph under consideration, hence the high probability that he became familiar with the narrative form through psychoanalytic contributions rather than through classical psychiatric and/or neurological case histories.

One doesn't need do much more than closely read texts in order to grasp *formal affinities* of the kind just mentioned. But doing studies in the history of the sciences requires more – among other things: looking for traces of laboratory and/or field work, searching administrative documents of all kinds and on all levels of science administration, describing apparatuses and instruments that were used by individual researchers and/or research groups, gathering information on informal power relations both within discipline and cross discipline networks, etc.

Let's take merely one example of what is at stake here. In the last decade before he died, Luria published (among other texts) a short monograph on the incredibly vast mnestic capacities of one of his subjects he and other reserchers such as Vygotsky had examined and closely followed during many years. The Russian title he chose for this book is *Malenkaya knizhka o bolshoy pamyati (um mnemonista).*[31] The title is highly ironical. Indeed, the material gathered for the case study of Shereshevsky, the subject mnemonist and 'hero' of this this text, fills files and files of notes, reckonings, and observations. The noun *knizhka* is the diminutive form of *kniga*, the word meaning 'book.' Hence, *knizhka* may be rendered as 'booklet.' If you add *malenkaya* to *knizhka*, you turn a little book into a little little book (to suggest a somehow clumsy, but correct translation). And the antagonism between the sheer incredible vastness of the mnemonist's memory and the sheer incredible tininess of the text not only signals the irony of the publication as such,

---

28 See Luria, 1960 [1932], e.g. pp. 99–102.
29 See Luria Ibid., p. XI.
30 On the Burghölzli studies see Marinelli & Mayer, 2003, pp. 25–38; Mayer, 2012, pp. 210–213.
31 See Luria, 1968a. For the English translation, see Luria, 1968b.

but also the disproportion between the hidden quantity of empirical data and the *visible* outcome of the case study itself.

The modest space chosen by Luria for the narrative of an extraordinary case did not permit him to address the work practices on which the examination of the mnemonist Shereshevsky rests. One may infer from the text that the mnestic capacities at stake were 'measured' by means of an Ebbinghaus type instrument. But Luria could not have applied the methods designed by Ebbinghaus[32] himself, for the latter used 2300 meaningless syllables written on paper cards and drawn by chance from some kind of container in order to form series of various lengths. The subject's task (Ebbinghaus acted first as his own experimental subject) was to store the series and to recall them correctly. The number of syllables of the series varied; the number of presentation of the series varied; the time needed for the faultless recall of a series was also measured. Luria knew the Ebbingausian paradigm of memory research (cf. supra). However, rather than resorting to meaningless syllables, he used mainly series of words as well as series of numbers, which were read to the mnemonist. Strangely, the mnemonist did not need to listen twice or more times to the stimuli; he could recall the series within a brief lapse of time or weeks later; he even was able to recall the series from the end to its beginning. Moreover, it turned out that the menmonist's memory could store endlessly, so that the psychologist (Luria or whoever took Luria's role as experimentalist or observer) never could *really determine* Shereshevsky's mnestic storage capacities since any series of words presented to him could have been longer than the prepared series.

All tests were properly stored; innumerable notes were written down; data were recorded throughout a few decades of a longitudinal study as if extended laboratory experiments were done. Yet this kind of necessary, hard, perhaps also tedious labor has remained in a state of latency in the "little little book" Luria devoted to one of his favorite subjects who reveals himself to have been an extraordinary person beyond, as one could say, human mnestic measurements.

The latent aspect of Soviet psychology: a Cold War story of official Pavlovization

Let me now pinpoint a sequence of events fit to epitomize the relevance of facts that remained officially (in print, in public lectures, etc.) unsaid but were nonetheless historically significant, especially for the historical unfolding of Luria's conception of psychology. The research program launched in the 1920s, associated with the names of its founders Lev Vygotsky and Alexander Luria, and conventionally called the *cultural-historical school of Soviet psychology*,[33] reached social visibility not only by way of publications, academic lectures, laboratory work, and the like, but also through face-to-face interactions with visitors who were invited to Moscow,

---

32 See Ebbinghaus 1913.
33 See Yasnitsky et al., 2014.

or through interactions that took place, sometimes informally, during international congresses or on other, similar occasions. A further expedient for reaching social visibility especially on the international level consisted of establishing more or less informal links to members of non-Soviet communist parties in the bourgeois West in order to enhance the academic reputation of Soviet psychology, be it that of Pavlovism, that of the cultural-historical approach, or that of the Tbilisi school of the so-called *set-theory* led by the Soviet Georgian psychologist Dimitri Uznadze. The analysis of the various ways to which Soviet scholars resorted when seeking firm reputation and securing venues for their research implies that traces of the interplay of official, non-latent, i.e. public action and latent, private, inofficial activity be found and subjected to comparative interpretation.

Take as a telling example of such public arena *vs.* latent sphere events the stay of three French speaking psychologists in Moscow in 1955. In order to grasp the significance of this episode, a preliminary narrative, however, is needed. This introductory narrative focuses on the fuzzy, complex, and intricately ambivalent bonds that established due to radical changes of the political situations concerning the fate of the teaching of the famous Russian and Soviet physiologist and Nobel Prize winner Ivan Pavlov (1849–1936).[34]

The researches inspired by Pavlov's teachings were perceived essentially as truly materialist, whatever the intimate, personal convictions and creeds of that famous scholar may have been. The dogmatic reading of Pavlov's theories and of those who were judged to be his true followers rejected subjective processes such as thoughts, feelings, expectations, and other mental events. Mental entities, they were convinced, did not belong to the set of possible *explananda* of animal and/or human behavior. But this rejection was perceived by several psychologists as a dangerous challenge to their research aims and institutional recognition. If Pavlov's teachings were true, psychology would be out – this is a trivialized recapitulation of the tensions that obtained between Pavlovism and psychology in post-revolutionary times. Thus, it was safe for psychologists of the early Soviet era to refer to Pavlov's (materialist, monist, close to Marxism) theorems, for they were building a new, monist, and materialist psychology, on the one hand. But on the other hand, Pavlovian theorems, if strictly applied, undermined psychology as an *autonomous* science, and particularly as a science that addressed social beings endowed with the capacity of planning revolutions, designing political systems devoid of exploitation, of scientifically administering industrial plants, etc. Hence, the virtually unending competition between divergent trends for material allocations and political recognition.

In the 1930s, many Soviet psychologists turned away from Pavlov's teachings. They contended that these teachings could advance psychology's understanding of genuine conscious activities in humans. To put it differently: Pavlov's teaching promoted at best a mechanistic, non-dialectical, and trivially materialist

---

34 On Pavlov's intricate relations to (and with) Soviet Bolshevism see Todes, 1995; Todes & Krementsov, 2010.

understanding of human mental life. This is not to say that all Soviet psychologists were anti-Pavlovians. Yet it *seemed* that the *autonomy of psychology* had come to be successfully and definitely recognized politically, ideologically, and epistemologically, whatever the ideological errors of this or that psychologist of this or that trend may have been.

In the late 1940s and early 1950s, in contradistinction, Pavlov's teaching (and those of some of his strong-willed and inflexible followers) enjoyed a *politically induced* renaissance. On September 27, 1949, Yuri Zhdanov[35] submitted a memorandum – it *did* reach Stalin himself – on bourgeois, idealist deviations that were said to damage Pavlov's true theories. In the conclusion of the memo, Zhdanov

> outlined what he believed needed to be done to improve Soviet physiology. He called for the restructuring of the higher-education curriculum to emphasize the importance of Pavlov's work for medical research and practice, particularly in psychoneurological clinics. But, most important, he called for a conference where Bykov should give a speech criticizing Orbeli and others while defining the parameters of Pavlov's work.[36]

Stalin endorsed Zhdanov's idea on October 6.[37] He also instructed the latter to organize the conference on Pavlov and its enemies in a joint meeting of the Academy of Sciences of the USSR and the Academy of Medicine of the USSR. A dogmatic Pavlovian, Konstantin Bykov, was politely ordered to prepare a speech, whose draft he sent to Zhdanov for approval – which shows that the conference was 'directed' by the innermost circle of (party, i.e. national Soviet) politics. The conference finally was held on June 28 to July 4, 1950, in Moscow. Both Andrei A. Ivanov-Smolensky (another hardliner of Soviet physiology) and Bykov denounced Pavlov's "scientific heir" and the official Soviet leader of his physiological school Leon A. Orbeli and several other physiologists and physicians as traitors to the true teachings of Pavlov.[38]

The Pavlov affair was not closed yet, for a follow-up conference was held, also in Moscow, on October 11 to 15, 1950. It was now Luria's turn to be attacked for his anti-Pavlovian attitude. He was in particular accused, among other failures, of having deliberately ignored Pavlov's theory of localization when dealing with issues of cerebral disturbances as well as of having relied on Goldstein, a bourgeois neurologist and advocate of a non-materialist approach to human neurology.

35 Yuri Zdanov (the son of the Soviet Communist Party top functioneer and the right-hand man of the Party leader Joseph Stalin, Andrey Zhdanov) was at that time in charge of supervising all scientific research in the Soviet Union and personally close to Stalin, whose daughter Svetlana (known in the West as Svetlana Alliluyeva) he had married in 1949.

36 Pollock, 2006, p. 145.

37 See Stalin, 2006.

38 See Banshchikov et al., 1952.

It may seem that this prelude to the episode on which I shall draw the readers' attention in the following lines is too long, and thus exhausting. But the point to be made cannot be made without the description if its antecedents.

In 1952, Anatolii Smirnov published an essay in which he took up the line of argument of the supporters of Pavlov's reborn teachings in an aggressive critique of those psychologists who showed signs of deviancy from a materialist approach to human behavior. Among those mentioned in this article (which was a speech given at a major public convention), there was Luria who, as Smirnov asserted, had omitted in his studies of psychological disorders caused by cerebral lesions to recognize the relevancy of Pavlov's conception. Moreover, Luria was blamed for having based his research on cerebral systems which he accounted for in anatomical rather than in neurological terms (the latter notion was meant to express Pavlov's theory of higher nervous activity).[39]

Now, three years later, three renowned Francophone psychologists, Jean Piaget, René Zazzo,[40] and Paul Fraisse[41] were welcomed as respected guests in Moscow. And gathered as much information as they could on the state of psychological research two years after Stalin's death and soon before the onset of what has come to be called the thaw, a short-lived stretch of time of a less illiberal regime. They visited various research institutions and met many psychologists. In his account of the Moscow visit, Fraisse reported:

> Am I going to conjure up the visit we, Piaget, Zazzo, and myself, have payed to the Soviet Union in 1955? The visit of the Institute of Psychology in Moscow had been the revelation of a highly complex situation. We had supposed psychology had been brought to crash, but nearly one hundred researchers were working in that Institute. We went from laboratory to laboratory, each of which presented its projects. The visit of each laboratory amused or annoyed us, depending on the person who introduced us to the research under way, by simplistic references to Pavlov. But then followed the comprehensive descriptions of the valuable researches based on appropriate methods. No mention was made any longer of conditioned reflexes and higher nervous activity, except when mentioning explanations of that type were objectively justified. The conclusion to be drawn: one doesn't stop science. One evening, we were having a conversation with the five great psychologists of that time: Leontiev, Luria, Smirnov, Rubinstein, and Teplov. Dried fruits and oranges were on the table. One of them seized two halfs of an orange which had been emptied of its fleshy content and said to

39 See Massucco Costa, 1977, p. 210.
40 René Zazzo was doing research on child psychology and education; during World War II, he joined the Résistance; member of the French Communist Party, he taught psychology at the École Normale Supérieure as well as at the École Pratiques des Hautes Études.
41 Paul Fraisse, a Belgian psychologist, studied first theology and then turned to experimental psychology at Leuven/Louvain (Belgium) under the guidance of Albert Michotte; he was later named head of the psychological laboratory of the École Pratique des Hautes Études in Paris.

me – aside –: "You see, Pavlovism, that's like this orange, it's so beautiful," and holding the two peels apart, he added: "you also see, it's empty inside." Inflated jest, of course, but encapsulating the prevailing mood.[42]

Fraisse did not mention who (among the five hosts, among them the same Smirnov who some three years earlier had *politically* and *scientifically* attacked Luria) explained to him what Pavlovism looked like in 1955. One may thus hypothesize that it was Luria, who spoke French. It could also have been Leontiev, who also spoke French (for neither Fraisse nor Piaget understood more than some rare bits of tourist-Russian, and I do not know whether Zazzo was fluent in Russian . . .). Given the linguistic skills of the three other hosts, one might as well believe that it was one of them. Guess who! Unless some diary entry, some letter, some other, more explicit record pops up, the episode will remain unsettled. Interestingly, Fraisse concedes that the one host who told him that Pavlovism was empty made an exaggerate claim. Did that host exaggerate a bit, or too much? As reported by Fraisse, the episode shows that it was *unclear to the hosts* as well as *to the guests* how (and where) to draw the demarcation line between theories derived from Pavlov that would make sense in the field of psychological research and theories dressed in Pavlovian jargon that would not.

There is a grain of irony in the episode couched in Fraisse's words. The episode is told in the preface of the French translation of Angiola Massucco Costa's history of Soviet psychology, published in Rome in 1963. The Italian author's stance is that of an historian who drew her knowledge from printed sources in various languages. Fraisse's point of view is that of a witness who gained knowledge from the latent inside made vivid in an informal gathering. This is not to say that *latency* is a characteristic solely of private life. The latent history of Soviet psychology is stored in private *and* public archives, correspondences, diaries, administrative files, etc. And concerning Luria, as long as the history of sciences progresses only on the surface of publicly available, print sources, the fully fledged story of his life and work is doomed to remain incomplete, devoid of tensions, and thus rather abstract.

Fraisse adds that, while staying in Montreal in 1954 and in Moscow in 1955,

> the Soviets didn't talk of Vygotsky. But I remember being surprised in 1959, at the congress held in Brussels, Luria and Leontiev told me: "You must by all means publish Vygotsky in France." Times had changed, or rather: old times had returned.[43]

Promoting Vygotsky: a fragment of Luria's science policy

This episode concerns primarily Luria and another Vygotsky and Luria close associate from the 1920s, Alexei N. Leontiev (1903–1979). Luria's and Leontiev's

---

42 Fraisse, 1977, p. 5.
43 Ibid., p. 5.

proposal to publish Vygotsky abroad was in no ways a trial balloon. On the contrary, Vygotsky – and now the name may stand for a talented psychologist who died much too young from tuberculosis and/or for *the* pioneer of the new, true Soviet *psychology* and/or for the emblem of a school of thought, theoretical approach, or research program – was *used* especially by Luria for purposes of science policy (in our case: of 'psychology policy'), and he did it in two ways. On the one hand, he honestly believed that Vygotsky needed to be remembered and honored as a scholar of excellence; on the other hand, he also 'pushed' Vygotsky in order to consolidate his own approach (and that of those colleagues who referred to Vygotsky without being among the very close followers) against other, competing approaches of Soviet psychologists. In his memoirs *Looking Back*, Luria evoked the "intimate meetings" he and Leontiev attended at Vygotsky's flat in the late 1920s and early '30s. The meetings were held once or twice a week. Their purpose was "to elaborate the general 'complexes' of the new psychology." At these meetings, "the leading spirit of Vygotsky played the decisive role, the other two in the 'troika' being mainly his followers and partly his instruments."[44] The expression "partly his instruments" either means that Luria and Leontiev happened incidentally to be instrumental for Vygotsky's theoretical thinking, or else that he used his visitors as sources for making progress in his own thinking. The passage seems to be a rare instance where Luria's attitude towards his genial friend and teacher is tinged with slight ambivalence.

However, as mentioned some lines earlier, Luria also *used* the 'posthumous Vygotsky' as a significant instrument in his own interest. He did so either alone, as in the brief obituary published in March 1935 in the international quarterly *Character and Personality*. Among other remarkable contributions to psychology-building in the Soviet Union, Luria mentioned that

> Vygotsky [. . .] did not confine himself to the study of theoretical problems, but devoted much of his work to the practical application of psychology. Unlike the psychologists of both the physiological and the idealistic (*geisteswissenschaftliche*) schools, Vygotsky tried to find a scientific solution of the practical problems of our daily life. [. . .] The psychiatric and neurological clinics owe to him a number of valuable contributions. He has shown that the disintegration of the complex mental functions plays an important part in the understanding of the mechanisms of nervous and mental diseases.[45]

A characteristic feature of this obituary is worth a brief comment. While Stalin and his fellow comrades had already decided that Soviet research had to be genuinely Soviet, that it had to rest self-sufficiently on Soviet sources, that it had to avoid foreign (i.e. non-Soviet) inputs, and that it conform to the party line, Luria published

---

44 Luria: *Looking Back*, ms. 1977, p. 43, private archive; my emphasis.
45 Luria, 1935, pp. 239–240.

this text in the USA, wrote it in Russian, and dealt with a scholar whose work was anything but taken for granted by the majority of Soviet psychologists (also, notably, because it drew from foreign sources). It also turns out in hindsight that Vygotsky's portrait drawn by Luria could likewise be seen as a sketchy self-portrait, at least as far as the outlook of the research program was concerned.

A similar *use* of Vygotsky happened in 1958 in the German Democratic Republic. The impact of Soviet psychology on her little sister in the GDR was undoubtedly important at that time. It was probably stronger than the impact of American (or, broadly speaking, Western) psychology on her academic sister in the Federal Republic of Germany. But many people doing psychology in the GDR either on the student level or in teaching positions did not closely follow Soviet output *in Russian*. Buying academic Soviet-Russian books and journals wasn't easy either.

Two years after Vygotsky's first posthumous book had been published in Moscow (it containing a variety of scholarly contributions[46]), the East German *Zeitschrift für Psychologie* carried the translation of the preface Luria and Leontiev had contributed to the Russian book. To put it simply: this amounted to obvious pushing of Vygotsky in the GDR psychology as the most significant and still highly relevant figure of Soviet psychology or even as the leading Marxist psychologist of the USSR. The presentation of (and introduction to) Vygotsky's works that *were not yet* available in German translation was structured like previous Lurian reminiscences of the dead friend and teacher: physiology and its psychological offspring on one edge of the academic field, idealist, *verstehende*, Diltheyan, humanistically oriented psychology (and its offspring) on the other edge of the field, and Vygotsky revising both approaches on the basis of Marx's historical and dialectical materialism, thus clearing the field for good for now and for future research.[47]

A footnote by the journal's (unnamed) editor stated:

> The publication of some of L. S. Vygotsky's already published writing constitutes a welcome enrichment of the psychological literature worldwide. A. N. Leontiev's and A. R. Luria's introductory article (published here in translation) introduced the reader to Vygotsky's psychological conception; it requires special attention, since it critically assesses Vygotsky's scientific thinking from a historical perspective and thus reveals the development of psychology in the USSR to the present day.[48]

The persons who did *not* act as censors in Moscow and/or in Berlin were convinced that *this* piece of scientific prose was not either ideologically or politically detrimental. It could have been otherwise some years later; it could also have been the same. But another case shows that political and ideological factors were not

---

46 Vygotsky, 1956.
47 See Leontiev & Luria, 1958.
48 Anon, 1958, p. 165.

always predictable, and from time to time quite aleatory. Child psychology was an important field of research both in Eastern and Western Europe. Two French speaking psychologists, Henri Wallon and Jean Piaget, both doing research on the mental development of children, were read and studied outside France: Piaget in the USA (where a considerable number of translations of his works were published) and Wallon in the USSR. And both obtained some attention in the two German states: Piaget in the 'bourgeois' Federal Republic of Germany (FRG, or West Germany), because he was accepted by American scholars as a serious theoretician of children's mental development, and Wallon in the 'progressive' GDR, because he was a member of the French Communist Party and still an outstanding specialist of child psychology. In later years, Piaget was also well received in the GDR. And he was known to Soviet psychologists (especially to Vygotsky, Luria, Leontiev, and others) in the late 1920s and early '30s long before mainstream psychologists became aware of him in Germany and the USA.[49]

Thus, in retrospect, Luria's and Leontiev's efforts of promoting Vygotsky in the West might have played an instrumental role for them: first, as a means of advocating for their own research agenda within the Soviet Union and, second, as a major vehicle to overcome the domestic and dogmatic 'Pavlovians' and, thus, to defend the status of psychology as an independent and truly Soviet scientific discipline.

Luria's life-writing

In the preceding parts of the present contribution, priority has been given to the early years of Luria's career and to some still unsettled questions. In the remainder of this contribution, I focus on his autobiographical texts. However, I prefer the term 'life-writing' for the denotation of what has come to be seen by most readers as a true expression of Luria's authentic account of his scientific career (or intellectual life, as he also called the subject matter of his autobiographical contributions).

Close study of the sources indicates that Luria was not at all the solitary author who calmly set out to narrate his academic-scientific career. As it turns out, several persons have been materially involved in his life-writing, so that what we know today by way of the 'autobiographies' is due also to the marks left by amanuenses.[50]

It was the famous psychologist and one of the foundational historians of this discipline, Edwin Boring, who invited Luria, a stellar scholar having an acknowledged international reputation of a one of the founders of *neuropsychology* (the specialized field of research at the intersection of brain studies and psychology), to contribute a chapter to volume V of the series *History of Psychology in Autobiography* on January 20, 1964. Luria's response was fast. On February 1, he wrote among

49 See Métraux, 1990.
50 This is not the place to discuss the issue of auto-, hetero-, or simply biographical genres. Though dealing with early modern life-writing, Stewart's remarks on this issue are easily transferable to the present time; see Stewart, 2018, pp. 5–7.

other things that, feeling honored by the invitation, he would be glad to contribute to the project.

Up to this point, everything seemed to have been transparently clear. Some slightly embarrassing complications occurred nonetheless. For Luria had also suggested his friend Alexei Leontiev and his colleague Boris Teplov be asked to contribute; it would be good to have different research fields of Soviet psychology represented in the volume in the making, viz. developmental psychology on the one hand, and physiological psychology on the other, with Leontiev and Teplov as the figureheads of these two major branches of Soviet psychology, respectively.

Since Boring depended on the majority vote of a committee that would choose the psychologists to be present in the series, he could not approve of Luria's suggestion alone: the members of the committee hardly knew Leontiev, and Teplov not at all. Luria finally agreed, a bit reluctantly, to start working on his self-portrait in prose. He informed Boring on August 14 that it would be the historical reconstruction of his ideas and findings, to which he would add a biography of his friend Vygotsky.

A motif that appears many times in Luria's work and upon which he drew attention with devotion (which looks like having bordered on obsession) – Lev Vygotsky the genius, the teacher, the friend – thus was etched into his own account, turning the chapter into a double (biographical and autobiographical) narrative. Boring politely expressed annoyance because he didn't know whether such a blend of two lives would be suitable for the project under way. He therefore informed Luria that the piece could not be published under the given circumstances in volume V, and that it would be taken care of by Frederick Skinner who would hand it over to the editor of volume VI in due time – where this first piece of Lurian life-writing figured in 1974 in print and in English translation by Michael Cole (Luria, 1974).[51]

This chronologically first composed self-portrait was followed by another autobiographical text, published in the *International Social Science Journal* in 1973 in English and in French (Luria, 1973). The making of this second narrative has not been thoroughly examined yet. A seemingly insignificant but surely relevant detail of the second autobiographical text sheds light on the third, and ultimate, piece of Lurian intellectual life-writing. Luria considered his historical self-reflection as being part and parcel of his scientific output. As a matter of fact, he sent Luciano Mecacci a handwritten table of contents for a collection of articles in Italian translation. And that volume was thought to comprise, in addition to scientific contributions, the autobiographical sketch of 1973 (see Figure 6.1). The conclusion may be drawn now that Luria deemed his life-writing (due to its stubborn focus on *academic work*, on *theory building*, and on *making psychology and neuropsychology progress* the best one could do, on the *intellectual* aspect of his career) to count as well as *scholarly contribution*, or to put it the other way round, that this kind of life-writing was but another

---

51 Cf. Luria 1970. The original typed version with handwritten addenda by Luria may be consulted *sub* http://luria.ucsd.edu/HistoryFragments.pdf, accessed July 12, 2019.

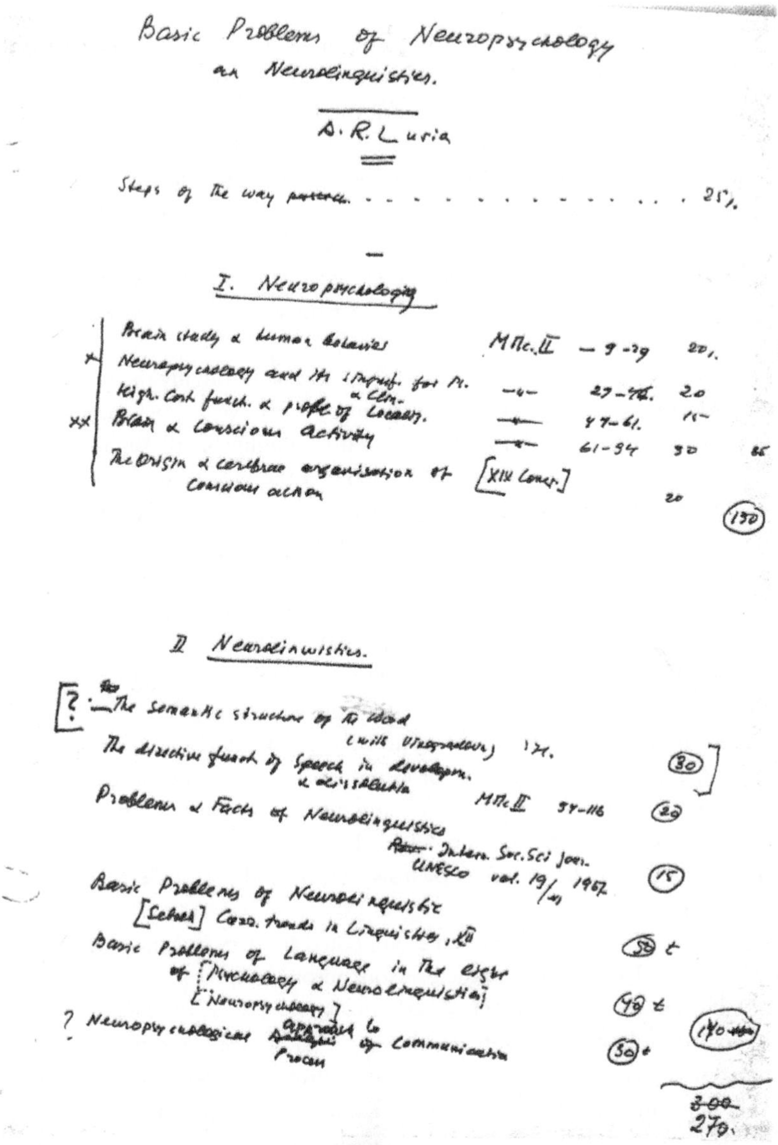
Basic Problems of Neuropsychology
an Neurolinguistics.

A. R. Luria

Steps of the way passed. . . . . 25 p.

I. Neuropsychology

Brain study & human behavior MПс. II — 9–29 20 p.
x Neuropsychology and its significance for Ps. & Clin. —"— 27–46. 20
High. Cort. funct. & probl. of Localiz. —"— 47–61. 15
xx Brain & Conscious activity —"— 61–94 30 85
The origin & cerebral organisation of conscious action [XIX Congr.] 20
(130)

II Neurolinguistics.

[?] The Semantic structure of the word (with Vinogradova) 17.
The directive funct. of Speech in developm. & dissolution (30)
Problems & Facts of Neurolinguistics MПс II 54–116 (20)
Intern. Soc. Sci Jour. UNESCO vol. 19/1 1967 (15)
Basic Problems of Neurolinguistic [Sebeok] Curr. trends in Linguistics, XII (50) t
Basic Problems of Language in the light of [Psychology & Neurolinguistics] [Neuropsychology] (40) t
? Neuropsychological Approach to Communication Process (50) t (170)
~~300~~
270.

FIGURE 6.1 The Table of Contents prepared by Alexander Luria for the collection of his writings in Italian translation, published as *Neuropsicologia e neurolinguistica*, edited by Eduardo Bisich and Luciano Mecacci, Rome: Editori Riunit, 1974.

Source: © Courtesy Luciano Mecacci, Florence.

aspect of his scientific achievement (and that this way of reading him was the right one for the Italian readership).

The third piece of Lurian life-writing consists of *The Making of Mind*. Or rather: it consists of a text published in 1979 in Cambridge, MA, but initially entitled in the *English* typed version as *Looking Back: The Life of a Soviet Psychologist in Retrospect*. In a letter dated March 2, 1976, Luria had written to Michael Cole: "I started to make notes for the Phillip Blake's Interview, – and it developed in a new book. It will be a Retrospect of my whole life in science, *half scientific, half lyric*."[52] This letter and the archival document *Looking Back* corroborate Cole's assertion according to which he and his wife Sheila did *not* translate, but rather *edit* the draft they received from Luria. And they edited it under the author's guidance and with the latter's repeated agreements (see also Appendix 1).

The structure of *Looking Back/ The Making of Mind* is roughly the same as that of the two previous self-portraits. But the primary incentive to start working on this piece of life-writing was a project submitted by Phillip R. Blake, a director and producer of scientific films. Luria had welcomed the project with pleasure, but it had to be officially approved also by the Soviet News Agency. The outline (sent by Blake) of what Luria called 'interview' (rather than 'film') in the letter mentioned above was too sketchy, however. Hence his request sent to Blake on December 10, 1975: "I should prefer to have [a] more detailed plan of the film so that I can work beforehand. Please do discuss it with Prof. Michael Cole."[53]

By comparison with the extent of the two other self-portraits, that of *The Making of Mind* evidently differs in some respects. It is incomparably more detailed, it is more lively, and there are vibrant sections. The overall structure remained unaltered, which is to say that, in spite of Luria's thoughts, recollections, impressions, assessments having been put down in writing, his other life – the non-intellectual parts or aspects of his life – remains silent. He seems to have had devised a stable narrative scheme for the accounts of his scientific and/or intellectual life for the public at large.

The fact that the narrative scheme embodied by *The Making of Mind* led to a more vivid and dense story than the previous autobiographical contributions is due to the editorial work performed by Sheila and Michael Cole on the draft of *Looking Back*. The latter, however, is appreciably longer and not so elegantly worked out – not surprisingly after all, since Luria, although probably more polyglot than any of the colleagues and friends of his generation, did not write in his native tongue. This entails that *The Making of Mind* is in effect *not* purely Lurian in character, though its origin is, notwithstanding, purely Lurian (see Figure 6.2).

The editors' work on *Looking Back* unfolded in all likelihood in parallel with Luria drafting the text. Author and editors stayed in close touch throughout the

---

52 Alexander Luria to Michael Cole, March 2, 1979; private archive; courtesy Michael Cole.
53 Alexander Luria to Phillip R. Blake, December 10, 1975; my emphasis; private archive; courtesy Michael Cole.

making of both texts. No wonder that Cole could suggest that, at one point, Luria address more than in passing the 'romantic science' aspect of his work (also see Appendix 1). The typed draft, with some handwritten corrections made (as the occurrences of Luria's handwriting testify), was completed before his death, whereas the edited version of *The Making of Mind* was still in the making in the USA. This is to say that the final outlook of *The Making of Mind* reveals itself to be by all means a piece of life-writing in that the biographical genres (autobiography vs. biography or, more to the point, heterobiography) were blended with one another.

Considering the Lurian self-portraits, some more or less urgent questions arise, which point to several lacunae in current Luria studies:

- The Russian near-equivalent of *The Making of Mind*, *Etapy proidennego puti*,[54] published in 1982, differs also from its English sibling. Or, to put it the other way round: both *The Making of Mind* and *Etapy proidennogo puti* resemble each other much more than they resemble Luria's original draft written in English. Now, the last part of *The Making of Mind* was not yet completely edited when Luria died. Since no evidence has shown up that he began rewriting the version edited by Sheila and Michael Cole in Russian, one wonders who provided the Russian version for the publication in Moscow. But let's make the counterfactual hypothesis that Luria had somehow produced a handwritten or typed translation of the parts already edited for *The Making of Mind* before he died; one would still have to ask: *Who* completed and delivered the Russian version for the remaining, i.e. posthumous, parts for publication?

- Given the fact that the Italian translation of Luria's self-portrait consists of, as one could say, a synopsis of both *The Making of Mind* and *Etapy*, and that the contribution to volume VI of the *History of Psychology in Autobiography* was available to the English speaking public in common with *The Making of Mind*, historians of science (in particular historian of psychology) would have to study the varying social representations of Luria in various countries, since this aspect does also belong to the study of the history of Soviet psychology.

- As mentioned by Cole (see Appendix 1), Luria consented to add more than just some lines on the 'romantic science' aspect of his work. A large part of chapter 10 of *The Making of Mind* is thus devoted to the two case histories that have had a lasting impression upon the general public much more than any other contribution by Luria – to such an extent, one should add, that Peter Brook and Marie-Hélène Estienne audaciously adapted the story of Shera-shevsky, the man with the miraculously unlimited memory, for the stage.[55] In that chapter of *The Making of Mind*, one reads: "At the beginning of this

---

54 See Luria, 1982.
55 See Brook & Estienne, 2013. Note that the hero's name is spelled 'Sherashevsky' in *The Making of Mind*, whereas it is usually written out as 'Shereshevsky.'

century, the German scholar Max Verworn suggested that scientists can be divided into two groups according to their basic orientation towards science: classical and romantic."[56] The reference to Verworn has been reiterated innumerable times by other authors who quoted or mentioned the 'romantic science' aspect of Luria's work. Yet no one seems to have verified whether Luria may have forgotten to check the source to which he resorted when introducing the distinction between 'classical' and 'romantic scientists.' Indeed, the German scholar who elaborated on this typological difference was not (with a very high degree of probability) Verworn, but Wilhelm Ostwald.[57] As the preceding quote shows, Luria's interpretation of what he believed to derive from Verworn went beyond the idea set forth by Ostwald. The distinction spelled out in *The Making of Mind* was more often then not taken to denote a style or a pattern of science writing (the narrative form) rather than a person's disposition of, or an attitude towards, doing research. But if Luria had the narrative approach in mind, it would be misleading to focus, as he did in that book, merely on the two case histories (the mnemonist Shereshevsky, on the one hand, and Zassetsky, the man with the shattered world, on the other hand), instead of also considering the role of clinical single-case reports for Luria's conception of concrete psychology as embodied in the neuropsychological monograph on memory,[58] or even in the vignettes in *The Nature of Human Conflicts*.[59] To put it differently: Luria's *concrete* psychology has certainly been often appreciated, but hardly ever reconstructed in detail. So, how did he and his collaborators collect data, how and where were these data stored, how were they assessed, by which means did general psychological or neuropsychological propositions emerge from the data?

These questions indicate a range of interesting avenues for future researchers, which means the reader of this text will not have the right answers to them, not yet. At the same time, they are reminding us about the ever 'hidden,' latent, unofficial story of private life and personal story of virtually any subject in the history of the Soviet Union. And this is definitely true of Soviet history's public figures, especially of Alexander Luria, the brilliant scholar and international scientific broker.

Conclusion

It seems that research explicitly focusing upon the history of psychology – in any country, continent, of any school or approach – gets underway for good only after

56 Luria, 1979, p. 174.
57 See Ostwald, 1909, pp. 370–388. The typology of scientists was first outlined by Ostwald in an article authored for *Deutsche Revue*, see Ostwald, 1907; on Ostwald's typology see Simmer, 1978.
58 See Luria, 1976, pp. 236–250 (patient Rakch.) or pp. 213–226 (patient Snyatk.); note that this patient was studied by T. O. Faller and L. I. Moskovichute under Luria's supervision.
59 See Luria, 1960 [1932] e.g. pp. 99–102 (case n° 1) and pp. 109–114 (case n° 4).

a temporal hiatus of one or two generations (the term 'generation' being used here in an unspecific way). By 'history of psychology' I mean to denote full-fledged studies of the political, socio-economic, institutional, and administrative conditions of psychological research and teaching practices beyond the realm of theories, ideas, methods, instruments, and rhetorics. Thus, Ulfried Geuter's history of psychology in the Third Reich (i.e. Germany in the brief, but devastating epoch of the national-socialist regime) was published in 1988.[60] Two critical and highly enlightening monographs on the cognitive revolution of psychology on the North American Continent were completed in the early twenty-first century, i.e. roughly four decades after the onset of the cognitive turn (by which the then ruling trend of behaviorism was supplanted).[61] And some twenty years had to elapse after the end of the Soviet Union before a revisionist approach to Vygotsky's life and work became attainable.[62]

I venture just one hypothesis (perhaps a too ill-founded hypothesis) that might explain historiography's punctuated awakening for encompassing inquiries into the past of psychology: most of everyday psychological research presupposes the allocation of funds that constitute the object of sometimes severe competition between actors, public or private institutions, and academic governances. The political dimensions of such competition are either kept strictly invisible to the outsiders or are rhetorically hidden. But archives are like talking machines that, sooner or later, permit historians to listen to what the files and folders of paper saved there have to say.

The case of Alexander Luria illustrates the transition from the public *persona* (defined as an actor in the academic milieu, as an author of publications, as a member of a scientific academy, etc.) to (a) the private Alexander Romanovich and (b) to the inofficial figure who defended his status and his reputation against competing figures who also acted in more or less hidden ways. The gap between these two 'Lurias,' if I may say so, is likely to be progressively bridged by further discoveries of archival sources. To put it differently: the one, the public Luria is present in his printed works; the other, the still latent Luria, in contradistinction, needs to be awakened from the yet unread notebooks, diaries, letters, drafts, experimental data, reading notes, administrative, and other records, etc. – much more extensively than I have done in the present contribution.

Take the example of Soviet politics at the background of Luria's life. When drafting the *Epilogue* to Luria's *The Making of Mind*, Michael Cole approached Vladimir Zinchenko. When reading the draft, the latter crossed out the lines that recalled in a passing, historically harmless remark the epoch of Stalin (see Figure 6.2). 'No politics, no mention of Stalin': this was the rule also for authors who,

---

60 See Geuter, 1988, 1992.
61 See Cohen-Cole, 2014; see also Crowther-Heyck, 2005, 2006a, 2006b.
62 See Yasnitsky & Van der Veer, 2016.

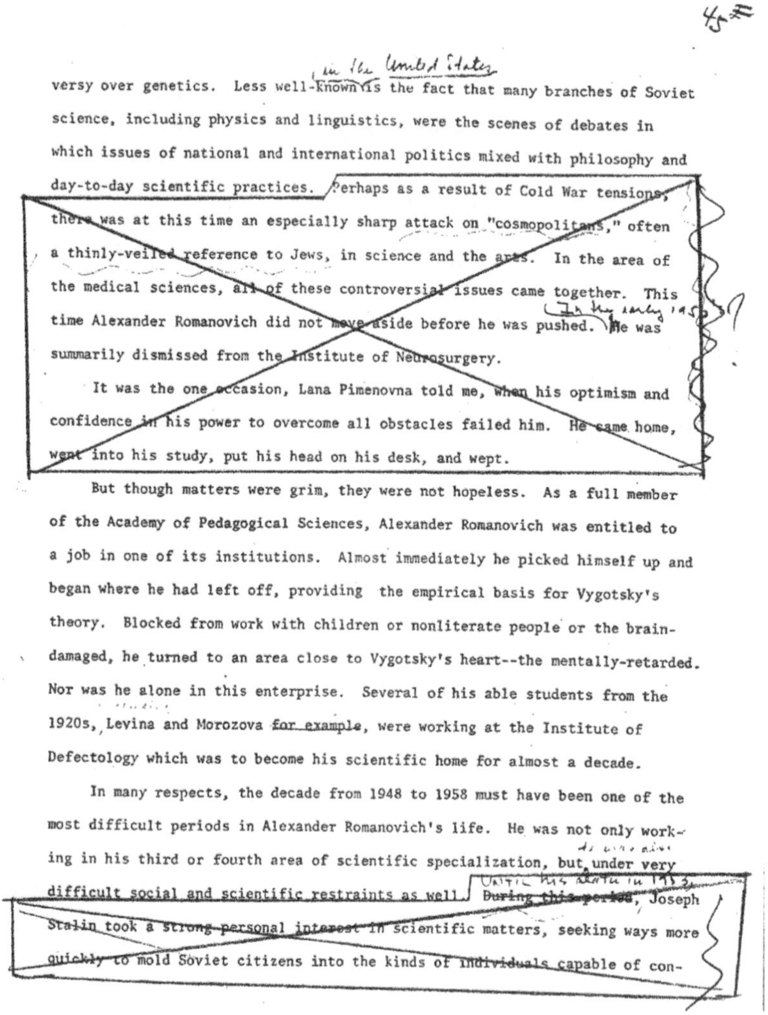

, in the United States

versy over genetics. Less well-known is the fact that many branches of Soviet

science, including physics and linguistics, were the scenes of debates in

which issues of national and international politics mixed with philosophy and

day-to-day scientific practices. Perhaps as a result of Cold War tensions,

there was at this time an especially sharp attack on "cosmopolitans," often

a thinly-veiled reference to Jews, in science and the arts. In the area of

the medical sciences, all of these controversial issues came together. This

In the early 1950s,

time Alexander Romanovich did not move aside before he was pushed. He was

summarily dismissed from the Institute of Neurosurgery.

It was the one occasion, Lana Pimenovna told me, when his optimism and

confidence in his power to overcome all obstacles failed him. He came home,

went into his study, put his head on his desk, and wept.

But though matters were grim, they were not hopeless. As a full member

of the Academy of Pedagogical Sciences, Alexander Romanovich was entitled to

a job in one of its institutions. Almost immediately he picked himself up and

began where he had left off, providing the empirical basis for Vygotsky's

theory. Blocked from work with children or nonliterate people or the brain-

damaged, he turned to an area close to Vygotsky's heart--the mentally-retarded.

Nor was he alone in this enterprise. Several of his able students from the

1920s, Levina and Morozova for example, were working at the Institute of

Defectology which was to become his scientific home for almost a decade.

In many respects, the decade from 1948 to 1958 must have been one of the

most difficult periods in Alexander Romanovich's life. He was not only work-

ing in his third or fourth area of scientific specialization, but under very

difficult social and scientific restraints as well. Until his death in 1953, Joseph

Stalin took a strong personal interest in scientific matters, seeking ways more

quickly to mold Soviet citizens into the kinds of individuals capable of con-

FIGURE 6.2   A page of Michael Cole's draft of the epilogue to Luria's *The Making of Mind* with traces of Vladimir Zinchenko's critical reading.

Source: © Courtesy Michal Cole, San Diego.

in post-Stalin times, dealt with Luria's life and work. Hence, it was politically correct to silence politics.

Or, to put it in slightly other words, time has come to get rid of Cold War mythology which urged one to perceive Soviet psychologists either as innocent victims of a dictatorial regime or as brutally uncompromising villains prone to eliminate, if not physically, at least symbolically their enemies from research and teaching in the science of psychology. This is not to say that Soviet life was easy, or that costs for surviving in academia and also in everyday life were low. The point is simply that it's worthwhile to first enter, as far as possible, the real life of Soviet psychologists and to grasp the events that shaped their career, their successes, and their failures.

This is all the more needed since Luria's work has undergone a posthumous trivialization. Luria is, for a lot of people, just the Luria of the *Luria-Nebraska Neuropsychological Battery* (*LNNB*); for other people, he is nothing but a conventional, regular neuro-psychologist who made some discoveries that are outdated now; and for again other people, he is the narrator of extraordinary neuro-and-brain-stories that also look like those told by Oliver Sacks. The conjunction of collecting experimental findings, of gathering clinical data, and of concreteness in the description of individual subjects and groups – a conjunction which is paradigmatic for Luria's historical materialism in psychology and neuropsychology – has more and more faded away. Thus, if the notions both of historical materialism and Marxism are well understood according (a) to the expectations Luria had in his attempt to build a new psychology in the Soviet Union and (b) to the potential these notions had for his building theories during the Stalin and post-Stalin era, there is a good deal of hope that further Luria studies, straightforward or revisionist in the best sense of the word, will yield inspiring results.

★ ★ ★ ★ ★

APPENDICES

Both interviews below were conducted in June and July 2019 while the present contribution was in the making. The appendices are meant to complement the preceding account by eyewitness testimonies.

Appendix 1

Q: Of the various autobiographical texts Luria contributed in the later part of his academic life, in which of these three version have you been involved (either as translator, or as critical reader, or in some other function)? And with regard to *The Making of Mind*, did you suggest to Luria to author this text?

MICHAEL COLE: *The Making of Mind* arose because two documentary film makers wanted to do a biographical documentary about Aleksandr Romanovich . . .

Q: . . . do you remember their names?

M.C.: . . . no . . . and I advised him to write down his own account, so that he could provide his framework and have some control over the process. They were interested in more than a recounting of his scientific work. They were starting to interview him and I told him then he better write it down before they make it up by themselves. . . . No, I really do not recall who the film makers were – they were from the United States and academically connected, as I recall now.

Q: In which language did all this happen?

M.C.: Alexander Romanovich almost always spoke with me in Russian, except when English speakers were around. That and daily work in his and two other Moscow laboratories with non-English speakers resulted in my spoken Russian being stronger than my reading and way stronger than my writing (I spell poorly in English, never mind Russian!). As to the editing process, I saw Luria on a visit to Moscow and was able to confirm our editing through about three or four chapters before he died. The remaining chapters we carried out in the same style, he had had few corrections to suggest prior to his death. However, those changes were rejections of the introduction of personal information about his life. For example, he did not want to include the fact that he was Jewish in his brief treatment of his early life.

Q: So let me summarize now what's there in the making of *The Making of Mind*. Your first encounter with Alexander Romanovich took place in Moscow in 1962. In 1964, he wrote the autobiographical essay for Edwin Boring. One may recall that the subtitle of this account already contains the wording of the title of the later Russian autobiography – I mean here the posthumously published Russian version of *The Making of Mind*. In 1973, another autobiographical sketch was published in the UNESCO journal. In 1974, the essay authored in 1964 finally appeared in your English translation in volume VI of *History of Psychology in Autobiography*, edited by Gardner Lindzey, Boring having died in the meantime. *The Making of Mind* was published in 1979, and five years after Alexander Romanovich's death, the Russian near-equivalent was finally available in the Soviet Union and Warsaw Pact states. All this is pretty complex, and it seems that Luria's life-writing activities were auto-biographical and at least in part also hetero-biographical. We are miles away from the lonely author recalling without external input what seems to have been important to him or her and writing all that down in near secrecy. How do you now perceive the past events relating to *The Making of Mind*?

M.C.: I was just an American candidate with my own lady love on our travels to exotic Russia when all this began in the fall of 1962. I have in my ancient folders what I believe to be an original final draft from Alexander Romanovich of the complete manuscript that Sheila and I then began to edit. But before that, I was asked by Edwin Boring to translate the text Luria had sent him for the *History of Psychology in Autobiography*. I do not know why it took so long to appear in print.

Q: And later on the making of *The Making of Mind* was initiated. As I understand it, the project began with English speaking film makers preparing a documentary, roughly in 1973. Luria agreed to be filmed. And then, Mike Cole, who was visiting Moscow at that time, intervened . . .

M.C.: . . . yes. While being briefly interviewed by the film makers, Alexander Romanovich talked to Sheila, my wife, and about the film project. I suggested that he take control of the script, which is to say that he start thinking of the film to be shot in terms of presenting his life history as he wished. And since the film makers are native English speakers, he wrote the entire text in English. The film was never made. I do not know what put an end to it, but I suspect that Alexander Romanovich's refusal to delve into his life experiences made the project unappealing. But the autobiography went beyond anything he had written before and Harvard Press was happy to publish it. The manuscript was written entirely in Alexander Romanovich's English so we began to edit it and send the results to him. It was Sheila's role to edit Luria's English. It was my job, as it had been in previous publications, to suggest edits where more, or less, material seemed needed for an American audience. We got the whole manuscript at the start. It was written in English. I have no idea who translated it into Russian, it may have been Alexander Romanovich.

Q: The chapters edited step by step by the Coles raised questions about some details of Luria's life and work, but he kept his line and wanted to come up with an intellectual biography without the romantic science aspect?

M.C.: No, I had already edited publications of his romantic science books, the second of which I had to fight for and cut. Luria had been preoccupied with neuropsychology for several decades and the manuscript was top heavy repeating things he had written elsewhere for a more specialized audience. He was perfectly happy with that. I noticed that the contribution for the *History of Psychology in Autobiography* volume had ended with neuroscience. That earlier version of his autobiography had been written before those books came out. So I was very pleased that he had added a "Romantic Science" chapter, which is very interesting: an elderly scholar putting together his early clinical aspirations à la Freud but in a framework marked by the cultural-historical cum Vygotskian approach as a fundamentally important methodology. When Alexander Romanovich died, we concluded *The Making of Mind* in the same spirit that had already been established previously. My own work has taken up the thread of romantic science, but in non-clinical, developmental settings and over long periods of time.

Q: And there's also an epilogue. . . . As far as I know, Vladimir Zinchenko was somehow involved in that, but I haven't seen anything of that part of the story mentioned in print.

M.C.: If you examine the book you will see that it is made up of three parts. An introduction by me, the text of the autobiography, and the epilogue. I wrote the introduction exactly as I imagined he would want it, by providing the scientific context that his work had grown up and developed in. Nothing personal. In the Epilogue, which was my attempt to provide social context that he would never have written about himself, making it as clear as I could that this was my personal interpretation filtered through my own, naïve encounter with Luria and the USSR.

The Soviet copyright agency (VAAP) accepted the core manuscript and the introduction, but at first rejected the book because of remarks made about the difficult and dangerous circumstances of his work from the 1930s through the 1950s. They enlisted Volodya Zinchenko, to intervene. I had become friendly with a number of members of the Luria-Leontiev group in 1962, but got to know Volodya mostly over the course of the next twenty-five years. He and Vasiliy Davydov were a close pair, both of whom influenced my later work. Volodya was the most senior of his generation and should have been the director the Institute of Psychology of the Rossiiskaya akademya nauk (RAN), but the politics of the time ran against the Vygotskians and the job was handed to Boris Lomov and then Andrei Brushlinsky. Volodya and I remained intellectual and personal friends until his untimely death (Davydov, too, died as the result of medical incompetence). At the time the Luria manuscript was being negotiated through VAAP, Volodya was their 'go between' in psychology.

Q: Was it Luria's wish that he do the job of accompanying you in the making of the epilogue, or was he Luria's assistant, or possibly one of his many assistants, and thus possibly his 'monitor' reporting about the manuscript?

M.C.: Either Luria, who had been the 'go between' for VAAP himself previously, suggested him, or Volodya was chosen because he was known as senior academic and a party member. But I do not know any detail. Volodya was exceedingly well educated. I myself had worked earlier with a lady at VAAP about translating Luria's books.

Appendix 2

Q: You were called "Italy's effective 'afferent channel' in matters of the history and content of Soviet psychology" in a review of 1978 written by Josef Brožek; in addition, you were said to have worked in the Moscow psychophysiological laboratory of Vladimir Dmitrievich Nebylitsyn (see Figure 6.3). In this review, there is no mention of your encounters with Aleksander Romanovich Luria. How did you meet him? And which projects did you pursue with, or on, him in the subsequent years?

FIGURE 6.3   Luciano Mecacci (left) and Vladimir Nebylitsyn at the entrance of the Moscow psychophysiological laboratory.

Source: © Courtesy Luciano Mecacci, Florence.

LUCIANO MECACCI: In January 1972 (I was 25 years old) I went to work for a semester to the Laboratory of Psychophysiology of Individual Differences at the Institute of Psychology of Moscow. The Laboratory was directed by Nebylitsyn, a student of Boris Teplov (see Figure 6.3). The so-called Teplov-Nebylitsyn school was developing the Pavlovian typology, both by extending it to human beings and by applying new electrophysiological techniques (I did research with Vladimir Rusalov, one of Nebylitsyn's students, and later well-known for his studies on temperament; our research – on attention and EEG correlates – was published in *Voprosy psikhologii* in 1973). At the same time I began to be interested in the history of Soviet psychology. What we knew about it in Italy appeared to be quite different from what I was discovering during my stay in Moscow. For this reason I asked for permission to visit other institutions, and to meet the most important people in psychology and neuro-physiology. One evening (around mid-January) I received a phone call (I was staying at the hotel of the Academy of Sciences) from Alexander Luria who had been informed of my intention to meet him as well. He lived on ulitsa Frunze, close to the Lenin (today National) Library, but invited me to the place where he was staying for a period of rest. This was in the former datcha that belonged to Pavel Tretyakov, the founder of the famous Tretyakov Gallery in Moscow. This was the beginning of a close relationship; it was crucial for me on both the personal and the professional level. I was many times invited at his apartment for dinner, I also was friendly with his wife Lana and daughter Elena – that is, in the first half of 1972 as well as at the end of 1975. The Italian translation of Luria's book on the mnemonist, with my preface, published in the summer of 1972, was the first of a long series of works devoted to the spreading of Soviet psychology in Italy, and I was strongly encouraged to pursue this line of action by Luria himself.

Q: Alexander Romanovich was a member of the Communist Party, whatever his intimate political and ideology-bound convictions may have been. If my information is correct, the Italian C.P. was promoting Soviet psychology (and other contributions to the social sciences) in Italy. Would you mind elaborating on this topic?

L.M.: This is an important chapter in Italian-Soviet relationship relating to the field of culture and science from the late 1960s to roughly 1980. Remember this: at that time, the main channel to Western countries of works and authors diverging from the official political and ideological lines of the Soviet Union was Italy. The first edition of Pasternak's *Doctor Zhivago* and Evgenya Ginzburg's *Journey into the Whirlwind* appeared in Italy both in Italian and Russian; the first Western translation of Bakhtin's book on Dostoyevsky was Italian, and the same happened to the philosopher Ilyenkov's works. A key figure of mediation was Giuseppe Garritano (1924–2013), a member of the Italian Resistance, a historian and journalist. For many years, he was the Moscow correspondent of the newspaper of the Italian Communist Party, *l'Unità*. He was fluent in Russian and translated many Russian works. He personally knew Pasternak, Ehrenburg, Bakhtin, and others, and was a close friend of Ilyenkov (I was introduced to Ilyenkov by Garritano). His name appears in the so-called "Pasternak affair" and "Ilyenkov affair" that had to do with the complex problem of the Western publication of their works. Garritano was also the director of Editori Riuniti, the publishing company of the I.C.P., and I was doing many translations or much editorial work in the field of Soviet psychology (I should add that I was a Party member from 1977 to 1980). These publications of Editori Riuniti were a component of the new programmatic orientation defended out by the Party secretary, Enrico Berlinguer, who aimed at distancing the I.C.P. from Soviet politics.

Q: Luria established lots of contacts with so called Western scholars until the attack of the USSR in 1941 by the German Wehrmacht and again after the end of World War II. The list of his colleagues and friends in Western countries is impressive. It seems to me that his work as well as his research was constantly reflecting what happened in academia outside his country, and it also impinged upon research in the West. Please, elaborate on the "international" or "blended", Soviet as well as non-Soviet work of Alexander Luria.

L.M.: Luria's scientific work after World War II was increasingly focusing on neuropsychological issues. On the one hand, this allowed him an international audience and to assure frequent contacts with Western colleagues. It created a kind of neutral territory where one could work without ideological and political implications. And on the other hand, he distanced himself from the other exponents of the traditional historical-cultural approach, although they continued to constitute a coherent group on a formal plane (editorial boards, congresses, handbooks, and so on). We must not forget that the new Institute of Psychology of the powerful Academy of Sciences of the USSR, which was founded in 1973, its first director being Boris Lomov (Josef Brožek and I wrote on this in the *American Psychologist* in 1974), had a trend completely opposite to that theory, but this controversy within Soviet psychology did not affect the activity of Luria's neuropsychological group.

★ ★ ★ ★ ★

Acknowledgement

Wholehearted thanks for help, information, suggestions, and documents to Michael Cole (San Diego, CA), Matthias Horstmann (Basel), Carlos Kölbl (Bayreuth), Andres Mayer (Paris/Berlin), Luciano Mecacci (Florence), Henning Schmidgen (Regensburg), Serena Vegetti (Rome), Anton Yasnitsky (Toronto/Kharkiv), and The Reference Staff, Harvard University Archives.

★ ★ ★ ★ ★

References

Anon. (1922a). n.t. [Note on the foundation of the Kazan association]. *Internationale Zeitschrift für Psychoanalyse, 8*, 380.

Anon. (1922b). n.t. [Note on the Kazan association with list of members]. *Internationale Zeitschrift für Psychoanalyse, 8*, 525.

Anon. (1958). *Zeitschrift für Psychologie, 162*(2/3), 165.

Artemov, V. A. (1925). Problema odarennosti i marksism [The problem of aptitude and Marxism]. In. K. N. Kornilov (Ed.), *Psikhologia i marksizm [Psychology and Marxism]* (pp. 93–112). Leningrad: Gosizdat [State Publishing Company].

Artemov, V. A. (1956). *Eksperimentalnaya fonetika [Experimental phonetics]*. Moscow: Izdatelstvo literatury i inostrannnykh yasikakh [Publishing Company for Literature and Foreigne Languages].

Bakhurst, D. (1995). Social being and the human essence: An unresolved issue in Soviet philosophy. A dialogue with Russian philosophers. *Studies in East European Thought, 47*(1/2), 3–60.

Banshchikov, V. M., Konovalov, N. V., et al. (Eds.). (1952). *Fiziologicheskoye uchenie akademika I. P. Pavlova v psikhiatrii i nervopatologii*. Moscow: Gosudarstvenoye Izdatelstvo meditsinskoy literatury MEDGIZ [State Publishing Company of Medical Literature MEDGIZ].

Brook, P., & Estienne, M.-H. (2013[1998]). *L'Homme qui, suivi de Je suis un phénomnène*. Arles: Actes Sud.

Cohen-Cole, J. (2014). *The open mind: Cold War politics and the sciences of human nature*. Chicago: University of Chicago Press.

Crowther-Heyck, H. (2005). *Herbert A. Simon: The bounds of reason in modern America*. Baltimore: Johns Hopkins University Press.

Crowther-Heyck, H. (2006a). Patrons of the revolution: Ideals and institutions in postwar behavioral science. *Isis, 97*(3), 420–446.

Crowther-Heyck, H. (2006b). Herbert Simon and the GSIA: Building an interdisciplinary community. *Journal of the History of the Behavioral Sciences, 42*(4), 311–334.

Ebbinghaus, H. (1913). *Memory: A contribution to experimental psychology*. New York: Teachers College, Columbia University.

Fraisse, P. (1977). Préface. In A. Massucco Costa (Ed.), *Psychologie soviétique* (pp. 3–6). Paris: Payot.

Geuter, U. (1988). *Die Professionalisierung der deutschen Psychologie im Nationalsozialismus*. Francfurt on the Main: Suhrkamp.

Geuter, U. (1992 [1988]). *The professionalization of psychology in Nazi Germany*. Cambridge, MA: Cambridge University Press.

Hogg, G. E. (1998). Bolshaia Sovetskaia Entsiklopedia. In A. Kent & C. M. Hall (Eds.), *Encyclopedia of library and information science* (Vol. 61, pp. 17–62, supplement 24). New York, Basel and Hong Kong: Marcel Dekker Inc.

Humphrey, G. (1920). The conditioned reflex and the Freudian wish. *Journal of Abnormal Psychology, 14*(6), 388–392.

Kornilov, K. N. (Ed.). (1925). *Psikhologia i marksism [Psychology and Marxisms]*. Leningrad and Moscow: Gosudarstvennoe izdatelstvo [State Publishing Company].

Krementsov, N. (1997). *Stalinist science*. Princeton: Princeton University Press.

Leontiev [Leontjew], A. N., & Luria, A. R. (1958). Die psychologischen Anschauungen L. S. Wygotskis. *Zeitschrift für Psychologie, 162*(2/3), 165–205.

Luria, A. R. (1926). Die moderne russische Physiologie und die Psychoanalyse. *Internationale Zeitschrift für Psychoanalyse, 12*(1), 40–53.

Luria, A. R. (1935). L. S. Vygotsky. *Character and Personality: An International Quarterly, 3*(3), 238–240.

Luria, A. R. (1960 [1932]). *The nature of human conflicts or emotion, conflict and will: An objective study of disorganisation and control of human behaviour.* New York: Grove Press.

Luria, A. R. (1968a). *Malenkaya knizhka o bolshoy pamyati (um mnemonista).* Moscow: Izdatelstvo Moskovskogo universiteta [Moscow University Press].

Luria, A. R. (1968b). *The mind of a mnemonist: A little book about vast memory.* New York: Basic Books.

Luria, A. R. (1973). The long road of a Soviet psychologist. *International Social Science Journal, 25*(1/2), 72–87.

Luria, A. R. (1974). A. R. Luria. In *A history of psychology in autobiography* (G. Lindzey, Ed., Vol. VI, pp. 253–292). Englewood Cliffs, NJ: Prentice-Hall.

Luria, A. R. (1976). *The neuropsychology of memory.* Washington, DC: V. H. Winston & Sons.

Luria, A. R. (1977 [1925]). Psychoanalysis as a system of monistic psychology. *Soviet Psychology, 16*(2), 7–45.

Luria, A. R. (1979). *The making of mind* (S. Cole, Ed.). Cambridge, MA and London: Cambridge University Press.

Luria, A. R. (1982). *Etapy prodiennogo puti. Nauchnaya avtobiografya* (E. D. Kohmskaya, Ed.). Moscow: Izdatelstvo Moskovskogo universiteta [Moscow University Press].

Marinelli, L., & Mayer, A. (2003). *Dreaming by the book.* New York: Other Press.

Massucco Costa, A. (1977[Italian publication 1963]). *Psychologie soviétique.* Paris: Payot.

Mayer, A. (2012). *Sites of the Unconscious.* Chicao: Chicago University Press.

Métraux, A. (1990). Psychologie. In J. Leenhardt & R. Picht (Eds.), *Au jardin des malentendus. Le commerce franco-allemand des idées* (pp. 326–329). Arles: Actes Sud.

Métraux, A. (1993). Zwei unveröffentlichte Briefe Freuds. *Psychoanalyse im Widerspruch, 4,* 7–13.

Métraux, A. (2002). Aleksandr Lurijas Briefe an Kurt Lewin. *Mitteilungen der Luria-Gesellschaft, 9*(2), 23–43.

Métraux, A. (2015). Lev Vygotsky as seen by someone who acted as a go-between between eastern and western Europe. *History of the Human Sciences, 28*(2), 154–172.

Ostwald, W. (1907). Zur Biologie des Forschers. *Deutsche Revue, 32,* 16–27, 43–55.

Ostwald, W. (1909). *Grosse Männer.* Leipzig: Akademische Verlagsgesellschaft.

Pollock, E. (2006). *Stalin and the Soviet science wars.* Princeton and Oxford: Princeton University Press.

Scheerer, E. (1984). The great Soviet encyclopedia as a source for the history of Soviet psychology. *Revista de Historia de la Psicología, 5,* 313–335.

Simmer, H. H. (1978). Ostwalds Lehre vom Romantiker und Klassiker. Eine Typologie des Wissenschaftlers. *Medizinhistorisches Journal, 13*(3/4), 277–296.

Stalin, I. (2006). Pismo Yu. A. Zhdanovy 6 oktyabrya 1949 goda [Letter to Yu. A. Zhdaov, October 6, 1949]. In *Sochineniya [Works]* (Vol. 18, pp. 535–536). Tver: Informatsionno-izdatelskiy tsentr "Soyuz". https://sovetia.at.ua/Stalin/Tom18.html#t243.

Stewart, A. (2018). *The Oxford history of life-writing, volume 2: Early modern.* Oxford: Oxford University Press.

Todes, D. P. (1995). Pavlov and the Bolsheviks. *History and Philosophy of the Life Sciences, 17*(3), 379–418.

Todes, D. P. (2014). *Ivan Pavlov: A Russian life in science.* Oxford: Oxford University Press.

Todes, D., & Krementsov, N. (2010). Dialectical materialism and Soviet science in the 1920s and 1930s. In W. Leatherbarrow & D. Offord (Eds.), *A history of Russian thought* (pp. 340–367). Cambridge: Cambridge University Press.

Velichkovsky, B. M., & Métraux, A. (1981). Mozg i soznanie [Brain and Consciousness: A review of Luciano Meccaci's *Cervello e storia*]. *Voprosy psikhologii [Problems of Psychology]*, *1*, 148.

Velichkovsky [Veličkovskij], B. M., & Métraux, A. (1986). Aleksandr Romanovič Lurija. In R. Harré & R. Lamb (Eds.), *The dictionary of physiological and clinical psychology* (pp. 143–146). Cambridge, MA: MIT Press.

Voloshinov, V. N. (1993 [1925/27]). *Freydizm [Freudianism]*. Moscow: Labirint.

Vygotsky, L. S. (1956). *Izbrannye psikhologicheskie issledovaniya: Myshlenie i rech: Problemy psikhologicheskogo razvitiya rebenka [Selected psychological works: Thought and speech: Problems of the mental development in children]*. Moscow: Izdatelstvo Akademii pedagogicheskikh nauk RSFSR [Press of the Academy of the Pedagogical Sciences of the Russian Soviet Federative Socialist Republic].

Yasnitsky, A. (2016). The archetype of Soviet psychology: From Stalinism of the 1930s to the 'Stalinist science' of our days. In A. Yasnitsky & R. Van der Veer (Eds.), *Revisionist revolution in Vygotsky studies* (pp. 3–26). London and New York: Routledge.

Yasnitsky, A., & Van der Veer, R. (Eds.). (2016). *Revisionist revolution in Vygotsky studies*. London and New York: Routledge.

Yasnitsky, A., Van der Veer, R., & Ferrari, M. (Eds.). (2014). *The Cambridge handbook of cultural-historical psychology*. New York: Cambridge University Press.

Zeigarnik, B. V. (1972). *Experimental abnormal psychology*. New York and London: Plenum Press.

Epilogue

SOVIET PSYCHOLOGY AND ITS UTOPIAS

Historical reflections for current science[1]

Luciano Nicolás García

Introduction

Pasts are not inert, as they provide us with perspectives to problematize both present and future. In the case of sciences, since the XIXth Century, they became unavoidable agents in the discussions of our present and possible futures. This is so, not because of a corporate zeal, but because scientists are related to governmental agendas, politics are inseparable from the roles assigned to scientists, by themselves or third-party agents. Therefore, if scientists would not be reduced to a mere instrument of the powers that be, they need to build up a conscious political thinking to navigate the public arenas of their conjunctures. From such a perspective, some historical outlines are here presented to guide a reflection on the present and future, a task enforced by the lack of promising perspectives in the current situation of world politics.

Typically, scientists are characterized, by themselves and by lay people, as experts or technicians, when they should be considered as public figures in the full sense. As Pinault (2003) highlighted, the reduction of scientists to "experts" blurs the fundamental role scientific thinking had in the imaginaries, politics, economy and culture of the last centuries, that is, the impact of science in the definition of institutions, power disputes and relevant problems, both in their local communities and distant times and geographies. As Livesey (2006) points out, two opposing perspectives usually add up to this mischaracterization: On the one hand, the members of scientific disciplines tend to consider the knowledge production as an individual endeavor, and thus exaggerate their capacities as individuals or their intellectual autonomy, following the "genius" model of

---

1 This chapter is a revised version of L. N. García, Utopía y pensamiento científico: reflexiones a partir del caso de la psicología soviética. *Revista Psicología Política,* 19, no 44, 2019, pp. 131–146.

desired identity. On the other hand, science, technology and society studies tend to minimize the capabilities and agendas of scientists as individuals or specific groups in order to integrate – sometimes subsume – them to broader cultural, political and economical processes. These opposing views hinder the possibilities of thinking scientific agency: or it is assumed without being thematized, or it is disregarded.

What is at stake here is how scientists, psychologists in particular, are thought, by themselves and others, of as intellectuals to intervene in the public sphere, yet not as mere specialized science communicators or guardians of professional interests, but as actors in the disputes for social imaginaries and future horizons. Actually, such a position would not be new; Charle (1990) has pointed out that the role of the contemporary intellectual, typically awarded to writer and essayist Émile Zola, has been directly preceded by Louis Pasteur and Claude Bernard, key figures in the legitimation of medicine as a socially relevant scientific practice, and to Hippolyte Taine and Ernest Renan, who used scientific thinking to address philosophy, history and literature. One could even trace the articulation of scientific and political thinking back to the physiocrats of XVIII century (Dostaler, 2008). Nevertheless, scientists' incursion in public politics has not been, and it is still not, direct, effortless and even necessarily positive, especially when it is about disputing a *status quo* to obtain a more inclusive and equitable future. Thus, a critical and historical examination of such interventions is required, which here will be exemplified with the experience of the Union of Soviet Socialist Republics (USSR), a rich conjuncture to examine the possible and actual ties between science and politics in a more recent history.

A regular feature in leftist politics is to produce visions of a future social organization to guide activism. XIXth and XXth century communism was exemplary in that gesture, with the peculiarity that tried to distinguish itself from other socialist trends by means of a scientific analysis of social and economic reality. Notably, Friedrich Engels (1878/1960) proposed a "scientific socialism", a political praxis based on systematic inquiry of social order, as opposed to "utopian socialism", which voluntarism would be inadequate to understand oppression mechanics and so give proper direction to activists. From this rationalist basis, communism, especially in the USSR, built a series of narratives oriented towards the unfolding of human potencies once it's freed from its economic and social yokes. Such narratives had a profound effect in the rhetoric and imaginary of political and military, authorities, civil activists, artists and scientists (Stites, 1988), and shaped a future horizon that could be justifiably considered as a utopia, not in the pejorative sense as a fantastic imagination detached from reality, but in its propositive sense, as a believable and desirable horizon of expectation that organizes and articulates the projects and practices of several social sectors towards a mediate future (Jameson, 2007). In the case of sciences, utopias are not just imaginaries of the upcoming times, but an inherent vector in the organization of research agendas and goal assessment. Recent research on the history of futures, predictions and projections, especially in social sciences (Andersson & Rindzevičiūtė, 2012, 2015), shows that those sciences aimed for mid and long-term effects on global politics and techno-economic management. That kind of study focuses on scientific knowledge geared towards the planification and control of future social scenarios, power effects, and the agency of institutions and actors in policy making. Military strategy, energy and natural resources exploitation, and macroeconomic management show the deep intertwining between science and political power in the XXth Century. Though these studies try to differentiate form the analysis of unrealistic utopias, and emphasize how certain actors defined future as "a field of action, intervention, management and protest" (Andersson & Rindzevičiūtė, 2015, p. 11), they also acknowledge that the distinction between scientific planification and utopia is not always unambiguous. What is of interest here is to highlight the links between utopias, as the unfolding of possible horizons, and future oriented science, in the specific sense of Andersson and Rindzevičiūtė.

The principles of scientific socialism promoted by Soviet psychologists can be synthesized as a socio-political utopia resulting from scientific and technical advances, as the social life can and must be rationally planned for the emergence of the "New Man". The analysis of this *idearum*, even though it is now deactivated, is useful for a reflection on how current scientific thinking can participate in public debates, avoiding both political ingenuity derived from futures dislocated from our conjunctures, and technical pragmatisms that hamper the understanding of the aims and consequences of science activities.

Psychology's utopias in the development of the USSR

One of the most notable cultural features of the Bolshevik experience was the broadening and transformation of the horizon of expectation together with an acceleration of political time (Koselleck, 2003; Pittaluga, 2015). A central part of that horizon directly involved sciences, as a driving force in the modernization of the backwards Tsarist economy and culture. Bolsheviks had their own version of positivism as rationalist understanding of the world and trust in the general progress of humanity (i.e. Joravsky, 1961; Todes & Krementsov, 2010), and, while that outlook quickly declined in the Western world after the First World War, in Russia it was revendicated as the safeguard of civilization form successive Barbarisms: Tsarism, Capitalism and Fascism.

Utopias, in a historical sense, have not been a mirage, an illusion incapable of grasping reality – as many communist theoreticians and propagandists claimed – but, as mentioned, provided programmatic meanings to present actions, that is, future visions defined the required means and the proper sequence of events. In this sense, Marx and Engel's communism was strongly utopian, yet with the Russian revolution that horizon gained a specific attribute, it became a feasible utopia, not just a potential future, but one that could be historically achievable with scientific knowledge and political direction. This kind of utopia had different moments and many actors in the history of communism, though this text will focus in certain authors and events in the USSR, in particular those related to psychology.

It is possible to define the constitution of that feasible utopia through Russian science fiction, a very fruitful source for the imaginary of the first decades of the XXth Century (Rispoli, 2016). In *Red Star* (1908/1984), a novel written by the physician and Bolshevik theoretician Alexander A. Bogdanov after the thwarted revolution of 1905, the protagonist Leonid, a mathematician and professional activist, was chosen by aliens to travel to Mars and became familiar with an already settled communist society. Bogdanov then shows the visions and promises, as well as the problems, of scientific socialism in a technically and culturally advanced society, eager to establish its social system in the Earth, to the benefit of both Martians and earthlings – at least those wishing to adhere to that process. After the Bolshevik Revolution, the writer Aleksey Tolstoy published *Aelita* (1923/1985) where he inverted the scenario: Bolsheviks are the ones who attempt to establish communism in a Martian society ruled by engineers, technically sophisticated but deeply classist and conservative. Russian science, freed form capitalist instrumentation, develops the machines for space travel with which to bring the revolution to a "universal" proletariat.

After the triumph of the Red Army in the Civil War, the *ethos* of scientific rationality offered a political and technical certainty almost omnipresent in the writings and discourses of revolutionary leaders, regularly associated with the coming of the "New Man"; Trotsky can be cited for the sake of an example:

> The problem of how to educate and regulate, how to improve and "finish" the physical and spiritual nature of man, is a colossal one, serious work on which is conceivable only under conditions of socialism. We may be able to drive a railway across the whole Sahara, build the Eiffel Tower, and talk with New York by radio, but can we really not improve man? Yes; we will be able to! To issue a new "improved edition" of man – that is the further task of communism. But for this it is necessary as a start to know man from all sides, to know his anatomy, his physiology, and that part of his physiology which is called psychology. (. . .) Only with socialism does real progress begin. Man will look for the first time at himself as if at raw material, or at best, as at a half-finished product, and say: "I've finally got to you, my dear homo sapiens; now I can get to work on you, friend!"
>
> *(Trotsky, 1924/1973, p. 140)*

Such horizon was materialized by a general restructuring of education and scientific inquiry. USSR organized a system of scientific production strongly centralized and fully financed by the state with the pretention of a complete planification of research. Bolsheviks assumed that planned science would avoid what they saw as profit driven or anarchic research of capitalist countries, which was superfluous for the working class. A large part of the scientific community did not support the revolution, yet Lenin, as well as his People's Commissar for Education, Anatoly Lunacharsky, had the objective of keeping and strengthening the Academy of Sciences, an institution created during Tsarism, so as to preserve researchers, as they were a hardly replaceable human resource. Universities, however, were tightly intervened in order that future generations of researchers would stick to Marxism-Leninism. During the 1920s and 1930s the USSR gave science and technology as much importance as the most developed Western countries (David-Fox, 1997). Nikolai Bukharin, the former member of the politburo and editor of the official newspaper *Pravda*, attended the Second International Congress of History of Science, held in London in 1931, where he stated: "It is not only a new economic system that has been born. A new culture has been born. A new science has been born" (cited from Graham, 1992, p. 70). One of the most well-known cases of direct political support to a non-communist scientific was Ivan P. Pavlov, whose physiological research captivated key party members such as Trotsky, Bukharin and Vyacheslav M. Molotov – in fact, he saw his research as a tool for a eugenic program, an instrument for the improvement of Russian society (Todes, 2014, pp. 614–616). Nevertheless, as it is well known, the cost of that political interest and the reorganization of scholarship was a profound bureaucratization and the loss of disciplinary autonomy.

Unsurprisingly, Soviet psychology followed that process; Lev S. Vygotsky was a result of both that scientific organization and rationalist *ethos*. As Yasnitsky (2018, 2019) has pointed out, Vygotsky openly embraced Trotsky's project of the "finishing" of man through science. During his youth, Vygotsky was committed to the Jewish cause in the Russian Empire, and when he adopted Marxism after the 1917 Revolution, he retained some of his previous emancipatory and utopian views, yet changed the religious approach for a scientific, rational one. For him, Marxism was a key for understanding man as it provided the epistemic frame, the rational mediation between reality and political aims. Vygotsky perceived himself as a maker of the revolution from his discipline, in a historical and institutional position where he could study not only actual people in his current context, but also contribute specifically to the development of the future "New Man". Within the framework of pedology, by then the attempt to create an integral science of childhood, he wrote in *Varnitso*, the journal of the All-Union Association of Workers in Science and Technics for the Furthering of the Socialist Edification in the USSR:

> *New generations and new forms of their education represent the main route which history will follow whilst creating the new type of man.* In this sense, the role of social and polytechnical education is extraordinarily important. As it happens, the basic ideas which underpin polytechnical education, consist of an attempt to overcome the division between physical and intellectual work and to reunite thinking and work which have been torn asunder during the process of capitalist development.
>
> *(Vygotsky, 1930/1994, p. 181, Vygotsky's emphasis)*

This statement is important, as it was made by an author who was a key organizer of three simultaneous research teams, in Moscow, Leningrad and Kharkiv (Yasnitsky & Ferrari, 2008). Vygotsky and his colleagues made psychological science well aware that they lived in a moment of deep transformations in education and health institutions, which were allowed to produce knowledge in an unprecedented setting, with new and very different aims than any other place. Vygotsky's political and academic position, as well as his contact with important figures such as Lunacharsky and Nadezhda K. Krupskaya, gave him the opportunity to transfer that research, with few mediations, into the ongoing changes of state policy. The first phase of the Russian revolution was accompanied by a first utopia, the possibility to develop human sciences that would push the powers of human beings to their self-improvement. As such, the development of a socialist society and science were one and the same process. In a more terrestrial and concrete direction than Russian science fiction imagination, Vygotsky and his fellow Soviet psychologists were part of a series of academic institutions in conditions to push forward, both by the politburo's exigency and their personal conviction, a politically oriented research where psychological sciences would not have a marginal place.

After World War II, the arms race put science in the center of political agendas, and after Stalin's death, a second feasible utopia was formed upon cybernetics, which became a general framework, almost a metadiscipline. Sketched in Russia by physiologists like Pyotr K. Anokhin and Nikolai A. Bernstein during the 1930s, cybernetics developed in the USA during the '40s, tied to some US military programs, and disseminated quickly in the following decade as a promising tool for understanding and controlling objects, artifacts and living beings. In the USSR it was criticized during Stalinism for being the prototypical bourgeois knowledge: it was derived from military management in order to subdue the population with inhuman control. Nevertheless, as soon as the Khrushchev's Thaw started cybernetics were swiftly appropriated by Soviet scholars as the new promise for technical-political advancement (Rispoli, 2015). Form astrophysics to economy, including biology and psychology, cybernetics provided a new lexicon to formalize and quantify any knowledge, and aimed as a scientific tool for any kind of phenomenon. Though some partisan philosophers questioned its compatibility with Dialectical Materialism, to politicians the pledge was irresistible: practical results in engineering, astronomy, defense and communication systems, and most of all in economy, where cybernetics seemed to offer a promising technology to sustain and extend economic planification while diminishing the bureaucratic burdens entailed with constant supervision and control of production and commerce (Gerovitch, 2002).

With support from the *politburo*, the Soviet Academy of Sciences formed a scientific council for cybernetics in 1959; two years later the Communist Party of the Soviet Union itself (CPSU) proposed cybernetics as one of the main tools for building a communist society, as it was considered a key knowledge in the military, space and sports competition with the West, and scientific achievements such as the

Sputnik satellite launch and the civil use of atomic power became part of the official propaganda. The Czech mathematician Ernst Kolman, once very close with Stalinism – and nevertheless arrested for several years – became an ardent and authorized promoter of cybernetics, and broadened its scope to neurophysiology and psychology. He suggested that the new possibilities of formalization and quantification would offer a renewed conception of memory and cognition through, for example, computing devices. For him, cybernetics could be an extension of the psyche, as tools and machines were extensions of the body (Kolman, 1956). The 1962 All-Union Conference on Philosophical Problems of the Physiology of Higher Nervous Activity and Psychology promoted this confluence with cybernetics, although many psychologists were wary of this trend, given the previous attempt of Stalinist Pavlovism for subsuming psychology to physiology (Graham, 1987, pp. 198–199). Nevertheless, the 1963 All-Union Congress of Psychology included a new session devoted to cybernetics (Razran, 1964). Cybernetic physiology, as developed by Pyotr K. Anokhin and Nikolai A. Bernshtein, had its impact in the reemergence of the topic of the unconscious, which had Filipp V. Bassin as its main figure. In his 1968 book *The Problem of the Unconscious*, the most important work on the subject since the 1920s in the USSR, he claimed that psychology ought to use cybernetic physiological theories in order to build *"a constructive, dialectical materialist, position towards the problem"* (Bassin, 1972, p. 345, author's italics; this and any other translation are mine), though he made it sufficiently clear that psychological issues could not be merely derived from neurological processes. Bassin's interdisciplinary stance accompanied the resolutions of the XVIII International Congress of Psychology held in Moscow in 1966, where cybernetics was again present in the program – even positively regarded by several authors, among them, Jean Piaget (1969). More important was that both Anokhin and Bassin stated that there was no solid theory of consciousness without a solid theory of the unconscious, a stance that openly challenged the primacy of consciousness of the partisan interpretations of Marxism-Leninism and led psychology directly to political discussions.

During the 1960s the figure of the "New Man" as a complete overhaul of the human being lost some of its initial glow in the soviet imaginary, by then more tempered after Stalinism and the Second World War. However, the promise of a scientific and technological unfolding of human potencies was still part of communist utopia; Roger Garaudy, an official philosopher of the French Communist Party, was enthusiastic about the possibilities of cybernetics, even stating, "The cybernetic mutation makes possible an unprecedented blooming of human subjectivity" (Garaudy, 1970, p. 54). This assertion is meaningful not only in its utopian tones, but also because it shows that politics cannot by then be considered detached from science, both natural and human sciences. The German philosopher Jürgen Habermas expressed the same idea in 1967:

> I suspect that the institutional changes brought about by scientific and technical progress exercise an indirect influence on the linguistic schemata of

worldviews of the same kind once exercised by changes in the mode of production; for science has become the foremost of the forces of production.

(Habermas, 1967/1988, p. 258)

It is possible to outline a third and final form of the political and scientific Soviet utopia towards the 1980s, under the label of "human factor" of productive forces. Though this formula was already established by the '60s, it became more prominent in the later years of the USSR, when two conceptions can be distinguished: a first one, since Mikhail S. Gorbachev assumed power until early 1986, when "human factor" was instrumentally conceived, as new techniques directed to motivate workers and accelerate, increase and improve production; and a second one, after the 27th CPSU Congress, held in March 1986, when that formula was broadened and it was discussed as a "collective mentality" that ought to be formed with the "hidden reserves" of Soviet citizens. That same year, the Presidium of the Soviet Academy of Sciences created a scientific council with the program "Man, Science and Society", aimed to give scientific and interdisciplinary basis to the notion of "human factor" (Rawles, 1996). Boris F. Lomov, by then director of the Psychology Institute of the Academy of Science, was specialized in engineering psychology and had ties with the Soviet space program, which made him a more than suitable researcher to promote such a program. To him, "the fundamental aim of industrial psychology is the humanization of technology", which meant the following:

When new technology is created or a new technological process is developed, the thought of how man will do the activity is, unfortunately, not always present. Later, during the process of production, it is discovered that such technology is "psychologically disturbing" to man. (. . .) Psychological problems also appear related to the improvement of the direction systems of popular economy (. . .), direction is not reduced to the simple organization of technology and the application of economic models. (. . .) The improvement of the direction system requires the knowledge about human activity and behavior, about psychological differences between individuals, about the interrelations among working collectives. (. . .) The need of results in psychological research emerges, one way of another, from all spheres of social practices, of working with man: industry, transport, direction systems of popular economy, teaching, healthcare, art, ideology and politics. Such need is tied with the urgency of the study and calculation of the so called "human factor" in order to solve practical problems. (. . .) The importance and need for the activation of the human factor were underlined once more in the programmatic documents of the XXVII CPSU Congress (1986), and the subsequent statements of the General Secretary of our party, M. S. Gorbachev.

(Lomov, 1989, p. 114)

The impassive partisanship of this quote does not hide the acknowledgment of a troubled economy that did not consider human individual and collective needs. To him, Soviet psychology, insofar as Marxist-Leninist, was still at the service of "the formation of a new man", an issue that was "accordingly addressed in the latest CPSU's congresses", though he was aware that "it would be a mistake to assume that the new social relations 'automatically fabricate' a new man" (p. 115). Nevertheless, Perestroika as a process had unexpected and conflicting effects that ultimately revealed there were no such psychological reserves to keep up with such utopia. Social psychologist Igor Kon, one of the more visible authors in a specialty that was neglected for decades in the USSR, considered perestroika as a kind of return to form to 1920s Leninism, in an attempt of leaving Stalinism definitely behind, yet to him, by 1988, that was a problem in itself: "One cannot forget the deeply-rooted custom (. . .) of approving any suggestion that comes from the top and which fulfilment doesn't need, consequently, any intellectual effort". To Kon, the reform should aim to new forms of social responsibility through "broadening real and actual democracy, and self-management" (Kon, 1988/2002, p. 114). He questioned the yearnings and utopian undertones of Soviet authorities, in particular those that required psychological technology, and rejected the idea of the complete transformation of man altogether: "It is necessary to overcome the idealized image of the 'new man', the man that only has virtues, and on the contrary, be able to look ourselves with criticism and sobriety" (p. 101). By then, the communist utopia that would bring the "new man" after the Bolshevik triumph stopped appearing as feasible; what was left was the analysis of the "ordinary man" that resulted from seventy years of Soviet socialism. Thus, an acid skepticism on decades old promises of Marxism-Leninism as worldview and Socialist state driven science became a common humor in late '80s psychologists – as narrated by Razdzikhovskii's chapter in this volume.

In practice, scientific institutions did not follow Perestroika's spirit; towards the mid-1980s the USSR had the largest scientific community in the world and one of the biggest funding, though the military–industrial and the energy system had 87% of the total budget for research and development, and more than half of the researchers. Such imbalance derived from the strong centralization with which Soviet science was organized for decades and was expressed by the important advances in military and aerospace technology, in contrast with the reduced research aimed to domestic industry and the production of consumer goods, which were problematic for several decades. Scientists were not interested in the latter, nor were there the necessary mediations to transfer the basic and applied results of military and spatial research to daily civil life. At the same time, science investment did not generate enough returns and the Chernobyl disaster revealed the inefficiency of scientific management and policies. There were approaches to industrial production and social problems, and some decentralization policies in science were promoted; the 1987 and 1988 laws of individual activities and cooperatives related to science allowed for some initiative by researchers, and for 1990 there were around 10.000 cooperatives related to science and technology. However, the experience was chaotic due to the difficulties for obtaining supplies and scientists' lack of experience for working outside highly structured environments. Besides, scientific authorities kept the monopoly of funding and insisted on centralizing research during the late 1980s, although more centralization did not mean producing better science, as shown then by the North American and Japanese cases. In 1989 there were protests organized to demand reforms in the Soviet Academy of Science, which led to the creation of the Union of Creative Scientists and a Russian Academy of Sciences, parallel to the Soviet one, yet those initiatives did not succeed. As soon as the USSR was dismantled, both academies were unified, and scientific funding was reduced by around 1000% (Graham, 1992, 1998).

Is there a place for utopia in scientific politics?

As is well known, the fall of the USSR and socialism in central and eastern European countries was not only a historical defeat of communism, but also a closure of alternatives to capitalism and its political and economic pathologies. Certainly, "the end of History", Fukuyama's infamous formula, proclaimed the global empire of capitalism, as well as the closing of horizons of expectations – a geographical extension correlative to a historical narrowing. A decade later, with the resuming of military intervention and the struggles for the control of the global economy, what became apparent is that we had negative futures ahead. To this day, the world economic system does not offer substantial improvement to populations, not even in the "first-world" countries; the ecological deterioration is evident even for lay people, and science has been "disenchanted" as it has lost the ability to evoke the hopes and promises that rose until the 1970s. Then again, science fiction shows this change, as it was by then that the genre, both in literature and other arts, in the USSR and in the West, became almost completely dystopian, as science's role was subsumed to political and economic oppression (Moylan, 2000; Fitting, 2010). While in the Soviet imagination the socialist project required science as a social and economic driving force, to present population science is more a threat than a solution, both for common citizens and political leadership – albeit for very different reasons, of course.

As a consequence of such a lack of perspective and the dead end of capitalism, communism began to be reconsidered, and the theme science and utopias has gained new traction. In this matter, there is a whole range of positions. One side can be exemplified by French philosopher Alain Badiou, who tries to get rid of both references:

> The real untiringly disproved scientific pretensions, so that is mandatory a critical distance with them. Only an understanding of societies stripped from the burden of the scientistic paradigm shall allow us to forge a will capable of leading them in the sense we consider more appropriate. (. . .) The

communism I advocate is exactly the opposite to a utopia, even though is not "scientific" in any sense. It is simply a rational possibility of politics, and there are others, for example, the destruction of humanity due to the disastrous effects of globalized capitalism.

(Badiou & Gauchet, 2014, pp. 73–74)

Italian historian Enzo Traverso took a somewhat middle ground, not rejecting both categories, yet modifying them through the addition of the issue of memory, that is, the past as a source for the future:

Once cut short of its utopic dimension, Marxism stopped acting as a trans-mission vector of class memory, of emancipatory struggles and revolutions. (. . .) Science did not promise socialism, but this could rest on its results to satisfy the ancestral wish of happiness. Even reinterpreted as utopia – or *possible* alternative to barbarism –, socialism was still the historical *telos*, that is, the objective fixed by an action and fed by an ensemble of wishes that memory had cultivated. If we must summarize in one formula the Marxist conception of memory, we may take the definition proposed by Vincent Geoghegan, 'remembering the future'".

(Traverso, 2014, pp. 154–165, author's italics)

Nevertheless, he also states that "the world can't live with utopias, and it's going to come up with new ones", without offering more elements for that wish.

At the other side of the spectrum, authors like Argentinian historian Ariel Petruccelli considers that "it is essential re-think calmly and thoroughly the prob-lems of *ethics* and *utopia*, without abandoning the ones of *science*. The socialism of our time should keep a multiple commitment to ethical reflection, utopian imagination, scientific rigor, and political responsibility" (Petruccelli, 2016, p. 23). Moreover,

if we are to be faithful to the legacy of Marx, then we should pack in our backpacks the clothing of a rigorous scientist that try, productively yet per-haps without success, reach the truth, as well as the attires of the passionate revolutionary, willing to do the utmost sacrifices for his/her ideals. Thus, science and utopia.

(p. 287)

Actually, Petruccelli is far from being an orthodox communist, yet he represents the idea that science and utopia can and should be together in a post-Soviet socialism, as far as it does not repeat well-known dogmatisms.

Besides Marxism, with its understandable ambivalences towards the heritage of the "real socialism", other political trends also decidedly included science in the search for future horizons. Some of them are reactionary, as the uses neoliberals and conservatives give to the new classical macroeconomics or sociobiology (Gómez, 2003; Rose & Rose, 2000). Others are antiestablishment, such as feminism which finds science as a necessary component for the subversion of the *status quo*. Philosopher Donna Haraway, in one of her most-known articles clearly stated: "Science has been utopian and visionary from the start; that is one reason 'we' need it" (Haraway, 1991, p. 192). That is, women need science because they have been historically excluded from the production of knowledge and been unilaterally defined – and still are – by scientists incapable of realizing that they take as natural and mandatory what actually are their gender prejudices and ignorance. Feminist psychologists have critiqued, many times during the XXth century, the "natural" roles of motherhood and couplehood assumed by psychology and psychiatry (Rutherford & Granek, 2010). Naomi Weisstein's assertion that "psychology has nothing to say about what women are really like, what they need and what they want, essentially because psychology does not know" (Weisstein, 1968/1992, p. 63) is still meaningful in that what psychology typically produces – including, I might add, Vygotskian inspired psychologies, as gender issues are not part of Vygotsky's agenda and therefore are not regularly considered in this literature – does not seem productive or relevant for a future without gender oppression. Science then is a disputed domain because of the evidences, technologies and legitimation it provides, and therefore feminist psychology struggles against the androcentrism and patriarchy both in their discipline as well as in society at large to provide knowledge and practices that would change the current relations among genders.

Contrary to revolutionary Bolshevists, feminists seem to have been quite aware that their political aims are to be obtained in the long-term, not merely in a few decades. As mentioned before, utopian thinking can be accepted as an inherently positive value. Philosopher Claire Colebrook (2010) sensibly considers that a moderate hope towards the future can lead one to consider accomplished objectives beforehand, and so limit changes to very specific spheres. On the other hand, a radical utopia that implies an absolute break with the present situation leaves us without the present elements with which to build a future, and leads to dejection, cynicism and demands dislocated of present possibilities. According to her ideas, feminism should unfold a vision of a desirable future negatively inspired in the present, where specific attainments do not mean that the broad scenario became acceptable, but they provide a hopeful imaginary that continues to drive activism through time. Can psychology, feminist or not, provide us with a sensible utopianism, this one described or any other? In any case, it is apparent that we cannot accept ingenuity or ready-made narratives when considering the possible futures our discipline is shaping.

Perspectives and definitions

Utopias, far from being mere ideal fictions, are active elements of political thinking and discourses: they define how present is assessed in relation with the future, which values and results are expected from scientific knowledge, which dangers, intrinsic or accidental, are foreshadowed in the accomplishment of that future. The previous outline of the subject through Soviet psychology allows for the following conclusion: the scientific and political utopia inspired by Bolshevism, is no longer feasible, not even desirable. XXth century leftist revolutions have shown their own considerable limitations, not necessarily attributable to the siege of the "Free World", and many of them no longer endure. Too many things have changed in these more than a hundred years from the Russian revolution, especially in the way science is thought and managed. We need a critical memory of those experiences to give us alternatives to analyze the present without assuming past utopias can be still fruitful. Vygotsky tried to build a psychology oriented by and towards the "New Man", geared through social renovation and the perspective of a wide-open future. Now, current psychology has to offer solutions of the "old" human being, in historical scenery increasingly hostile to profound renovations and with specific and general challenges unimaginable for the communist worldview. Both Vygotsky and Lomov adhered to Bolshevist imaginary, yet for the latter that meant a disjunction from the reality of Soviet institutions and population. Perhaps Bassin, a barely known figure in the West, had a more thoughtful stance, as he balanced a political critique to psychology with a scientific critique to politics, where disciplinary autonomy was valuable because of the experience with Stalinism. Nevertheless, we do not have, and we would not desire, a political and scientific system that resembles that of the USSR from the 1920s to 1960s, not even present-day socialist countries. The Soviet experience can shed light on the productivity of the past for giving us topics to reflect upon, even when that past does not provide acceptable or replicable models.

Psychology has had an impoverished relationship with the future, usually stuck in a constant present of struggles between "schools" or specialties eager to monopolize the "genuine" idea of science and human being, if not an irreflexive confidence in some kind of automatic growth by means of evidence gathering and publishing, or worse, reducing the future to a mere control of variables for "prediction". Yet epistemological precision does not inform about the historical conditions necessary for the change and reproduction of a discipline. History is not just a reservoir of past knowledge, but a tool for acknowledging the historicity of our situated activities and a source to consider the kind of horizons we can provide ourselves. Part of that exercise requires debating what kind of relation we as scientists want to have with our governments according to our immediate objectives, why and in what situations disciplinary autonomy is a value worth defending, which past models are still viable and productive to propose feasible and desirable horizons. A discussion of our present and our futures can be informed by the past, not to find there a guide ready to be reactivated or metahistorical principles for a "good" science beyond political distortions, but to critically detect what kind of project we are investing in, which are its inertias, how our knowledges have been legitimized, their impact in the public arena, and actually how much they hold up to the promises and values they invoke. Such analysis may perfectly result in a negative outcome. Perhaps, the first step to that stance is to recognize psychology has theories and technologies that have proven to be irrelevant, instrumental to inequality, or even dangerous, independently of the good intentions of the practices. The acknowledgement that psychology, Vygotskian or not, is not an inherently positive and valuable body of knowledge becomes necessary to revise aims, sense of belonging and effects in order to gain perspective and renew disciplinary imagination.

In this century, it's almost unthinkable a future that does not include sciences as a key political actor, both for their productivity and social uses. Discussing a future beyond immediacy always implies a utopian dimension, and in order to be realizable it cannot leave aside the central place of science, for better or worse, the management of governments and the authorization of political thinking. In face of the increasing technification of economy, finances, propaganda and repression forces, the challenge seems to be to reincorporate in the discipline an anti-establishment tradition with a critical and productive regard that may offer desirable and feasible horizons, without reviving projects or teleologies similar to soviet Marxism-Leninism. The role of science in politics has to be reconstructed in regard of our conditions and not from the mold of a "good science" somehow inherited from an idealized past or assumed universal because of the results it gave in other contexts – which can perfectly be valid, yet not immediately suitable elsewhere. But to be able to make such reconstruction, we need to be historically aware of our situatedness.

Nowadays, when political and economic leaders adhere to creationism, dismiss climate change and vaccination, resurrect racial and gender prejudices, and condemn social and human sciences as unprofitable and lacking clear effectivity, it may seem that science has lost terrain in the public arena. But that is not true; both "hard" and "soft" sciences are still key for the exploitation of natural resources, work management and global economy, the control of diseases, and the promotion of ideologies and agendas through media. Anti-scientific rhetoric is mostly promoted by conservatives and rejects only those sciences that are able to dispute their means of legitimation and effective power. In other words, most current governments do not want scientists who can show the errors and undesirable effects of their management, even less those with concrete alternatives that mean a shift in power and resources. They only want a science that would make more efficient the decisions taken behind their populations' back.

The potency of sciences resides in the generation of means to know and intervene with natural, social and cultural reality, the obtention of evidence which contrasts our values and objectives, and the definition of a certain margin of predictability about our future. It resides in the hands of the forces that question the *status quo* to appropriate that potency and dispute the future – in fact, provide a future in the first stance as conservatives do not offer one, they only propose a continuous present of mere survival. Obviously it is a tough challenge for anti-establishment sectors to regain science and, at the same time, be aware of its ethical, political and technical problems and limitations, yet the option of using it without a critical stance is no longer acceptable. In other words, there is no worth in defending science itself, as if it were a self-sustaining activity or general good. We need a revindication of human emancipation, which requires a reformulated science so that, instead of being additional shackles or new blinders, it becomes part of scripts driven towards a pacific, equitable and sustainable coexistence.

References

Andersson, J., & Rindzevičiūtė, E. (2012). The political life of prediction. The future as a space of scientific world governance in the Cold War era. *Les Cahiers Européens de Sciences Po, 4*, 1–25.

Andersson, J., & Rindzevičiūtė, E. (Eds.). (2015). *The Struggle for the Long-Term in Transnational Science and Politics. Forging the Future.* New York, NY: Routledge.

Badiou, A., & Gauchet, M. (2014). *Que faire ? Dialogue sur le communisme, le capitalisme et l'avenir de la démocratie.* Paris: Philo éditions.

Bassin, F. (1972). *El problema del inconsciente.* Buenos Aires: Granica.

Bogdanov, A. (1908/1984). *Red Star: The First Bolshevik Utopia.* Bloomington, IN: Indiana University Press.

Charle, C. (1990). *Naissance des intellectuels (1880–1900).* Paris: Les Éditions de Minuit.

Colebrook, C. (2010). Toxic feminism: Hope and hopelessness after feminism. *Journal for Cultural Research, 14*(4), 323–335.

David-Fox, M. (1997). *Revolution of the mind: Higher learning among the Bolsheviks, 1918–1929.* Ithaca, NY: Cornell University Press.

Dostaler, G. (2008). Les lois naturelles en économie. Émergence d'un débat. *L'Homme et la société, 170–171*(4), 71–92.

Engels, F. (1878/1969). *Anti-Duhring.* London: Lawrence & Wishart 1969.

Fitting, P. (2010). Utopia, dystopia and science fiction. In G. Claeys (Ed.), *Cambridge companion to utopian literature* (pp. 135–153). Cambridge, MA: Cambridge University Press.

Garaudy, R. (1970). *El gran viraje del socialismo.* Caracas: Tiempo Nuevo.

Gerovitch, S. (2002). *From newspeak to cyberspeak. History of Soviet cybernetics.* Cambridge, MA: MIT Press.

Gómez, R. (2003). *Neoliberalismo globalizado. Refutación y debacle.* Buenos Aires: Macchi.

Graham, L. (1987). *Science, philosophy and human behavior in the Soviet Union.* New York, NY: Columbia University Press.

Graham, L. (1992). Big science in the last years of the big Soviet union. *Osiris, 2nd Series, 7*, 49–71.

Graham, L. (1998). *What have we learned about science and technology from the Russian experience?* Standford, CA: Standford University Press.

Habermas, J. (1967/1988). *On the logic of the social sciences.* Cambridge, MA: MIT Press.

Haraway, D. (1991). Situated knowledges: The science question in feminism and the privilege of partial perspective. In *Simians, cyborgs, and women. The reinvention of nature* (pp. 183–201). New York, NY: Routledge.

Jameson, F. (2007). *Archaeologies of the future: The desire called utopia and other science fictions.* London: Verso.

Joravsky, D. (1961). *Soviet Marxism and natural science, 1917–1932.* New York: Columbia University Press.

Kolman, E. (1956). La cybernétique vue par un philosophe soviétique. *La Pensée, 68*, 14–34.

Kon, I. (1988/2002). Psicología de la inercia social. In M. Golder (Comp.), *Angustia por la utopía* (pp. 101–125). Buenos Aires: Ateneo Vigotskiano de la Argentina.

Koselleck, R. (2003). *Aceleración, prognosis y secularización*. Valencia: Pre-textos.

Livesey, J. (2006). Intellectual history and the history of science. In R. Whatmore y B. Young (Eds.), *Palgrave advances in intellectual history* (pp. 130–146). New York: Palgrave Macmillan.

Lomov, B. (1989). Psicología Soviética. Su historia y su situación actual. *Política y Sociedad*, *2*, 99–115.

Moylan, T. (2000). *Scraps of the untainted sky: Science fiction, utopia, dystopia*. Boulder, CO: Westview Press.

Petruccelli, A. (2016). *Ciencia y utopía: en Marx y en la tradición Marxista*. Buenos Aires: Herramienta-El colectivo, 2016.

Piaget, J. (1969). L'intériorisation des schèmes d'action en opérations réversibles par l'intermédiaire des régulations des feedbacks. In *Union internationale de la psychologie scientifique, XVIII Congrès internationale de psychologie, 4–11 août 1966* (pp. 6–13) Nauka: Moscou.

Pinault, M. (2003). L'intellectuel scientifique: du savant à l'expert. In M. Leymarie y J. Sirinelli (Dirs.) *L'histoire des intellectuels aujourd'hui* (pp. 229–254). Paris: Presses Universitaires de France.

Pittaluga, R. (2015). *Soviets en Buenos Aires. La izquierda argentina ante la revolución en Rusia*. Buenos Aires: Prometeo.

Rawles, R. (1996). Soviet psychology, perestroika, and human factor: 1985–1991. In V. Koltsova, Y. Oleinik, A. Gilgen, & C. Gilgen (Eds.), *Post-Soviet perspectives on Russian psychology* (pp. 101–115). London: Greenwood Press.

Razran, G. (1964). Growth, scope, and direction of current Soviet psychology: The 1963 All-union congress. *American Psychologist*, *19*(5), 342–348.

Stites, R. (1988). *Revolutionary dreams. Utopian vision and experimental life in the Russian revolution*. New York, NY: Oxford University Press.

Rispoli, G. (2015). The path of cybernetics in the Soviet Union: From rejection to celebration in the service of communism. *Paradigmi*, *3*, 149–162.

Rispoli, G. (2016). Sharing in action: Bogdanov, the living experience and the systemic concept of the environment. In P. Tikka, J. Biggart, M. Soboleva, G. Rispoli, & V. Oittinen (Eds.), *Culture as organization in early soviet thought* (pp. 1–13). Helsinki: Aalto University.

Rutherford, A., & Granek, L. (2010). Emergence and development of the psychology of women. In J. Chrisler & D. McCreary (Eds.), *Handbook of gender research in psychology* (pp. 19–41). New York, NY: Springer-Verlag.

Rose, H., & Rose, S. (Eds.). (2000). *Alas poor Darwin: Arguments against evolutionary psychology*. London: Jonathan Cape.

Todes, D. (2014). *Ivan Pavlov. A Russian life in science*. New York, NY: Oxford University Press.

Todes, D., & Krementsov, N. (2010). Dialectical materialism and Soviet science in the 1920s and 1930s. In W. Leatherbarrow & D. Offord (Eds.), *History of Russian thought* (pp. 340–367). Cambridge, MA: Cambridge University Press.

Tolstoy, A. (1923/1985). *Aelita or the decline of mars*. Ann Arbor, MI: Ardis.

Traverso, E. (2014). *¿Qué fue de los intelectuales?* Buenos Aires: Siglo XXI.

Trotsky, L. (1924/1973). A few words on how to raise a human being. In *Problems of everyday life and other writings on culture and science* (pp. 135–142). New York, NY: Monad Press.

Vygotsky, L. (1930/1994). The socialist alteration of man. In R. van der Veer & J. Valsiner (Eds.), *The Vygotsky reader* (pp. 175–184). Oxford: Blackwell.

Weisstein, N. (1968/1992). Psychology constructs the female, or the fantasy life of the male psychologist (with some attention to the fantasies of his friends the male biologist and the male anthropologist). In J. S. Boham (Ed.), *Seldom Seen, Rarely Heared. Women's place in psychology* (pp. 61–78). Boulder, CO: Westview Press.

Yasnitsky, A. (2018). *Vygotsky: An intellectual biography*. London: Routledge.

Yasnitsky, A. (2019). Vygotsky's science of superman. From utopia to concrete psychology. In A. Yasnitsky (Ed.), *Questioning Vygotsky's legacy: Scientific psychology or heroic cult* (pp. 1–21). New York, NY: Routledge.

Yasnitsky, A., & Ferrari, M. (2008). From Vygotsky to Vygotskian psychology: Introduction to the history of the Kharkov school. *Journal of the History of the Behavioral Sciences, 44*(2), 119–145.

INDEX